THE
LITTLE CLOWN

AN AUTOBIOGRAPHY

REG VARNEY

THE LITTLE CLOWN

AN AUTOBIOGRAPHY

Hodder & Stoughton

LONDON SYDNEY AUCKLAND TORONTO

In some instances names and places
have been changed

British Library Cataloguing in Publication Data

Varney, Reg
  The little clown.
  1. Jazz. Piano playing – Biographies
  I. Title
  786.1'092'4

  ISBN 0-340-52077-9

First published in Great Britain 1990

Published by Hodder and Stoughton
a division of Hodder and Stoughton Ltd,
Mill Road, Dunton Green, Sevenoaks, Kent TN13 2YA.
Editorial Office: 47 Bedford Square, London WC1B 3DP.

Photoset by Rowland Phototypesetting Ltd,
Bury St Edmunds, Suffolk

Printed in Great Britain by
St Edmundsbury Press Ltd, Bury St Edmunds, Suffolk
and bound by Hartnolls Ltd, Bodmin, Cornwall

To my daughter Jeanne
and her husband Robert,
and my two grandchildren Ryan and Leah,
without whom my book wouldn't have been written.

And to my wife Lily and her sister Ruby, as well as Jeanne,
who typed and corrected my appalling spelling.

And especially, acknowledgment to Lily for mastering the
word processor – even if a little late, perhaps.

Contents

ILLUSTRATIONS

Illustrations appear between pages 128 and 129.
All photographs are from the author's private collection.

THE
LITTLE CLOWN
AN AUTOBIOGRAPHY

1

THE LITTLE CLOWN

As I got to the bottom of the stairs, Mum was coming along the passage with a letter in her hand. I followed her into the kitchen and stood by the scrubbed wooden table looking up at her.

She looked at the envelope. "Ooh, it's from your daddy!" she said, then put her thumb behind the flap, ripped it open, took out the letter and started to read. Halfway down the page she stopped, peered inside the envelope, turned it upside down and out into her hand dropped a little celluloid clown. It had a red conical hat, a yellow jacket and blue trousers. "Ooh," she gasped again, "look what your daddy has sent you," then she gave it to me. "And isn't it pretty?"

I remember feeling very disappointed, as apart from moving its arms and legs, which just swung to and fro, it did nothing else. It was while I was swinging its little arms and legs backwards and forwards trying to make it do other things, that Mum shrieked with delight, swooped me up in her arms, giving my knee a nasty crack on the kitchen table, and danced me round and round, bubbling over: "Your daddy's coming home! . . . Your daddy's coming home!" We were both crying; Mum with joy and me from a dislocated knee. "We shouldn't be crying," she said, her face all aglow. "We should be happy, your daddy's coming home!" I couldn't fathom out why I should be happy considering I had never seen this bloke called Daddy. He had been posted to Egypt during the 1914–18 war not long after I was born in 1916. Wiping away my tears Mum looked me straight in the face, gave me a big kiss and said, "And wait till he sees you, he will be surprised." I didn't reply, there was no answer to that one.

After a while when Mum could see I'd lost all interest in the little clown, she dropped it in the old pewter coffee pot which stood on the front of the dresser and held bits of tangled string, buttons, pencil stubs, fluffy acid drops hidden away at some time or another and forgotten, my sisters' hair-curling rags, and other odds and ends a family household collects. It was never used for coffee.

I have two brothers and two sisters: Sid seven years older, Bella four years and Doris two years older, as well as a younger brother Stanley, who didn't come on the scene until 1922. We were all born and bred in a small terraced house, No. 7, Addington Road, Canning Town, London E16.

Gran, a very tiny woman, always spotlessly clean in her starched white apron, lived with us, so with my parents and us kids it was quite a houseful. Luckily we were a close family. Dad was a tubby man of around five foot six, with an infectious smile and laughing eyes. He brought us up in a strict Victorian manner – he made the rules and although he loved us dearly, woe betide us if we strayed from them. He never hit us. There was no need, because those same laughing eyes, when angered, would send a chill down our spines. He worked in Silvertown in a factory called the India Rubber Gutta-Percha Works. He was a rubber spreader, which sounded impressive; in fact it was only a semi-skilled job so his wages, £2 10s. a week, weren't all that good.

With so little money coming into the house, Mum had a job making ends meet but being a hard worker and a magnificent housekeeper, she coped. Nothing was ever wasted in our house . . . nothing. Her early training in needlework stood her in good stead because not only did she make all our clothes out of odd remnants of material but to earn a few extra shillings to eke out the housekeeping money, she took in other people's washing. It was when it came to the extra washing that Gran came into her own. I can see her now, in the steam-filled scullery, lifting the lid off the white hearthstoned copper in the far corner and poking down the washing with the chewed-up end of the wooden copper stick.

Separating the copper from the small china sink with its brass cold water tap above, was the scullery window which looked out on to our back yard, and against the wall facing the window was the wringer, a monstrous thing made out of cast iron, standing about five feet high. It had a sort of small capstan wheel on top for screwing the well-worn rollers tighter, and beneath the wringer, to catch the water when the clothes were wrung, was an oval tin bath. Mondays and Tuesdays were the washing days – Mondays for whites and Tuesdays coloureds. Monday was a very low-key day; a dreaded day, a smell of boiling clothes day, a cold meat and pickles day, an everybody's miserable day, a nothing to look forward to day, except the rest of a hard slogging week.

My second vivid recollection was of a Monday such as this. Mum had dressed me in my best clothes, making me feel very apprehensive and more so when she came downstairs dressed in her best frock, her favourite hat with a bunch of cherries on it, and smelling of cologne. She looked pretty but I liked her best in her everyday clothes and instead of cologne, smelling that lovely Mum smell . . . the smell that only my mum had. Looking at her dressed like that, I felt shy and distant, and I was scared . . . scared of what lay ahead of me because this was my first day at school.

After making a few adjustments to her cherried hat in the oval mirror which hung over the mantelpiece, she gave me a final check-over then called out to Gran in the scullery, who had just got started on the washing, "Won't be long, Mum." Then she took my hand and off we went.

Outside the infants' school gates, which were less than thirty seconds from our street door, were a number of other mothers with their children. Some of the mothers were already deep in conversation, while the rest were trying to console their crying kids. At five minutes to nine the school bell rang. All the children in the playground were rounded up into their classes by the teachers, then class by class, in military fashion, they were marched into the school. After the last class had gone in, a kindly little woman came out and addressing the mothers with a smile said, "The Governess will see you now." As we followed her into school the mothers became tense and they weren't talking any more.

The school hall was large, and twice as long as it was wide. Down the left-hand side of the hall as you entered were most of the classrooms, with another two at either end. Opposite the classrooms were windows running nearly the length of the hall and in the centre of this range of windows, which overlooked the playground, was a huge desk mounted on a dais, and sitting at the desk was the Governess. She was a terrifying sight. Her jet black hair had an upward sweep, making her angular sharp-featured face look even more angular. She had a hooked nose, beady eyes and a scrawny neck and her ears stuck out; in fact on her everything seemed to stick out except her chest and that was flat. The plain black dress she wore hung on her bony figure and sitting there, poised above us, she looked just like a vulture.

The kindly little woman who had led us in lined us up with our mums in front of her desk, then took up her position beside the Governess. Except for the odd nervous cough there wasn't a sound.

After what seemed an eternity, the vulture turned her head to one end of the line and fixed her gaze on the first mother and child. It was a piercing look which didn't waver; the child started to cry, then stuck her head into her mother's skirt. The Governess glared at each mother and child in turn and it seemed that only when she'd given each child the screaming abdabs did she move her gaze on to the next. It wasn't until she got to me that I realised just how disturbing her look was Our eyes met and like a magnet hers locked on to mine; I felt like a rabbit caught in the headlights of a car. I could have sworn those piercing eyes were on me longer than the others, but I don't suppose they were. My bottom lip began to tremble, then the tears started to well up in my eyes. Mum put her arm round my shoulder and as she gave me a comforting squeeze, the headlights were gone and on to the next mother and child.

When she'd finished giving us the terror treatment, she summoned all the mothers in turn and had a little chat with them, after which she said, "That will be all, mothers, your children will be in good hands." Her voice was just as chilling as her look. My mother kissed me on the cheek and whispered, "I'll be back for you at twelve." Then she was gone. It was only the lingering smell of her eau de Cologne that told me that she had been there at all.

I stood there petrified, as I suspected the other kids were. The vulture never uttered a word, she just sat there eyeing us up and down as though choosing one of us for her lunch. Suddenly, when we weren't expecting it, she froze us with: "Now pay attention – and this means you," she boomed at one of the kids who was inquisitively looking around the hall, "and stop picking your nose." The kid snatched his finger out of his nose and wiped it on his jersey. She gave us another perishing look, then carried on: "Now listen carefully; this is your teacher, Miss Atkins." The kindly little woman who had been standing next to her stepped forward. "Miss Atkins will be in charge of you from now on and will keep me informed as to your progress. That is all."

The kindly little lady – of course Miss Atkins now – lined us up in a column of twos saying, "Come on, children, follow me," and led us into the classroom nearest to the entrance hall. When we were all inside she closed the door behind us . . . we were trapped.

The classroom had rows of desks and each desk sat two. All the kids began to talk to one another now. I guess it was the relief of being away from that monster outside. Miss Atkins sat at her desk, which was in the middle of the classroom. She said, "Now pay attention." (It didn't take long to learn that phrase. I heard it God knows how many times a day from that first day at school till my last day at the age of fourteen.) "You can sit at any desk you like for today, I will place you where *I* want you tomorrow." At that, I think every kid in the classroom made a bee-line for the desk nearest the door, including me. There was a pushing and a shoving and a general screech of kids' voices. Suddenly a terrifying voice shrieked through the noise – "QUIET!" There was a deadly silence.

14

For a frightful moment I thought the vulture outside had come in. We all turned to where the shriek had come from. Miss Atkins was sitting at her desk, her face like stone. Was it her? No one else was there – it had to be. What had happened to the kindly lady, the one with the gentle voice and smiling face? I thought, she's more frightening than the one outside, and we've got her for keeps. She rose up from her desk and with her eyes blazing, roughly ordered us into the desks until we were spread out evenly over the classroom. This done, she went back to her desk and sat down. All this took place in silence. She finally opened a register in front of her and with no touch of the gentle voice said, "Now pay attention. I am going to call out your names from this register and when you hear your name you will answer me by saying, 'Present, Miss,' and speak up so that I can hear you, don't mumble."

"Andrews!" she called – a boy shrieked out, "Present, Miss." As she called each name the kids shrieked back like Andrews – "Present, Miss," "Present, Miss . . ." I was intent on listening for my name (God, I daren't miss it) when she called out, "Seymore!" No answer. Louder, "Seymore!" No answer. I was looking round at the other kids hoping whoever Seymore was, he would answer up because Miss Atkins' face was turning a funny colour, and she hadn't called my name yet. I looked at the kid sitting next to me. He was crying his eyes out; his mouth was open so wide I could see only the top of his forehead and the bottom of his chin, the rest was drenched in tears. No sound came from him but a smell did.

Miss Atkins' little ferret-like eyes were darting around the classroom when she saw the boy next to me bawling his eyes out. She looked at him for a second or two; finally she said, "Why are you crying?" The only sound that came from him was a strangled Aagh. "Come on, speak up, why are you crying – *why are you crying?*"

Suddenly he blurted out, "I'VE POOPED."

She said, "Oh," and paused. "Is your name Seymore?" He could only nod. She ticked his name off in the register then said, without a trace of sympathy, "Off you go home and get your mother to clean you up." Poor little Seymore got up from the desk and shuffled to the door with his fear running down his legs.

Although I felt sorry for him, I also envied him. I reasoned that because he had messed himself he was getting out of this nightmare – he was going home to his mother. My mind was miles away wondering if I'd be lucky enough to shit myself, when she screamed out, "Varney!" I screamed back in terror, "PRESENT, MISS."

The rest of the morning is a blank to me, though I clearly remember Mum meeting me at the gate as promised. She gave me a searching look then said, "How did you get on?"

"The teacher frightens me," I said, then told her about Seymore.

"You'll soon get used to her," she said as she put her arm around my shoulder.

I knew then that the days of "never mind, darling, let Mummy kiss it better" had gone for ever. I was no longer a baby – I was a boy.

2

SEYMORE

I never dreamt on that first day that Seymore would become one of my closest friends. It didn't happen until we were about seven, and then it wasn't an overnight friendship – we sort of drifted together. It began one day when the school bullies were on the rampage. Being a very timid boy, I was scared to death, so to avoid them I hid in the "Dubs" (Dubs was short for WC). Sitting there with my legs dangling and my hands holding either side of the pan to stop myself from falling in, I noticed another pair of legs hanging below the partition dividing the next cubicle from mine. Nobody ever used the Dubs after school for going purposes, because with everyone living so near they waited until they got home, so unless the other pair of dangling legs had really been taken short and had to go, he also was hiding from the bullies. I wondered who it could be. It had to be someone who possessed the cunning skills of avoiding trouble like me.

When the playground became absolutely quiet, making it safe to come out, the owner of the dangling legs next door eased himself off the seat on to the floor; no paper was used, and no chain was pulled, so now I was convinced that whoever it was had definitely been hiding.

Our eyes met as we cautiously peered round the Dubs doors. When I saw it was Seymore, although his name wasn't amongst those I had suspected, I wasn't at all surprised because our first morning at school suddenly flashed into my mind . . . hadn't Miss Atkins scared the daylights out of him then? At least this time he was in the right place should his bowels erupt.

It was this chance meeting in the Dubs which started our friendship, although I concede it wasn't a very salubrious place for it to begin. Nevertheless, as our friendship grew we discovered we had a lot in common; the same taste in make-believe games. Materially I had nothing to share with Seymore, whereas his father bought him magnificent and expensive toys, which I drooled over.

Seymore lived with his grandmother. No one had ever seen his mother so it was not known if she was alive or dead, or if indeed she ever existed. It was a mystery to the district and remained so.

I always knew when his father had visited him because the next day he would show me, with little and sometimes no enthusiasm at all, another incredible toy his father had bought him. His blasé and couldn't-care-less attitude towards these gifts never failed to amaze me. Make-believe games were his passion. His let's-pretend-this and let's-pretend-that routines were endless, with not even a mention of his toys. I was constantly thinking up cunning schemes to justify incorporating one of his toys into his pretend games.

I had discovered early in our friendship that being boss meant everything to him, and by allowing him to boss me about I could get away with some outrageous spoofing. On one occasion he wanted me to go out in his back yard and dig a big hole, pretending we were navvies. I was to be the one down the hole digging while he was up top playing the foreman. I considered this one of the lousiest pretends he'd ever come up with. He had the most magnificent Hornby steam train set, which I was dying to get my hands on, but with all my cunning there was no way I could think of to include it in his pretend navvies. It did cross my mind at one point to say that I would need the train with its trucks down the hole to cart the dirt away, but as gullible as he could be when playing pretend games, by no stretch of the imagination would I get away with that one. So, unable to think up a scheme, I put paid to the navvies idea by suddenly developing a limp and feigning a bad leg.

I recall another time when he showed me a superb miniature bike (not to be confused with a fairy cycle) that his father had brought him the previous day. I stood there enviously looking at it. Much to my surprise he asked me if I would like a ride on it, and as reluctant as I was to admit that I couldn't ride a bike, I had to. "All right, I'll teach you," he said. So for the rest of that week after school he had a wonderful time teaching me to ride. I was a quick learner and within a couple of days, although a bit wobbly, I could ride, and come the end of the week I was quite capable. All that was needed now to give me confidence was a good long ride.

Imagine my disappointment when I went round on the Saturday afternoon, expecting another lesson, and discovered he had lost all interest, not only in teaching me, but also in his bike. He wanted to return to his favourite pretend game . . . Cowboys and Indians. I looked longingly at his beautiful bike leaning tantalisingly against the railings daring me to touch it, but I knew I mustn't.

His front porch was our headquarters and in the make-believe story he was the goody of course. I as the baddie had given our position away to the Redskins and we were now under siege; in doing so I had hoist my own petard and was forced to fight back. Arrows were coming at us from all directions while we counter-attacked by firing our imaginary pistols, with a verbal "Bang-Bang" on each pull of the trigger. I continued this charade mechanically, my mind elsewhere, working overtime trying to come up with a scheme which included his bike. This was a challenge if ever there was one: how does one equate having a modern bike with a Cowboys and Indians game?

All of an hour must have passed with us still bang-banging away at the invisible Indians. Seymore was really acting it up by dodging and weaving about avoiding the invisible arrows; at the same time yelling to me, "Look out, they're coming again," and "Watch it, there's one trying to creep over the top, shoot him, shoot him," and when I didn't he gave a couple of bang-bangs and shot him himself. Suddenly he stood up, gave a big "Ugggh" and fell back in the porch gripping an imaginary arrow sticking out of his chest. "Help me . . . help me," he moaned, "I've been shot with an arrow."

I couldn't believe my luck . . . this was the opportunity I'd been waiting for. I immediately dropped to his side and with a performance worthy of an Oscar I pulled the imaginary arrow from his clutching hand, examined the wound in his chest and said gravely, "This is a serious injury." On inspecting the invisible tip I cried, "And what is more, it's a poisoned arrow . . . this is an emergency, I've got to do something quick or you'll die."

Hearing he was going to die he stepped his acting up a couple of notches, writhing about on the freezing cold stone floor of the porch and making uncanny noises whilst gasping for air. I watched him going for his Oscar and as his agonising cries of pain became more pronounced, and his writhings more violent, I thought it best to hold him down in case it developed into a fit.

"Keep calm," I said, mopping his brow with a dirty piece of a torn-up shirt Mum had given me as a hanky. "I'll help you."

"But you're a baddie," he gasped.

"I know, but now I turn goody and have to take your bike to get the magic medicine to save you" – with that I mounted his bike and pedalled off up the street, leaving him in his porch still trying for his Oscar.

3

Mental Arithmetic

Every morning after the register had been called, we had deep breathing and nose blowing exercises. Miss Atkins would throw all the classroom windows open, line us up in front of them, and those of us who hadn't got handkerchiefs (which was practically all of us) were given a square piece of paper. The routine was twelve deep breaths, then blow each nostril into the paper. Then, as she said, screw the paper up – so the germs can't escape – and throw it into the wastepaper-basket.

One morning after the deep breathing and the nose blowing Miss Atkins was giving us a mental sums lesson. "Now pay attention," she said. "I am going to call out two numbers. I want you to add them up in your head and if you know the answer put your hand up. Now listen – two and two?"

Most of the class, except me and a few others, put their hands up. Some were so eager they were halfway out of their desks, practically waving to her.

She pointed to one of the hands – "You."

The "you" said, "Four."

"Correct. Next – three and two?" Up shot the hands again – "Yes, you."

The other "you" said, "Five, Miss."

"Correct – four and three?" Up shot the hands again – but this time she ignored the show of hands, looked hard at me, came over and stood beside me.

Looking down she said, "What is four and three?"

I was amazed – why was she asking me? I didn't know! If I had known I would have put my hand up.

The other kids were still waving their arms and hands about and some, the fully confident, to catch her attention, were calling out, "Please, Miss, I know. Please, oh! PLEEESE, Miss."

Their voices grew louder in competition. Still looking at me she suddenly shouted, "Shut up, all of you, and *sit down*." The noise ceased immediately.

The silence was scary, and as she towered over me with her stony face and little eyes piercing right through me, I felt the blood drain from my face.

It seemed an eternity before she spoke again, and when she did, each word was clipped and separate. "What – is – four and – three?"

I was so paralysed with fright I couldn't speak. I felt my eyes fill up and the tears roll down my cheeks into the corners of my mouth, and as I licked my lips I could taste the salt. I managed to turn my head from her and look round at the others appealingly – but nothing came back from them, in fact they seemed to be enjoying the show – the sadistic little sods!

She snapped out, "Look at me when I am talking to you."

I turned my head back to her, hoping she would take pity on me and leave me alone, but when I looked at her expression I knew I might just as well stand in the middle of a field and cry for the moon. Her face started to colour up round her cheeks, and when she spoke again it was through clenched teeth. "What – is – four – and – three?" As she said each word she bent closer to me so that on "three" her face was nearly touching mine. She smelled of mothballs. The smell was so overpowering, it was like being shut in a wardrobe. My mouth was opening and shutting but nothing came out, and when she still got no reply her face turned crimson and she shook with temper. She yelled, "Don't be so insolent, answer me when I speak to you."

I was sobbing so much my head started to throb, and although my little mind was terribly confused, I kept thinking – why is she so angry because I can't add up four and three? After all, I had been best at the deep breathing and nose blowing exercises. Suddenly two bony fingers pincer-gripped my ear and pulled. My ear, head, and body, in that order, followed her out to the front of the class and over to the bead board.

As she was pushing the beads to one side of the frame, I looked round at the rest of the class, and when I saw their faces staring back, something seemed to come over me. I stopped crying, my fear left me, and a feeling of calm took its place. I don't know how or why it happened, it just did.

I turned back to the bead board just as she put her fingers on the first bead. Sliding it across the wire, she spat out, "How many is that?" I said, "One." Sarcastically she said, "So you have got a tongue?" When another bead came across the wire she didn't speak but her eyes never left mine. "Two," I said. The next bead came over faster. Quickly I said, "Three," as though in time with the speed of the next bead. This had not reached the other three when I snapped out, "Four." Her fingers went on the first bead on the second wire and slid it across. I said, "Five." Another bead flew across. "Six." The next bead was pushed over with such force that when it hit the other two it sounded like the crack of a whip. "Seven," I said. I had hardly got "Seven" out when, still looking straight into my eyes, she boomed, "Then what is four and three?" I shouted back into her face, "Seven – seven – seven!"

She ignored my lost temper and said, "Right, you can go back to your desk now."

Miss Atkins looked at the rest of the class, knowing she had achieved what she had set out to do. It was the oldest ploy in the world. Unfortunately I was the one she had chosen for the demonstration.

I learned one valuable lesson from it though. Whenever any questions are flying about, stick your hand up with the rest, and when you do it, do it with conviction – but don't overdo it, because that can be very dangerous. I remember one boy, when I was in the seniors, who was a master of the art. He would stand up enthusiastically with his hand high, but just that split second after the others; and when the question had been answered, he would sit down at exactly the same time as all the rest, with a look of "I wish you had asked me".

One day, unfortunately for him, his timing wasn't all that good and he sat down just a fraction of a second after the others. The teacher, seeing the look on his face, said, "Don't be disappointed, Jackson, here's a question just for you – how do you work out the area of a pyramid?"

Jackson's face drained of colour and after a pause he said, "Excuse me, sir, could I go to the lavatory?"

Arithmetic was the only subject that really mattered. Reading and writing were very close to it, but I always had the impression that if you were bad at arithmetic you were considered a dunce. It was my worst subject, and all through my schooldays it never improved. In fact I was so bad I can't ever remember getting a sum right, or come to that any marks either. The best I ever did was on one occasion when my examination paper was returned – as expected, all five problems, beautifully presented, were crossed out in red pencil – but I was delighted to see at the bottom of the paper that I had been given one out of ten, for neatness.

4

HOSPITAL

My chances of improving became very slim when about this time
Mum noticed that, compared with the other boys, I wasn't growing.
She took me to Great Ormond Street Hospital where the doctors
told her that it was the result of my having had double pneumonia
when I was only about nine months old; the tremendous strain of
the illness had left me with two twisted valves of my heart, and
only complete rest would straighten them out.

The morning Mum told me that she was taking me on a tram to
the hospital I wasn't overjoyed, to say the least, because my only
previous tram ride had led to a ghastly experience.

On that occasion Mum didn't mention anything about a hospital,
she just said we were going for a ride on a tram. I'd been dressed
in my best green jersey and my best short trousers – Mum had
made these from one of Dad's old navy blue suits. I thought it must
be something special, and began to get terribly excited and more
so when she made up some corned beef sandwiches, wrapped them
up, and put them with two clean white towels into her rexine
shopping bag. On seeing this my thought was – goody, goody,
we're going on a picnic.

When we got off the tram, the conductor yanked the cord twice;
I heard a bell "ding, ding", then the tram moved away. Walking
up the road holding Mum's hand, I was looking round for a park.
I couldn't see one, and when Mum turned into a gravel drive which
led up to a grey ugly building I sussed that things weren't quite
right – this didn't look like a picnic area to me. I was puzzled as
to why Mum was bringing me here. Perhaps it was after this –
whatever this was – that we were going to picnic.

The stone steps leading up to the high arched entrance were well
worn. A long corridor stretched out in front of us, and as we walked
along it, with its green glazed bricks halfway up the walls, there
was this very strong smell of carbolic.

At the far end a lady sat at a small table. She looked spotless
in her blue dress – but what stood out more than anything
was her beautifully starched white apron, cuffs and collar
and frilly headgear. What a contrast she was to the grubby building.

As we approached the table she looked up. Her face was smooth and shiny, and she had red cheeks. She said, "Good morning, mother. Name?" She spoke gently but with authority.

Mum said, "Varney."

The lady looked down the list and when she found our name, speaking more to herself than Mum, she said, "Oh yes," and without looking up took a buff-coloured card and began to fill it in. When she had finished she handed the card to Mum saying, "Now go along to the waiting room and when you are called give this to the nurse."

Mum said, "Thank you, Sister," and went in search of the waiting room.

As we were walking along the corridor looking for it, I said, "Mum, you called that lady 'Sister'."

Mum said, "That's what she is."

"Then what's a nurse?" I asked.

Impatiently Mum replied, "You have to be a nurse before you can become a sister, and then only if you are very clever."

My mind was very confused. This was turning out nothing like I thought it was going to be, so I said, "Where are we then?"

There was no reply. She had found what she had been looking for.

The door to the waiting room had four glass panes at the top, and the lower half was painted green, very faded, and badly scuffed at the bottom where it had been constantly kicked. The room was square, of medium size, with bare walls distempered in cream (a long time ago). The light came from a dormer window high up; and against the wall was a long form.

When we entered, the hum of mumbled conversation stopped and all heads turned in our direction, making us feel self-conscious. Mum closed the door and all the heads turned away again and the mumbling resumed. There was no room on the form to sit down so we stood at the end.

From the moment we had walked up the gravel drive everything had been a mystery to me. Mum, apart from telling me the difference between a sister and a nurse, had given me no explanation about this depressing place, or what we were doing there. Looking down the form at all the mums and kids, my curiosity got the better of me, so I said, "Mum." I didn't think I'd spoken any louder than I normally did, but it came out as though a shot had been fired; there was complete silence and all the heads twisted round again. Mum said, "Shush." At the same time that she shushed me, a door opened at the far end of the room and all the heads turned to the nurse standing in the doorway, saying, "Next!"

The first mother, with her child, went to her, the mother handing over the buff-coloured card. The nurse glanced at it, then said, "Follow me." They all went through the door and it closed behind them.

The rest of the people on the form moved along, and Mum sat down in the free place and sat me on her lap. She started up a conversation with the woman next to her; it was one of those conversations not meant for young ears. Mum would sometimes spell out a word, that is if she could spell it, but now, for the subject they were on, the words were being mouthed. I wasn't surprised, as one of the words not mouthed quite softly enough was . . . "adenoids".

As time passed and quite a number of mothers had gone through the door with their kids, I became more and more puzzled. Apart from the nurse, no-one else had come out of that other room, so where the hell were all the mums and kids going? We kept moving up the form until eventually we were next, and last, to go in. Now that we were alone I felt there was no reason why Mum should not answer me, so I asked, "Mum, where are we?"

Very quietly she answered, "In a hospital."

That was a shock. Although I had heard of "hospital", in my mind's eye it was a beautiful place where old people went when they were ill . . . not a dirty, grubby place like this. Suddenly the thought came into my head . . . Mum was old, Mum must be ill. Was she going to die? Oh please God, don't let her die! I began to panic. I was about to ask her if she was ill when the door opened and the nurse said, "Come this way, mother." She took the buff card from Mum then glancing round the empty room said, "Are you the last?" After that remark it was a racing certainty she'd never make it to sister.

When the door closed after us the nurse went behind a curtain, leaving us standing in this bare room; it reeked of chloroform. It was an alarming smell which made me even more frightened for Mum. I was staring at the curtain the nurse had disappeared behind, wondering what mystery lay beyond it, when out she popped again. Going straight to Mum, she said, "All right, mother, you can leave him with us now." As she was speaking she was ushering Mum towards the door. She opened the door saying, "Will you come back for him, or will you wait?"

Mum said, "I'll wait."

"Very well, you'll find a seat out here in the hall." She closed the door immediately, giving Mum no time whatsoever to look round at me and say goodbye. Not that I wanted her to say that! I wanted to run to the door Mum had just gone through but I could not move, I was petrified. What was happening? Suddenly the changes had been rung on me; what a turn-up for the book! This was definitely a case of the good and the bad news; the good news was that nothing was wrong with Mum, the bad news being . . . something *was* wrong with me. One minute I'm thinking, Oh God, please don't let Mum die! The next minute I'm thinking, Oh God, please don't let *me* die!

The nurse came to me and taking me by the hand, half walked and half dragged me towards the magic curtain. I had no wish now to see what lay behind it, but before I knew what was happening the nurse had swished it back and there before me was a small cubicle. In the centre was what looked like a long couch with white sheets spread over it, and with a red rubber sheet on top of them.

On the wall at the back of the couch were two shelves, on which rows of round bottles with glass stoppers stood. Examining these bottles was a lady in a long white coat. She had her back towards us, but as we stepped inside she turned round and seeing me asked, "Is he the last?"

"Yes," said the nurse as she sat me on the couch, put a blue and white striped cape around my neck and tied the two tapes at the back. I sat there helpless and very scared, wondering what they were going to do to me. The lady in white came round and stood by my side. She smiled at me, then turned to the nurse saying, "You can tell the doctor we are ready for him now."

On the word "doctor", my head flashed round to her. Seeing the terrified look in my eyes she said, "Now there's nothing to be afraid of." It was easy for her to say that, she didn't have a blue and white striped cape round her neck. Giving me a comforting "Shush" which didn't work, she said, "Now I'm going to lay you down here and see how many you can count up to," and with that she put her hands on my shoulders and gently pushed me down. When I was flat on my back she told me to start counting as loud as I could. As I said "One," a pad was placed over my face. I heard myself counting "Three," but I couldn't manage "Four" – everything went black.

When I opened my eyes Mum was sitting next to me with her arm around me; her other hand held a kidney-shaped basin under my chin while I vomited blood. Groggily I looked up at her, and although she was smiling I could see she had been crying.

She said, "Hello, darling, do you feel a little better?" I tried to nod, but my eyes closed as blackness came again.

The next time I opened my eyes, I was cuddled up in Mum's arms with a big white towel wrapped round my face. Looking down at me Mum said, "It won't be long now, we're on a tram going home." Although I was still a bit hazy, Mum's words kept going through my head: going home . . . so there was no picnic! Then why the towels and the sandwiches? A few questions later and the mystery was solved. The sandwiches were for Mum during her long wait while I had my tonsils out, and the two white towels were for my blood; the one already in the shopping bag saturated with half of it, and the one wrapped round my face trying to keep the other half in.

5

DISCOVERING MY GIFT

Eventually Mum agreed with the doctors from Great Ormond Street Hospital that, owing to my heart condition, I should be sent to a convalescent home where, under the supervision of a specially trained nursing staff, I would get the rest I needed. So it was that one Sunday morning, with my case packed, Mum and Dad took me to London Bridge station to see me off.

"Mr and Mrs Varney?" A sister from the home introduced herself, Mum handed her the letter she had received from the hospital. She quickly scanned through it, looked up and smiled at me. "So this is Reggie?" Turning to Mum and Dad she said, "Well I'm afraid that the train will be leaving very shortly, so you had better say goodbye."

Mum knelt down to my height, hugged me very tightly, and sobbing said, "Forgive me, Sister, for showing myself up like this, but you see this is the first time he's been away from me."

"Now don't you worry, Mrs Varney," and she patted Mum on the arm, "we will take very good care of him."

Mum reluctantly let me go and stood up; as she did so Dad picked me up in his arms, kissed me several times in rapid succession, and with a catch in his voice said, "Now you'll be a good boy, won't you?" Then he stood me down.

The nurse took me by the hand, put me in one of the compartments of the train, followed me in and slammed the door. As the train began to move slowly out of the station I leaned out of the carriage window and waved to Mum and Dad, watching them grow smaller as the train gathered speed to take me to my destination – Seaford.

My father, although he had never had a lesson in his life, was a natural pianist and played beautifully – his chord sequences were a dream. He'd sent my elder brother and sisters to have piano lessons, hoping he had passed on his talent to at least one of them – but apart from my brother Sid getting as far as "The Robin's Return", and my sisters Bella and Doris "The Maiden's Prayer", he knew that whatever else he had passed on to them, it wasn't his musical ability. Mum and Dad thought that at the age of six I was too young to be taught; also sixpence a lesson in those days was a hell of a lot of money, and with three already having tuition an extra sixpence for me would be stretching it for them. How ironical then that I was the one who had inherited his gift.

Dad's piano was his pride and joy, and unless my brother or sisters were practising he always kept it locked. If any of them, after they had finished their practice, were caught tinkering about on it, he would come straight in, lock it up and say, "Now listen! This isn't a bloody sixpenny Woolworth's toy for every Tom, Dick or Harry to bang about on, you know." As a result, my fingers had never touched a keyboard until I got to the convalescent home.

It was on my second day there that, after breakfast, and dressed ready for the nurses to take us all to the beach, I was given the disappointing news that I couldn't go out for the first week because I had to rest. After I had taken off my hat and coat I came back into the empty hall and saw a piano over in the corner. No one was around to forbid me, so I wandered over and opened the lid. I stood in front of it, and with my right hand picked out a tune I used to sing at our parties, for the aunts and uncles. It was called "Maggie – Yes Ma!" I then sat on the stool, and within minutes had picked out the right chords with my left hand. From that moment on there was no stopping me. Thrilled to know that I was going to be able to play like my dad, every opportunity I got, I practised. I discovered something new every day, and as Dad was the only piano player I had ever heard, I naturally copied his ragtime style.

The nurses were delighted to find that I could play and would let me stay up an hour later than the other children so that they could listen to me; they would also sing me the latest songs of the day, such as "Yes Sir, That's My Baby", so that at the end of my eight weeks' stay at the home, not only had my playing, for my age, become pretty good, but I had acquired quite a repertoire of tunes.

Mum was waiting for me at London Bridge station as my train pulled in from Seaford, and after the hugs and kisses she told me that my sister Bella, who suffered badly from St Vitus's dance, had been sent away to a convalescent home in Reading; she had been away for five weeks and was coming home that afternoon. "I've got to get you home, give you some lunch, and be at Paddington station by two o'clock to meet her," said Mum.

We got home just in time to have a snack, then Mum had to leave. As she was donning her hat and coat she said, "I should be home by half past three." Left alone, the first place I made for was the parlour where the piano was. Surprisingly it wasn't locked, so I adjusted the spiral stool, sat down and started to play.

What a joy to play on this lovely piano as against the duff one in the home. It was then I realised how much my playing sounded like Dad's.

I heard Mum tell the story many, many times – of how she turned the corner of our road, heard the piano being played, and thinking it was Dad said to my sister, "Oh my God, Bella, your father's home – it must be stocktaking at the firm. That means short time, and when your father's on short time he's like a bear with a sore head!"

"Then why is he playing the piano?" asked Bella.

"That's what's puzzling me," replied Mum.

I was gaily going through my repertoire when the street door opened and shut. As Mum and Bella passed the parlour door which was only slightly open, Mum said, "Is that you, Dad?" I didn't answer – but hearing Mum say that was the biggest thrill of my life, and I couldn't wait for her to see it was me.

I heard them go into the kitchen, and after they had taken off their outdoor clothes, Mum came back to the parlour. As she pushed open the door, she said, "The least you could do . . ." The rest of the sentence didn't come out – she just stood there dumbstruck.

I finished playing and when I looked at her she was crying. After a few seconds she dashed over to me and hugged me so tightly I could hardly breathe. "Wait until your father hears you – he'll be beside himself. Now don't say anything to him when he comes in – wait until he's had his tea, then when I give you the nod, you slip in here and play."

Dad got home from work at five thirty, and after he'd given Bella and me a kiss and told us how much he'd missed us, Mum said that tea was ready.

Every night after tea Dad would have his shave, ready for the morning. It was a regular routine, and tonight was no exception. When the kitchen table had been cleared, he took the pewter coffee pot off the dresser, placed it on the table, propped a small wall mirror up against it and started to shave.

When his face was well lathered Mum nodded to me, which was my cue to slip into the parlour. This was the moment I had been waiting for; up until then I could hardly contain myself. So with Mum keeping Dad occupied with domestic conversation, I slipped off to give him his surprise.

When I started to play (Mum told me afterwards) Dad was still lathering his face; he stopped the circular movement of the brush immediately, his head came up straight, his eyes opened wide, and he sat there staring at the passage door.

I had chosen a number he used to play himself, and since I had copied his style it must have seemed to him that he was hearing himself play. Motionless he sat there, with this incredulous look on his face – then finally turning to Mum he said, "Who's that?"

"Go and have a look," she said.

He got up from the table and walked slowly towards the passage; he stopped at the door and looked at Mum again.

"Go on! Go and have a look."

The parlour door was wide open, and when he appeared in the doorway, his face still thick with lather, he just stood staring at me in disbelief; he shook his head very slowly from side to side, then finally accepting that it was me, he flung back his head, and roaring with laughter, shouted back to the kitchen, "Jesus Christ, Mother, I've done it at last!"

6

Our Parties

The means of entertainment in my parents' day were parties. They would start on Saturday night and go on till Sunday. The uncles and aunts would come round with their kids and stay the night, the kids sleeping head to foot across the width of the beds. All the grown-ups chipped in a few bob for the food and the beer. They never drank spirits, therefore they weren't drunken affairs.

Our parties were eagerly awaited, mainly for two reasons: the excellent table laid on by Mum with the money subscribed and, of course, Dad's beautiful piano-playing. Each aunt and uncle had their party song, and after a few halves of ale and one or two port and lemons for the ladies, they needed very little prompting. Mum had a lovely voice and was always the first to be called upon by Uncle Jack. He would say, "Come on, Annie, give us 'Indian Queen'." Dad would strike up the introduction as Mum got up and stood by the piano. It was always a verse and a chorus solo, then all joined in on the second chorus. After Mum had broken the ice it was the turn of the aunts and uncles, and they loved it. So did I! Oh how I loved those parties!

Some of the songs in those days had an enormous number of verses. Uncle Fred sang one that was tuneless and slow, and with a chorus after every verse it seemed to drag on for ever. Uncle Jack couldn't stand it, and on one occasion before the party started, he was having a quiet chat with Dad in the scullery over a glass of beer. Not knowing I was within earshot (because they seldom swore in front of the children), he said, "Do me a favour, Sid – for Christ's sake don't play Fred's introduction till last."

"Why?" asked Dad.

"Well," said Jack, "by the time I've finished singing forty-five choruses of his bloody rotten dirge I've got no bleeding voice left for my own number. Not that that makes much difference really, because by the time Fred's finished with the poor sods those that aren't kipping are nipping outside for a piss."

As kids we had to play in the kitchen or the scullery because there was not enough room in the parlour for us as well, and what is more, it was definitely frowned on if we went in there.

One of our favourite games was "Fathers and Mothers" which we played under the table, the table being the "house". When I say *our* I really mean *their* – I was always the odd one out. I cribbed about this once, saying, "I'm fed up always having to play the visitor and popping in now and then for a glass of water. Why can't I have a wife?"

"Because you're too young," said one of the husbands.

Fortunately for me, being known as the little clown, I was the only one of us kids with a party piece. As always on these occasions, I eagerly awaited Dad's call: "Reggie! Come and do your bit."

My party piece consisted of singing "Maggie – Yes Ma!" Then Dad would play the introduction to "Whistling Rufus" which was the cue for me to go into my act, a Chaplinesque dance (although at that time I was too young to have seen him), and as I danced around in a circle in the centre of the parlour I would, every now and again, kick myself up the arse. The company would roar with laughter each time I did this, and the more they laughed the more arse kicks I would give myself.

When the music came to an end they would all clap and call out "more", especially Uncle Jack; still laughing he would say, "Come on, Riggie" (he never called me Reggie), "let's have it again." But Dad always said, "No, don't laugh at him any more, Uncle Jack, otherwise he'll start being silly." I used to think that was a cruel thing to say: after all the adulation I was crushed by those few words and at that moment wished the floor would open and swallow me up. Actually he was very proud of me, and loved me very much. He was afraid that I might become precocious and, as he would say, "big-headed".

Two weeks after the discovery of my ability to play the piano Mum and Dad arranged a party at our house for all the friends and relations. They didn't tell me, but later I found out that they had kept secret the fact that I could play the piano, and knowing how much everyone appreciated my little song and dance routine, were anxious to see their reactions to my piano-playing. My older brother Sid often says what a joy it was to see Mum and Dad standing in the parlour doorway, flushed with pride, watching the stunned faces of all and sundry as I flashed up and down the keyboard.

It was a joy for me also because I knew that never again would I hear those dreaded words – "No, don't laugh at him any more, Uncle Jack, otherwise he'll start being silly."

7

THE WIG

Actually I had two Uncle Jacks. One was as tall as the other was short. Uncle Jack (the taller) developed alopecia during the 1914–18 war. This left him completely bald, so he wore a wig. It was supposed to have been issued to him by the Army, but how true that was I'll never know. Where he got it is of no consequence – all I know is that it was a wig and it was ginger.

Some of today's hairpieces leave a lot to be desired, so you can imagine what a 1920s wig looked like. When outdoors, Uncle Jack always wore his cap on top of it, and when he removed it his head resembled the head of a ventriloquist's doll. His hairpiece fascinated me so much I couldn't take my eyes off it, and I used to get terribly embarrassed, especially when he sat me on his lap, as he often did, to ask me how I was getting on at school. The trouble was I couldn't stop my eyes wandering to his wig. I would force my eyes back to his face, but within seconds there I was staring up at his "rug" again.

It was obvious he was very self-conscious about his baldness because to my knowledge nobody ever saw him without a covering of some sort on his head. He never slept in the wig. Because he and his wife lived some way away, if they came to one of our parties, they would stay for the night. Before retiring to bed he would ask Mum for a small saucepan of hot water. It was a regular routine for Mum so she'd give him the one already heated on the stove. He'd thank her and disappear into the scullery. After a few minutes he would emerge and in place of the wig would be his white breast pocket handkerchief, knotted at each corner.

"Well, I'm off to bed," he'd say, wishing Mum and Dad good night, and before they had time to reply, he'd be gone. Dad said to Mum once, "When Jack comes in from the scullery with that handkerchief on his head saying, 'Well, I'm off to bed now,' I feel like saying, 'Don't you mean the beach?' "

Looking back on our parties, it seems a miracle, in such a tiny house as ours, that so many people found somewhere to sleep, considering we only had two small bedrooms and a boxroom upstairs. The one on the left of the landing was Mum and Dad's room, known as the front room. The one to the right was the middle room. Although this was called Gran's room, my sisters had their bed in it too. Opposite Gran's bed a door opened into the small boxroom. This room with its single bed shared by my elder brother Sid and me, was always referred to as the "boys' room".

The house was lit by gas. The kitchen and parlour had gas brackets with mantles and fancy glass shades. The scullery and each bedroom had just a pipe sticking out of the wall which turned up at the end with a nozzle, and when lit, produced a blue fan-shaped flame. The light was adequate, but when the gas was turned down low for sleeping, the room changed its character, becoming sinister and menacing, with weird shadows created by the dim flickering light.

I remember as a kid staring at these shadows and, after a while, in my imagination they would turn into cloaked monsters moving slowly towards me and, just as they were about to pounce, I would dive under the bedclothes, my heart pounding away with fear. My sister Doris was even worse . . . she was petrified, especially on Sunday nights. Her fear stemmed from the Sunday morning drill when all of us had to take our opening medicine . . . liquorice powder. It was vile stuff to take, with vicious after-effects. The griping stomach pains would start soon after lunch. It also blew you up with wind, always making you feel you wanted to pass it, but you soon learned not to give way to this urge because if you did, by the time you'd discovered it was a mistake it was too late – you had followed through.

Wanting to go to the lavatory was a feeling that lasted all day and all night. During the day we used the outside toilet but having no toilet inside the house, at night we used the pots – we called them "pos". Two of these pots were always kept underneath the foot of Gran's bed. Gran had all the luck!

You can imagine my sister Doris' dread of Sunday nights, having to get up in this dimly lit room to use the po. To overcome a certain amount of her fear, before going to bed she would safety-pin her nightdress to Bella's so that when she, or Bella come to that, had to use the po the other one was forced to follow. Really, there was no cause to feel alarmed . . . with the two of them at it, no self-respecting ghost would go anywhere near them.

However, back to Uncle Jack's wig. It was the night after one of our parties. Both Uncle Jacks were given the girls' bed. All the children were sleeping head to foot in Gran's bed, which was next to it. Before retiring tall Uncle Jack, as always, draped his wig over the brass knob of the bed, using it as a wig block. During the early hours of the morning it slipped off on to the floor. Not long after, sister Doris, wanting to wee-wee, went to the foot of the bed and pulled out the po. Just as she did so, Uncle Jack's wig caught her eye. To her it looked like some hideous furry creature. She screamed and tore back to bed, shaking brother Sid. She was so hysterical she could hardly speak.

Sid woke up with a start. "What's the matter, what's the matter?"

"It's a thing, it's a thing," she spluttered.

"A thing! Where!"

Pointing to the foot of the bed she cried, "There, there! On the floor . . . next to the po." Leaping out of bed, he grabbed his boot, saw this thing in the poor light and without hesitation lashed out at it with the steel-studded heel of his boot. When the thing made no attempt to escape, Sid, beginning to doubt, peered at it more closely, and on realising he'd been knocking hell out of Uncle Jack's wig, carefully picked it up and placed it back over the brass knob.

With the hilarity of the night's singing and dancing, coupled, of course, with a nice drink or two, when the grown-ups finally found somewhere to put their heads down, they went out like a light, so this schemozzle went unnoticed.

The following morning revealed the damage done to Uncle Jack's hairpiece. When Uncle Jack returned from the scullery having put it on, it didn't bear the slightest resemblance to a wig. The steel studs covering the heel of Sid's boot had cut it to shreds. It looked like a camouflage net draped over his head. Knowing something was radically wrong, he picked up Dad's shaving mirror from the dresser, took one look and immediately went back into the scullery. When he reappeared the knotted handkerchief was back on his head and without a word he walked through the kitchen and out into the passage. Within seconds he was standing behind the kitchen table wearing his cap, the knotted white handkerchief back in his breast pocket.

Mum and Dad were mystified as to how the wig became so mutilated. Uncle Jack never did query it. Perhaps he was glad it had come to pass. He never wore another wig. Anyway I liked him better in his cap.

8

THE CRYSTAL SET

It was one Saturday afternoon about two o'clock. Sid had just got home from work. He placed three paper bags on the kitchen table, two brown and one white.

"What's in the paper bags, Sid?" I asked, at the same time reaching out for the little white one.

"Don't you dare touch that," came the reply, as though it was something that would go off any second. I snatched my hand away like I'd touched a red hot cinder.

Mum placed the dinner she'd been keeping hot in front of him. He picked up his knife and fork saying, "Thanks, Mum," and ravenously got stuck in.

I was curious now . . . what secret did the bags hold to make him snap so? I pulled a chair up to the table next to him and furtively slid on to it. I sat there not saying a word, just eyeing the bags I was dared not to touch. Every so often I glanced up at him and then at the bags, hoping the movement would attract his attention. I wasn't going to give up. I was determined to find out the mystery of the bags, especially the little white one.

After a while it worked. He flung down his knife and fork and said, "Now look here, it's no good to keep looking at me and the bags because I'm not doing a thing until I've eaten my dinner, washed and changed."

So he was going to do something – that was interesting – but what? I had to know, I'd burst if I didn't. Wheedling, as a seven-year-old would, I said, "Is what's in those bags anything to do with what you're going to do when you've had your dinner?"

He turned to Mum. "Gawd, this kid, he never gives up does he?"

"You might as well tell him, you know what he is, he'll drive you mad until you do, besides I'd like to know too."

Sid munched away at his dinner. "If I tell you, you won't know what I'm talking about."

"Do you think we're daft . . . of course we will."

Sid swallowed what he'd been chewing and leant back in his chair. "Well if you must know . . . I'm going to make a crystal set."

"A crystal set!" we said together. "What's a crystal set?"

37

He threw up his hands in despair. "What did I tell you?"

"Well we wasn't expecting it to be something we had never heard of," said Mum. "What is it?"

Sid resigned himself to his fate. "It's very difficult to explain, because although I know what it does, I don't know enough about it myself to tell you how it works; it's scientific . . . it's to do with the waves in the air."

Mum thought about that, then very puzzled she said, "D'you mean marcel waving?"

"No Mum, not *hair*, air – like in the atmosphere." He looked at Mum's vacant expression, shaking his head. "I knew you wouldn't understand."

"All right, what does it do?"

"It enables you to hear what is being transmitted!" He pushed his plate away.

"What does?" asked Mum.

"Oh Gawd," he said, "the crystal set!"

"Well what is being transmitted?"

Sid was becoming exasperated. "Oh Mum, this is ridiculous . . . how the hell do I know what's being transmitted?"

"Now don't you start losing your temper with me. It was you who said it lets you hear what's being transmitted, whatever that means."

Sid had no intention of attempting to answer that. "Look, Mum." He paused, trying to think how best he could put it; then, making up his mind, said, "You can't hear what's being transmitted until you have what's called a receiver . . . A receiver is a crystal set . . . that's what is in those bags."

Immediately he said it he knew he had made another mistake, so quickly before Mum could say a word he went on, "What I mean is, when I've made the parts up which are in those bags, then it will be a crystal set, and with a bit of luck you'll be able to hear what is being transmitted with these." And from the largest paper bag he produced a pair of earphones.

"Now watch . . . you put the earphones on like this," he said, demonstrating. Then showing Mum the two brass tags at the ends of the leads, "You attach these to the crystal set and when you find the right spot on the crystal with the cat's-whisker, then you can hear what's being transmitted through these." He touched the earphones. "Now do you understand?" he said with a smile, thinking he had explained it quite well.

Mum eyed Sid and you could tell by the incredulous look on her face that she didn't believe one word of what he said, but it was his deliberation in explaining she misconstrued. She was convinced he was ridiculing her; and that she could never tolerate.

Mum was very sensitive about her lack of education and would have loved to have studied more. Her idea of an educated person was someone who used big words. She loved big words and when in the company of people who she thought were educated she would come out with all the big words she knew. We used to sit there and cringe listening to her, thinking to ourselves . . . what a load of rubbish she's talking. It was only in later years, when reminiscing about her, that we looked up all the words she used and discovered, much to our amazement and shame, that most of the time she was right; the laugh was on us . . . we were the ignorant ones and not her. Naturally she made the odd faux pas now and again.

I remember one occasion in the summer of 1949, my first season at the Lido, Cliftonville. I had just begun to attract the attention of the powers-that-be in show business and one night after the show I invited Mum and Dad out to dinner. Ted Kavanaugh, the famous scriptwriter of the equally famous radio show *ITMA*, came to see me work. After the show I introduced him to Mum and Dad, at the same time inviting him to join us for a meal. He declined, but being the gentleman he was, accompanied us to the hotel, singing my praises to them on the way. When we reached the hotel, he said, "Well Mr and Mrs Varney, it has been a great pleasure meeting you, goodbye." Mum very graciously said, "Granted." As he walked away Dad said, "He was only saying goodbye, he hadn't shit himself!" Any other time Mum would have counter-attacked, but in this situation she was in no position to do so. Dad, realising he'd unwittingly hurt her, took her arm and linked it through his and as we entered the hotel I saw him squeeze her hand.

This time, with Sid, it was different. Fuming, she tore into him: "No, I don't understand. How dare you make a laughing stock of me, just because I've never heard of a crystal set. As far as we're concerned you can take your bits and pieces elsewhere. I wish we'd never asked . . . and what's more, we are no longer interested." With that she picked up Sid's plate and stormed out to the scullery.

Sid sat there aghast at Mum's tirade. As for me, I was astonished at what she said. I mean, since declaring my ignorance of a crystal set, I hadn't opened my mouth. But what really shattered me was the way she kept saying, we're not this, and we're not that. Well I *was* this and I *was* that and I didn't want him to take his bits and pieces elsewhere. I wanted to be there watching him make the crystal set – yes, and driving him mad with questions.

Sid knew really, and understood that what he had just been trying to tell Mum must to her have sounded outrageous, especially as he was lost himself when it came to the technical side of this new invention.

He went to the scullery door. "I'm sorry, Mum, I wasn't trying to make a fool of you, honestly. The reason I can't explain it properly is because truthfully I don't understand how it works myself . . . I just know it does. When I've made the crystal set up, then you'll see."

Her back was towards him as she washed his dirty plate and without turning round she said flatly, "I have just told you. I am not interested."

"All right then," he said, "I'll show you," and with great determination he turned, went to the table and took out all his bits and pieces.

"What's that?" I said as he took a piece from the bag and placed it on the table.

"That, oh yes, that's what's called a condenser."

"And that?" pointing to another piece he'd taken out.

"Yes," he said, "now that's a vari-meter; these are coils and these here are just ordinary coils of wire, this one's for wiring up and this larger one is the aerial."

But it was the little white paper bag I was interested in, and just as I was thinking, I'll scream if he doesn't show me soon, he picked it up. I knelt up on the chair so as to get a closer look, and leant forward, my eyes full of wonder, as he put his hand inside the bag and very gently took out a small object and placed it on the palm of his other hand. "Ooh," I said in awe, "what is it?"

"This is the cat's-whisker," he said, as though it was the answer to the world's problems. It was a little glass tube held in place by a nickel-plated stand, with a miniature knob protruding from one end.

Pointing with his little finger to the glass tube he said, as a lecturer would, "Now you see that very fine wire gently touching that tiny sparkling piece of stone?" I nodded. "Well, that fine wire is called the cat's-whisker, and the tiny piece of stone is known as the crystal."

"What's the little knob for?" I asked.

"Ah yes, well you see the cat's-whisker is attached to that and the knob is for manoeuvring the cat's-whisker over the crystal."

With that he carefully placed it on the table and took a folded piece of stiffish paper from his overalls. He opened it out, flattening the creases with the palm of his hand.

"What's that?"

I could tell he was losing his patience with me the way he said, "Oh that's the plan, it shows you how to wire it up."

I was about to pester him with another question when he stopped me, exasperated: "Look, if you want to do something useful go out in the yard and bring me back the lid of that old Libby's box."

The Libby's box had at one time been filled with tins of Libby's milk. The grocer in the corner shop had given it to Mum for firewood, but as it was made of two-ply no-one could break it up so it had been stuck out in the yard for ages.

I brought the lid back saying, "What's this for then?"

He threw up his hands in desperation. "Now look here, this is the last question I'm going to answer. If you ask one more I'll turf you out, have you got it?"

"Yes," I said sheepishly.

"Right now, listen carefully," he said. "I am using this lid as a panel . . . I bore holes in it according to this plan, then I fix the condenser, coils and vari-meter to it so that I can wire it up at the back. The panel should be a Bakelite one, but as I couldn't afford it I am making do with this lid . . . now do you understand?"

"Yes," I said, but of course I didn't.

I sat there watching fascinated as he, totally absorbed, began deftly to twist the wire with his fingers round the small screws and terminals of the parts he'd attached to the Libby's lid.

We must have been there hours because Mum, without saying a word, had given us tea and cleared away and still he hadn't finished making the crystal set. Several times he'd wired it up wrong and had had to retrace his steps and start all over again. I marvelled at his patience and as much as I was dying to speak to him, after what he had said to me last time, I knew I daren't.

He surprised me suddenly by saying, more to himself than to me, "I've only got to fix this wire to the cat's-whisker, then, this time, I think I've got it."

Just then my sisters Bella and Doris came in. They took one look at Sid and all the things wired to the Libby's lid and said to Mum, "What's Sid doing?"

Mum, still with the hump, said, "Don't ask me, ask your brother."

It was obvious to them that something had upset her but they knew better than to ask, so they turned to Sid. "What're you making?"

I couldn't wait to tell: "He's making a crystal set!"

"We didn't ask you," one of them said.

Ignoring their insult I carried on. "When he's finished making it you put these earphones on, fiddle about with the cat's-whisker and you can hear what's being transmitted."

They didn't query it, but turned to Sid. "Ooh, is that right?"

Tetchily Sid said, "Yes it is, so don't you two start," and nodding his head towards me continued, "I'm fed up having to put up with his questions all afternoon." At that he picked up the aerial and marched out to the yard with me following him like a faithful little dog. I was so happy, I'd never known such an exciting day.

I watched him as he climbed the clothes-line pole at the end of the yard and fixed the aerial to the top. When he slid down he said, taking the other end of the aerial, "I've got to keep it as high as I can before I pass it through the kitchen window." He gave me the other end of the aerial to hold while he took the tin bath off the rag nail on the outside of the scullery wall, hooked the wire over the nail and passed it through the top of the kitchen window.

"Right, well that's that," he said, muttering to himself. "Now to earth it." Everything he said went right over my head, but I didn't care, it wouldn't be long now before we would be hearing whatever there was to be heard.

He connected the earth wire to the gas pipe, came back and then connected it to a terminal next to where he had attached the aerial. He stood back admiring the finished job, clapped and rubbed his hands together saying, "Now comes the moment of truth."

He sat down in front of the crystal set with a sigh of satisfaction. Immediately we closed in on him, pushing and shoving to get the best view. We were all terribly excited; the girls were gabbling on, falling over their words . . . "Ooh isn't it marvellous!" "Yes, I wonder if it will be somebody talking."

"It might be music" – I had to be part of the excitement.

Sid raised his voice: "Stop pushing and shoving; stand back, I can hardly breathe, and shut up, the lot of you."

We quietened down, but not a lot – the importance of the moment was too great. He put the earphones on and as he bent forward and delicately manoeuvred the cat's-whisker over the crystal you could have heard a pin drop. It seemed like he'd been sitting there for ages twiddling the knobs with negative results. I could see the blades of the condenser moving backwards and forwards in response to Sid tuning the dial.

"Can you hear anything yet, Sid?" I asked.

Slowly shaking his head, his face full of disappointment, he said, "No, nothing, not even a crackle." He stood up, took the earphones off and for the umpteenth time checked everything that should be checked. He must have made some adjustment because when he returned he said, putting on the earphones, "Well, let's try once more."

We no longer crowded him; we sat, our legs too tired to stand. His turning the knob with one hand and twiddling the cat's-whisker with the other had lost its magic, and as nothing was happening our interest was rapidly diminishing. Just as we had given up all hope he yelled out, "I've got it, I've got it!"

We jumped up as though we had been given an electric shock and rushed to him, nearly knocking him off his chair. "What is it? What have you got? Is it talking or is it music?"

"Let me listen, Sid!" I was nearly crying.

"Will you be quiet, all of you, I can't hear if you keep making all that noise." We fell silent, frightened he might lose what he'd got. Impatiently we waited, watching him, his eyes staring into the distance. At last with his face beaming he said, "It's music, I think it's a foreign station . . . It's a bloke playing some instrument!"

We were banging our heads together trying to get them closer to the earphones. Whimpering I said, "Oh please, Sid, let me listen."

"Shush," he said, then he listened; after a second or two he said in awe, "It's a bloke playing the mandoline."

Our faces lit up; we could hear a mandoline as well. Unable to control our excitement we screamed out, "Yes, we can hear it too!"

"Now be quiet, I'll try and get it louder because at the moment it's very faint." As he put his hand on the dial and cat's-whisker he paused, lifted his head, cocked it to one side as though in thought, then slowly turning to us he said in amazement, "You can hear it too?"

"Yes," we said with our heads still close to his, listening to the mandoline.

"Yeah, and it's ever so loud," I said.

"That's funny. I can barely hear it and I've got the earphones on." Suspiciously he removed the earphones and listened. We watched him as he began to realise what it was, and when he turned his head we turned ours too, following his gaze as he disgustedly stared at the kitchen wall listening to the man next door, Westie, playing his mandoline.

He sat there looking at the wall, then seeing the funny side of it began to laugh. We were amazed – we expected him to smash the set up, but no, there he sat with tears streaming down his face, his laughter so contagious we started to laugh with him until eventually we were hysterical.

Mum had got over the hump and was sitting in her chair next to the kitchen range, darning socks. Hearing the screams of laughter she looked up. "What's so funny?"

Sid was holding his side. "Oh Mum, I thought I'd got a foreign station . . . Spain, I thought . . ." He went into fits of laughter again.

Mum said, "For goodness' sake control yourself."

In between his outbursts of laughter, he finally got the story out. "Listen, Mum, can't you hear him, Westie, he's still at it."

Mum, listening, said, "Oh yes," and went on darning. She didn't think it was all that funny; perhaps she hadn't quite got over the hump.

Dad came in from visiting a sick workmate.

"How's Gimlet then?" asked Mum. (That wasn't his real name, he was nicknamed Gimlet because he was tall and thin.)

"Oh he's not too bad now." He hung his hat and coat up in the passage. "He'll be back at work on Monday," and seeing the Libby's lid with all the bits and pieces wired to it, he asked, "What's all this paraphernalia, Bogey?" (Bogey was Dad's pet name for Sid, had been since he was born, and he never called him anything but Bogey all his life.)

"It's a crystal set, Dad." Dad, unlike Mum, didn't ask what it was, so it was obvious he had heard of crystal sets. "It's taken me all afternoon to make it and now I can't get the damned thing to work!" Then he told Dad the funny story about Westie and his mandoline, which Dad thought was hilarious.

"Have you checked it with the blueprint?"

"Yes, Dad, over and over again, it's wired exactly as the plan."

Pointing to the window Dad queried, "Well what's that wire coming in through the top there?"

"That's the aerial, which is attached to this terminal here."

"Well what's this one leading to the scullery?"

"Oh yeah, that's the earth wire . . . that has to be fixed to the gas pipe."

Dad thought for a while, then said with a twinkle in his eye, "Well if we don't trip over this one and break our bloody necks, we stand a good chance of hanging ourselves with this one coming through the top of the window."

Sid didn't laugh, he was too engrossed in the blueprint. "It doesn't necessarily have to be the gas pipe," he said, reading from the plan. "It says here, 'It can be the water tap, or anything that goes to earth, making sure that it's free from grease or any other substance that will impair the contact.' " As he read the last bit he shot up and dashed out to the scullery saying, "That's it . . . yes, that's it . . . it must be." We shuffled after him. "I thought I was right, see? It's been painted . . . the gas pipe, it's been painted."

Quickly he took the potato knife from the drawer, got a piece of emery-paper from Mum's household cleaning bag and frantically set to work. Satisfied the pipe was now thoroughly clean he tore back to the set, with all of us falling over in pursuit, including Dad. Quickly he put the earphones on, having difficulty in adjusting them, so close were our heads to his. He had hardly touched the dial of the condenser and the crystal when he yelled out with delight, "I've got it, I've got it!"

Everyone was talking at once.

"What have you got . . . is it music?"

"Oh come on, tell us."

"Where's it coming from . . . is it loud?"

"Oh please, Sid, let me listen."

"No," he was emphatic, "I want Mum to hear it first."

So standing up and taking the earphones off and holding them out to Mum he said, "Come on, Mum, come and listen to the music." She came over and put the earphones on and as she listened a big smile spread across her face. "I was right wasn't I, Mum?"

Handing him back the earphones she said humbly, "Yes, you were right." Then with a wicked glint in her eye she carried on, "But I still don't understand it, and by the way, how about washing yourself and taking off those dirty overalls."

When Sid came down from washing and changing Dad was sitting at the table with the earphones on. "Is it still music, Dad?"

A big grin split Dad's face as he said, "You're never going to believe this, Bogey . . . but it's a bloke playing the mandoline."

9

THE BREAD PUDDING

It was Mum's magnificent management of the weekly income that kept us solvent. This meant her getting the value out of every shilling – which she did.

Never get yourself in debt, she used to say, if you do you'll regret it. Always wait until you can afford things before you buy them, and whatever you do, don't have anything on tick; you'll find out, when it's too late, that the tally-man is always knocking on your door.

She drummed this into us all the time. It wasn't a case of her not doing what she preached, she *did* what she preached. For instance, on the top shelf of the dresser were four tins, each tin marked as to its purpose: "Coal Money", "Boots and Shoes Money", "Gas Money", and the fourth tin, tucked away in the corner, labelled "Christmas Money". Each week she put a little in the four tins to provide for the larger bills when they came round. Occasionally she would have to juggle the money from one tin to another, sort of rob Peter to pay Paul. Many's the time I've heard her say to Gran, "Don't forget to remind me, Mum, to pay back the Boots and Shoes Money that I borrowed to pay the Gas bill."

Every so often she would have what she called the "settling up time". When this was due, down came all the tins from the dresser on to the kitchen table. Having got them arranged she would say, "Now let me see, Coal owes Boots and Shoes three shillings. Boots and Shoes owes Gas two and sixpence, Gas owes Coal two shillings. Coal and Gas owe Christmas tin four shillings," and so on. Each time you'd hear the chink of money as it was passed from one tin to another. When the tins were finally balanced, she'd return them to the dresser feeling very satisfied with herself. "Well that's settled," she would say.

This routine never failed to amuse Dad. He would say, "Boots and Shoes owes this, Gas owes that, how the bloody hell you get them to tally I'll never know."

Mum's answer was, "You don't have to – so long as I do, that's all that matters."

It was this tremendous struggle each week to make ends meet which created what my parents called "crimes": like leaving lights on, fires roaring up the chimney when not necessary, or wasting hot water. I can hear Dad's voice now, bellowing out after some crime had been committed, "Who's been in the parlour and come out leaving all the bloody lights on?" His complaints always ended up with the same old cliché – "Jesus Christ, d'you think I'm made of money?"

Wasting food was the biggest crime of all. That wouldn't be tolerated at any price by either of my parents. Should we ask for something to eat and then find our eyes had been bigger than our belly, we'd go to all lengths to hide it from them, fearing the consequences.

The outcome of fear can be either tragic or comic – like one occasion when Mum had badly sprained her ankle. The doctor advised her to go to bed and rest it. Mum argued that she could rest it just as well downstairs, but the doctor was adamant, saying, "No, Mrs Varney, if you stay downstairs you'll be tempted to hobble about on it, then God knows how long it will take to mend." He did say, however, that she could get up in the evening when plenty of help was available.

On occasions like this, when Mum was forced to go to bed, which was very rarely, the whole house was in a turmoil. Although we were brought up to be very domesticated, we lacked organisation; the administration therefore was carried out from her bedroom. Orders were shouted down from upstairs, and queries shouted up from downstairs. With the exception of the times when we took her meals up or brought the dirty dishes down, all conversations were carried out from a distance.

Mum's temporary disability meant someone had to be her legs. Gran, being in her late seventies, couldn't cope with the running of the house on her own without some assistance, so one of us had to be kept away from school. Sid had been out to work for some time now, so that left Bella, Doris and myself to choose from – our younger brother Stanley was far too young. The others had in turn performed this duty in the past, so this time Mum chose me. I was delighted, I didn't like school anyway.

My first morning started pretty quietly but by half past eight the house was alive with chatter and the hustle and bustle of the girls getting themselves, and young Stanley, ready for school. The street likewise was filled with noises of all description made by masses of children also making their way to school. At nine o'clock the noises ceased, the house became strangely quiet and the street outside was deserted, like a ghost town. This was all new to me. I had never experienced this type of quietness before – it was unreal. Gran had left to go shopping when the others went to school, so I stood there in the kitchen alone, feeling awkward, and not knowing what to do. I felt as though I had suddenly been placed in a vacuum. Mum's voice pierced the silence: "Reggie" – the house became real again.

I shouted back with relief, "Yes, Mum?"

"Have you cleared the table and washed up yet?"

"No, not yet. I'm just about to," I called.

"Well before you do, come up and get my cup and saucer, then I'll tell you what I want done."

Mum was renowned for her bread puddings. Everybody loved them, and on this particular morning, as I stood beside her bed, she told me this was what she was going to make.

The next half hour I spent running up and down the stairs with all the ingredients needed to make the bread pudding. I lost count of the number of trips I did, but during the dashing up and down I remember thinking that school wasn't such a bad place after all. After the umpteenth time I said, "Is that the lot, Mum?"

"Yes, but before you start cleaning the kitchen, light the gas oven – by the time I've finished mixing the pudding the oven should be just the right temperature for it."

Halfway through my chores I was called up and given my next lot of orders, which were to take down the things she'd finished with, and after doing the necessary washing up and putting away, to go back and collect the bread pudding.

I stood by the side of the bed watching her as, with a damp cloth, she wiped the excess bits of pudding from the rim of the dish. Finally she picked it up and, handing it to me, said, "There." She said "There" as if she expected me to give her a round of applause. The passing of the pudding was like a ceremony in itself and as I slowly walked down the stairs with it held in front of me, I wondered if I should be saying a few words over it.

I reached the bottom of the stairs with a sigh of relief. Only the kitchen to negotiate now. Slowly, step by step, I moved towards the scullery and just when I thought I'd got it licked, disaster struck. The toe of my boot caught in the torn piece of lino at the top of the scullery steps. Everything happened in a flash. My treasured charge was wrenched from my grasp and, as I went flying through the air, I could see the stone floor of the scullery rushing to meet me.

I braced myself, waiting for the crunch, but I was lucky – my fall was broken by my head hitting the wringer. I lay there for a moment concussed and unable to think. As my head slowly cleared the horror of what had just happened hit me. The pain from the bump on my head and my bruised body left me immediately. My only thoughts now were for the bread pudding. I looked around and when I saw the bottom of the meat dish staring up at me, with its contents hidden beneath it, I was struck with terror: to waste a crust was a punishable offence, but a whole bread pudding – this could be a lynching job! I started to panic. What could I do? I prayed to God, saying, "Oh please God help me, help me," but I got no answer. Perhaps he was busy doing a miracle for somebody else.

Finally I came to the conclusion that I had no alternative but to go upstairs, throw myself on Mum's mercy and tell her – but tell her what? How could I tell her that her beloved bread pudding was not in the oven, but having an affair with the coconut matting in the scullery?

My thoughts were broken by Mum's voice calling out, "Reggie, have you put the pudding in the oven yet?" That made up my mind. How could I tell her now? She sounded so happy.

"I'm just going to," I shouted back. I went to the drawer, took out a big ladle and scraped up every bit of the gooey bread pudding from the coconut matting, and put it back in the dish. This done, I quickly put it in the oven, calling out, "It's in, Mum."

"There's a good boy. I'll tell you when to take it out."

Then, like a criminal removing the evidence, I set about getting the embedded bits of pudding out of the weave of the matting. It was a painstakingly difficult job getting all the bits out by hand, so I finally decided to wash them out under the tap. The water left a dark patch but luckily it was a beautiful day and it wouldn't take long to dry over the line in the back yard. Then I checked the scullery and, satisfied that all was in order, flopped into Dad's armchair. After a while the shock started to have its effect. I sat there trembling.

The time passed with my mind conjuring up all sorts of un-pleasantnesses should the saga of the bread pudding come to light. What plausible excuse could I make? Would the truth be believed?

"Reggie." Mum's voice interrupted my thoughts.

I went to the foot of the stairs. "Yes, Mum?"

"It should be done by now, take it out of the oven. Stick a knife into it and bring the knife up to me."

"All right, Mum." This was it then. Yes, this was going to be the test. I went to the scullery, turned the gas off, took a tea towel from the hook on the back of the door, wrapped it round my hands, pulled the dish out of the oven and placed it on the stove. When I looked at it I couldn't believe what I was seeing. The pudding was a beautiful golden-brown. My eyes welled up with tears of joy. I looked up at the ceiling. So He had heard me after all! Excitedly I called up to Mum, "Mum, oh Mum, it's beautiful." With that I stuck the knife in it and tore up the stairs.

For the rest of the day I was in high spirits with the knowledge that my misdeed would go undetected, no one would ever know what happened to the bread pudding . . . It was my secret . . . I was safe.

Unfortunately for me, that evening Isabel paid us one of her rare visits. Isabel was my cousin and she adored Mum's bread pudding, so naturally Mum gave her a piece. Isabel took it, saying, "Oh thank you, Auntie, it looks delicious, I can hardly wait." And before you could say knife a large portion of it disappeared into her mouth. As she chewed it, with "ums" of pleasure, a look of ecstasy upon her face, we watched her.

Suddenly the "ums" stopped – her eyes wandered to the top of her head, as though thinking, then she started to twist her face into grotesque shapes. We wanted to laugh but daren't in case she was having a fit. After a while the funny faces stopped, and she opened one side of her mouth, pulled something from it, and placed it on the side of the plate. She continued this comedy routine as we watched fascinated, wondering what the hell it was she kept pulling from her mouth.

I went cold. In a flash I realised what it was – the coarse hairs from the scullery matting. Mum couldn't quite see what was happening. Her view of Isabel was obstructed by brother Sid, who had not long arrived home from work, and was sitting eating his dinner at the table. She could, however, see enough to gather that something was not quite as it should be, so leaning forward she said, "Are you all right, Isabel?" Isabel could only nod.

To make matters worse, Sid, watching her decorate the plate with these hairs, said, "Before you eat any more of that, Isabel, I'd nip it round the barber's and get him to give it a short back and sides."

Immediately Mum heard Sid's facetious remark she said sharply, "Don't eat any more, Isabel, spit out what you have in your mouth and give me the plate." Mum took one look at what Isabel had been trying to eat, turned, looked me straight in the face, and with a voice that sent a chill right through me, said, "Get up to bed, I'll speak to you in the morning." Full of guilt and shame I got up and walked out of the room.

I lay in bed unable to sleep, so tortured was my mind. It had been one catastrophe after another. Hundreds of disturbing thoughts ricocheted around in my head. Oh why did Isabel have to come round? If she hadn't, no one would have known. Then I realised how silly that was . . . the hairs were there, somebody would have found them. My brain was full of, if this hadn't happened, or that hadn't happened. Whatever I brooded on, it always came back to the punishment – what would it be? – and what could I say to lessen it? Finally nature overcame my despair. I dropped off to sleep.

The next morning, downstairs, nothing was said, even though I knew that my sisters were dying to know what crime I had committed. It was just after they had gone to school that I heard what I'd been dreading all night. "Reggie, come up here at once." There was no compassion in her voice.

I stood as far away from her as I could. She was sitting up in bed with her arms folded, staring at me, her eyes expressionless. She let me roast for a few seconds, then it came. "Well, I'm waiting." For a moment nothing would come out. "Well come on, out with it," she boomed.

"Well . . . well . . ." I started to stutter.

She cut in. "I'm not a complete fool. I know you dropped it on the floor – what I want to know is how?" Not allowing me time to answer she carried on, "Do you realise, because of what you did, how ashamed I was? Now come on, I'll ask you once more – what happened?"

With all the tension that had built up, I started crying bitterly. I tried to explain, in between sobs, how careful I had been carrying it downstairs. How, just as I thought I had it made, I caught my foot in the bit of lino sticking up on the scullery steps (Mum was perpetually on at Dad to tack it down – he always said he would but never did). As the whole truth of the catastrophe poured from my lips I broke down and sobbed uncontrollably.

I must have looked a pitiful sight standing there, my face awash with tears and my eyes swollen from sobbing. She watched me for a few moments, then holding out her arms to me, said, "Oh come to me, don't cry any more. It's all over now." I ran to her, burying my head in her bosom. She stroked my head saying, "There, there," as my tears released me from my misery and yesterday's torment.

10

THE RAGGED BOYS' SCHOOL OUTING

It was a gloriously sunny morning in July. The air was full of expectancy. Everything looked beautiful, even the back yard with its three chicken runs, which was always a depressing sight, and my excitement was such I could hardly contain myself. Mum said, "Listen, if you don't quieten yourself down you'll be ill, then you won't be able to go on the 'Ragged Boys' School Outing'." That subdued me for a while, but only until I was told to go and wash; this meant it was time to get ready for the outing.

When I washed I made sure that the back of my neck and my ears were done thoroughly; if not I knew Mum would whip me back to the scullery and, with a well-soaped flannel, make sure that not only the back and front of my neck were done but the ears as well, inside and out, not forgetting the creases round my nostrils; and she wasn't gentle. With her left hand on top of your head, it was amazing how she could screw it round to whatever position she wanted. "Never mind about the Ooh Mums," she'd say, "if you think for one moment I'm letting you go out like this, you've got another think coming."

Having satisfied herself that I had washed up to her standard, she said, "Take those dirty coms off and put these clean ones on."

"But why, Mum? These are clean, I only put them on on Sunday."

"Never mind about that, today's Wednesday, so do as you're told and put these clean ones on. I mean, supposing you get knocked down and someone has to undress you . . . how d'you think I'd feel knowing strangers were looking at you laying there in filthy coms."

Coms – short for combinations – were for infants. They were a two-in-one garment; vest and pants all in one that buttoned up down the front with a slit in the back which you pulled aside when necessary. By the age of about six most boys had outgrown them, but as I was such a titch I wore them until I was gone fourteen. In fact I was still small enough to wear them when I first went out to work.

I hated them because the last two inches of the legs were ribbed and always showed below my short trousers. As much as I hitched them up, after a while the ribbed part would wriggle its way down below my trousers again, making me an easy target for the boys at school. They'd shout out with sadistic delight, "Eh look, Varnish is still wearing coms!"

Happy now that I'd got on nice clean coms, Mum gave me my best trousers and best green jersey to put on. Next, she pinned a clean white hanky on the right side of my jersey, which I thought was very babyish but I didn't voice my opinion for two reasons; first, it would be easy to undo the safety pin and put the hanky in my pocket as soon as I was out of sight, and secondly, I didn't want a clump round the ear to send me off to my outing. But what really mattered was the next thing: pinned on the opposite side of my jersey was the pièce de résistance, my cherished round blue ticket with letters in bold black printed round the circumference . . . THE RAGGED BOYS' SCHOOL, and right across the centre in even bolder type, OUTING. Oh how proud I was!

I went to the mirror to see for myself what it looked like hanging on my chest and I wasn't disappointed. To me it was everything, and as I stood there a feeling of pride swept over me, knowing that I was one out of many to be chosen to go on the outing. I couldn't wait to get to the school gates where we were to meet, so I could swank to those who hadn't been chosen. Yeah, I'd show 'em. I'd flaunt in front of them with my ribbed coms down . . . let them call out now, "Varnish's wearing coms." Sneeringly I'd say, "Yes and Varnish's wearing a Ragged Boys' School ticket too! So there!"

My imaginings ended abruptly when Mum said, "Don't stand there admiring yourself, otherwise you're going to be late for the outing." She took a penny from her purse, gave it to me and as she followed me to the street door she said, "Don't forget to say goodbye to Mrs West." I knew her meaning. Mrs West who lived next door might give me a couple of coppers for my outing. I didn't like doing it. It wasn't that I minded saying goodbye; it was knocking on her door, knowing that I was begging, that I really didn't relish. Besides, you never knew what mood she'd be in, whether good or bad.

Many's the time she'd got us into trouble with her sarcasm. Like on the odd occasion on a Sunday evening when Mum and Dad went out. Brother Sid would be in charge of us kids and naturally we'd play childish games which called for a great deal of running around, causing screams of laughter and noise in general. The next morning when she saw Mum, she'd say craftily, "Did you have a nice time last night, Varney?"

Mum, puzzled as to how she knew, would say, "Oh yes . . . me and Sid went out for the evening."

"Yes, I guessed you'd gone out," she'd say with a snigger. "Well, the walls are so thin aren't they?"

Immediately we got home from school we knew Mrs West's tongue had been wagging by the way Mum tore into us, especially brother Sid.

Luckily, this morning she was standing at her street door as I came out into the brilliant sunshine, followed by Mum. "Hello Reggie," she said, "I see you are going on your outing." A big smile of satisfaction spread over my face. Not only was she in a good mood, she had also noticed my ticket without my having to draw her attention to it. "I must say you keep your children beautiful, Varney." She always called Mum "Varney". I suppose it gave her a feeling of superiority.

It was Mum's turn to take the praise, saying coyly, "Well I try."

Turning to me again she said, "Yes, I must say you look very smart." Then as quickly as the compliment was passed she took it back with one of her sly digs. "But for how much longer I wonder, eh Varney!" I thought, here we go again, the mixing old cow; then she gave me twopence.

My hopes of jeering at the boys who hadn't got a ticket were dashed to the ground, for, when I arrived at the school gates, all those already there had tickets pinned on them. After a little while I discovered that I wasn't one of a few, but of many, and those who hadn't been chosen weren't going to school anyway. I checked my coms immediately; they were going to be a bone of contention for the rest of the day.

Apart from its being a novelty, the train journey left a lot to be desired. Well it did for me, although I do remember being fascinated by the telegraph wires by the side of the track moving up and down past the carriage windows and wondering how that happened. The compartments were bare but adequate, with wooden seats and partitions reaching only halfway up, so by standing on the seat you could see the occupants in the next compartment. As the journey trundled on with nothing to do, the boisterous ones became restless and started to stand on the seats chi-hiking the boys in the next compartment. This led to climbing backwards and forwards from one compartment to another. Some of them egged me on to have a go, but I couldn't afford to indulge in such physical games for fear of my coms wriggling down. I sat very quietly until, relieved, we reached Loughton.

On arrival we were taken to a huge hut with a corrugated iron roof. It was like walking into an oven. Trestles with forms either side, which we sat at, ran the length of the hut. On the trestles, at intervals, were plates of bread and jam swarming with wasps. We were told we could help ourselves, but who was going to stick their hands into those nests of poison? I'd been stung on the neck when a tiny boy and was scared stiff of them, so as far as I was concerned they could keep their bread and jam. The one or two brave ones who did take a chance ended up tearing around the hut like lunatics yelling their heads off, arms flailing about, trying to get away from the pursuing pests.

We were given a mug of tea; it resembled coloured water. The older boys referred to it as gnats' piss. I couldn't corroborate that as I had never seen, or come to that, tasted gnats' piss.

Entertainment provided for our benefit consisted of a man who ran the donkey rides and a woman, most probably his wife, in charge of the swings and a stall where one could buy cold drinks. Although limited, it was adequate for the amount of money any of us had to spend. A donkey ride, a go on the swings, a bottle of pop, and I'd blown my threepence.

The wasps were nearly as bad outside as inside the hut, so to sit around was asking for trouble. The other boys, like myself, having spent their money, were chasing around the parched field kicking a football about. Once again, my activities were governed by my coms, so running around with them and the football was definitely out.

Conk, my closest school friend (he was called Conk because of the size of his nose), looked very tough but actually he was quite gentle; it was one of the reasons we became so close. Looking so rugged, nobody took advantage of him, which suited me as I was so timid; being his friend gave me a certain amount of protection.

Above all, me and Conk loved climbing; so we decided, as there were another two or three hours to be killed before tea, to climb one of the tall oaks on the far side of the common. We chose the tallest tree but the first branch was out of my reach, so Conk had to lift me up until I could get a grip and cock my leg over. He had no difficulty in reaching the branch and soon we were sitting side by side planning our ascent.

When we'd agreed on the best route, Conk said, "I'll go first, you follow me." Which I did, getting the odd slap across the face as he passed through the leaves. The higher we climbed the cooler it became. I said, "No wasps up here, Conk." "No," he said, "and it's better than kicking a ball about with that lot an' all."

The cries from below were gradually being shut out by the

density of the foliage. Up and up we went; it was very exhilarating and a marvellous sensation: no sound at all from below, only the rustling of the leaves as we continued upwards. There was no conversation now, we were too busy concentrating on our climb. I thought we must be near the top as faint shafts of sunlight kept piercing through the leaves. I shouted up, "Are you at the top yet, Conk?"

"Not yet," he said. The grunts of exertion coming from him told me I was not far behind. I heard more rustling as he pulled himself higher, then excitedly he called down, "Eh, I'm nearly at – "

He didn't finish the sentence. I heard the loud crack as his foot trod on a dead branch and Conk's terrifying yell as he fell. I gripped the trunk of the tree tightly to me as my whole body turned icily cold. As Conk's body plunged past me, his arms were frantically trying to grasp hold of a branch, or anything, and his eyes full of terror looked at me, searching for some help . . . I could give none. That look in his eyes and his fearful screaming will be with me always.

I clung to the tree terrified, listening as he crashed from one branch to another on his way down. His screaming suddenly stopped but I could still hear his body relentlessly smashing its way through, until I heard the sickening thud as he dropped, senseless, the last six feet to the ground.

It was eerily quiet. His screams must have chilled the blood of those below as they did mine. There I stood, high up; the leaves of the oak brushing my face, shaking from head to foot, unable to move. The stillness seemed endless, then suddenly pandemonium broke loose. Sounds of pounding feet running, voices hollering and shouting, getting louder as they drew closer to the tree. One voice above the others drifted up to me. "Quick, somebody call for an ambulance."

Someone else shouted, "Now be quiet, all of you." It was one of the teachers addressing the boys who had crowded round the base of the tree. "Does anyone know if he was up there on his own?"

One of the boys said, "No sir, I saw Varney walking with him towards the tree."

Boys just arriving were saying, "What's happened?"

"Someone's fallen from the top of the tree."

"Who?"

"Conk," said another.

The teacher, beginning to lose his temper, said, "Now I don't want to have to tell you again . . . be quiet!" Silence fell over the crowd. "Are you up there, Varney?"

Fear was affecting my throat, so my "Yes" came out so feeble he could hardly hear me. He called up again, "Are you up there, Varney?"

This time I managed to screech out a "Yes".

He heard that and said, "Are you all right?"

With the same screech I said, "Yes sir."

He knew I wasn't. "Now I know you must be scared, but try and make it down, there's a good lad."

No-one could help me, yet I knew I had to get down. If only I wasn't shivering so much.

"Come on, lad, if you take it slowly you'll be all right."

I knew that once I got on to the branch below I'd make it.

"Can you hear me, Varney?"

"Yes sir."

"There's a good lad," he said coaxingly. "Take it nice and easy and you'll make it." So, plucking up all the courage I could muster, I pushed the leaves away from my face and lowered myself on to the branch below. I perilously made my way down and as I did so I could hear the bells of an ambulance ringing in the distance.

As I hung from the bottom branch someone took me by the waist and lowered me to the ground. All the boys now started to push and shove, trying to get a better view. Another teacher blew a whistle then yelled out at the top of his voice, "Now this is definitely the last time you'll be told . . . GET BACK!" and with that he started pushing them away, a few in the front feeling the back of his hand in the process.

When I saw Conk lying crumpled up on the ground, his face lacerated and bleeding, and blackened with dirt from the tree as he fell, my shaking turned to hysteria. A lady, one of the organisers from the Ragged Boys' School Outing, came to me quickly and tried to console me, failing miserably. The more I looked at Conk lying there helpless with no-one seeming to do anything for him, the more hysterical I became. I tore myself away from her arms to go to Conk, but like lightning she grabbed me back saying, "No, no, you mustn't touch him."

Tears were gushing down my face. "But nobody's doing anything for him," I said, but so garbled, I doubt if she understood. "No, no, I want to stay with Conk."

Just then an ambulance bumped its way across the field to where we were. Two attendants jumped from the front of the vehicle and with great speed opened the doors at the back, pulled out a stretcher and placed it beside Conk. One of them went to Conk, lifted his eyelids then put an ear to his mouth. Gently he unfolded Conk whilst the other man placed a red blanket over him. When they'd put the stretcher in the ambulance, one of the teachers joined them, then they drove away.

Me and the lady from the Ragged Boys' watched as it slowly but carefully bumped its way back over the field to the asphalt road. Once on the road it sped away with its bells ringing furiously. The inquisitive crowd slowly began to disperse. For them the excitement was over, although it was an experience they couldn't wait to get home to tell.

I had quietened down considerably and was now in control of my speech.

"Let's you and me go and have a nice sweet mug of tea, eh?"

As I walked with her to the hut timidly I said, "Is he dead?"

"Good gracious me no. He's been badly hurt but he's in good hands now; he'll be all right, you'll see."

The hut was still baking hot and plagued with wasps. She sat me on a chair just outside the kitchen saying, "Now I'll get us that nice sweet mug of tea I promised."

My hands and knees were grimed with dirt from the climbing, and as I looked down at the filthy bit of coms hanging below my trousers, I thought of Conk and wondered if his mum had made him put on clean underwear.

11

DUCKS FOR CHRISTMAS

Out of all the school holidays, to me Christmas was the most exciting. I even liked school itself a fortnight prior to breaking up, because every day had something to do with Yuletide; sums, my dreaded subject, never came into it. You were either making paper chains or painting Christmas scenes. The paper chains decorated the windows and the longer lengths were draped from the green electric light shade . . . which always reminded me of a coolie's hat . . . to the four corners of the classroom.

The Christmas scenes, painted or done with pastels, were drawing-pinned to the tongued and grooved wooden panels and were placed around the classroom in order of merit. For instance, the scenes that were indistinguishable – in other words, just a mess – were pinned to the wall next to the door so that anyone entering wouldn't see them, but as the paintings progressed in standard so they were moved round the walls to a more favourable position. The best efforts were exhibited on the wall behind the teacher.

This particular Christmas I had painted three scenes. One was of Father Christmas on a snow-covered roof making his way to the chimney, his sack of toys over his shoulder with a fairy doll sticking out of the top. The second one was a Christmas tree in the corner of a room by a window showing a snowy winter scene outside. The tree was decorated with crystal balls hanging from its branches, glittering tinsel wound its way down and around to the bottom, and on the floor haphazardly placed round the foot of the tree were fancily wrapped parcels of different shapes and sizes. The third was a still life of a richly browned turkey, surrounded by baked potatoes, on an oval dish. These paintings were given the honoured position, centre of the wall immediately above the teacher's desk, and were framed with paper chains.

My teacher was very good at art and therefore he encouraged me, teaching me a lot. He also knew that my secret dream was to go to the College of Art in the Romford Road, so he suggested to Mum and Dad, one open day, that I should be allowed to go. They willingly agreed so he put my name forward for entry. Unfortunately, as I was such a dunce at arithmetic I failed the simple sums test I was given, so that was the end of my dream.

I painted the turkey, I suppose, because that was the nearest I

59

would ever get to eating one. We never could afford a turkey so Mum used to fatten up a couple of cockerels for Christmas.

At one time Mum had three chicken runs in the back yard, one either side and one at the end making them into a U-shape. They weren't posh efforts, just made from old doors and second-hand pieces of wood, all scrounged of course. The design was simple . . . two sides, a back, which was the fence, and a sloping roof covered with asphalt. The front, apart from the door, was mainly chicken wire. It was a miracle how they fitted in our back yard when you consider it was only twenty feet by fifteen.

Mum had started off with one hen, a Barney Feldy breeding bird, and a cockerel, but after two seasons she had twenty-five laying hens and a few cockerels, which when you come to think about it was quite an achievement. She was very resourceful and used to sell the eggs to the neighbours, thirteen for a shilling. That was very cheap for new-laid eggs compared with shop prices, so it did them a good turn and for Mum the extra few shillings every now and again helped her to battle through the week.

Mum kept one cockerel in the run with the hens for fertilising the eggs, so that when the Barney Feldy, the mother hen, became broody she was ninety per cent sure that the dozen she put under her would take. Mum loved her chickens and nursed them like babies, treating them for cramp and all the other complaints chickens suffer from.

My younger brother Stanley, although only seven, used to help her. They had names for all the chickens and if Mum noticed one was going down with something she would say to Stanley, "Go out and get me Lizzie. She looks a bit sluggish to me, I think she needs a tonic." Out he'd go and back he'd come with Lizzie. He would hold the bird between his knees and open its beak while Mum, with a little spoon, gave it its medicine. They worked as a team; he was the assistant. He loved the chickens as much as Mum, but for a different reason. He loved them as pets, but his favourite was the Barney Feldy, the mother hen.

Every morning as regular as clockwork, when he came downstairs he'd make a bee-line for the back door and Mum would say, "Stanley, come back here and have your breakfast first" – she knew where he was going. He'd come back, gulp down his Quaker Oats and dash out to his Barney Feldy. It was marvellous too how she knew him. Immediately he entered the yard she would cluck-cluck excitedly and come to him when he called, fluffing up her feathers. He would pick her up and cuddle her and as he rubbed his face against her feathers he would say, "And how is my beautiful Barney Feldy today?" His adoration of that lovely old bird was very touching. Mum used to say to Dad, "I hate to think how that boy will take it if anything happens to his Barney Feldy."

Mind you, all of us in turn had to help with the feeding of the chickens. One of my jobs when I was old enough was to boil up all the old potato peelings, cabbage leaves and any other vegetable waste in a big iron saucepan and when cooked strain it and mix in, by hand, half bran and half middlings till the mixture became crumbly – it used to smell delicious. It was then measured out equally into three bowls, one for each run. Another part of their diet was corn and maize which was scattered over the floor of the runs, with an occasional handful of grit thrown in for toughening up their shells.

We always knew when Mum was going to spend an hour or so with her chickens because she used to put on a terrible pair of old plimsolls caked with chicken droppings. She suffered badly with her feet and one day after attending to the chickens she came in, flopped in a chair, stretched her legs out in front of her and said to Dad, "Oh Gawd, my feet are killing me."

"Well if you will walk about in those bloody rotten slippers half soled and heeled in chickens' shit, what do you expect!"

The runs were kept spotlessly clean; at the slightest sign of red-mite they would be creosoted. I remember one occasion in the summer holidays she said to me, "I want you to creosote the big run for me, do you think you can do it?"

I was thrilled that Mum had asked me to undertake such a responsible job. "Of course I can, Mum."

From underneath the sink, she took a tin of creosote and an old round-headed brush kept especially for the job, filled an enamel basin (no longer in use for household purposes) with creosote and handed them to me, commanding, "There you are – now be careful, don't get it in your eyes. And let me know when you have finished it."

I went inside the big run and shut the door behind me. The hens began to cluck-cluck excitedly around my feet thinking I had brought them their food. I shooed them away with my foot and put the basin of creosote on the roost. Immediately a few flew up on to the roost to investigate and as soon as I put them down others flew up and took their place, so I had to take the basin off the roost and hold it in one hand while I painted the run with the other.

The fumes coming from the creosote were so overpowering . . .

I could feel them attacking my throat and after a while they began to make me cough; at the same time it seemed to me the chickens were clucking at half speed . . . like a gramophone running down.

Nevertheless I stuck at it and within about an hour I had completed my task. I put the creosote brush in the empty basin, stood it in the outside sink and dashed up to Mum, who was cleaning the bedroom windows, exclaiming excitedly, "I've done it, Mum, I've done it, come and have a look, it don't 'alf look nice."

"All right," she said, "I'll come and look." I was so eager for her to see I dashed down the stairs expecting her to be following me, but she wasn't.

Disappointed I called up the stairs, "Oh come on, Mum, please, come and have a look."

"All right, all right, I'm coming," she said impatiently. As soon as she reached the bottom of the stairs I grabbed her hand and pulled her after me in case she found something else to do.

We stood looking through the wire of the run, shocked at what we saw. The chickens looked as though they had been at the bottle all day – they were smashed out of their tiny minds. Some were lying down paralytic and every time they tried to get up their legs buckled under them and down they went again. Those that were just about able to stand were cross-legged and cross-eyed reeling about all over the run, taking one step forwards and two quick ones backwards to keep themselves upright. It was the funniest thing I'd ever seen and I stood there screaming with laughter; the more I looked at them the more I laughed. I glanced up at Mum expecting her to be laughing too. On the contrary . . . she was livid. "Why didn't you let the chickens out?" she yelled.

Her anger had an immediate sobering effect on me, just the tears of laughter remained on my face. I wiped them away with the sleeve of my jersey. "I'm sorry, Mum, but I didn't know I had to let them out . . . you didn't say."

Still furious she said, "Well don't stand there whimpering, help me get them out quickly."

We dashed into the run and within seconds got all fifteen or so chickens out into the yard. I was terribly worried as I watched them flapping and falling about all over the place. What had happened to them? Then suddenly I remembered how the fumes had made me cough and how odd the chickens' clucks seemed. Yes, that must be it, I thought – the creosote fumes were the cause. I realised then why Mum was so cross, and understood her concern. She could have lost the lot, the chickens and the extra shillings the eggs brought in. "Oh Mum," I said anxiously, "will they be all right?"

She nodded. "I think they'll be all right now." As she spoke I noticed they weren't reeling about quite so much and although still a bit wobbly, most of them were on their feet.

Earlier in the year, when the Barney Feldy became broody, Mum hadn't put the customary twelve eggs under her – this time she put ten and, for an experiment, two duck eggs. She said that if the experiment was a success we would be having duck for Christmas for a change.

The end of the three weeks – the hatching period – was a marvellous time. We used to love to watch the chicks peck their way bit by bit through the shells and when the final piece of shell fell away, they'd still be all wet. It was wonderful, too, watching the way the mother hen gathered them to her; she would half squat down and with a gentle treading movement and a wiggle of her bottom they would disappear beneath her. The next day they would be beautiful little golden balls of fluff.

As always we watched the chicks hatch out, but this time we were more interested in looking and listening anxiously for any sign of movement from the two little foreigners. At first Mum was convinced that her experiment with the duck eggs had failed, but lo-and-behold the next day, when she went to look, the mother hen was off the nest pecking around, with her cute little babies bustling about her scratching legs cheeping with delight. This gave Mum the opportunity to have a look at the duck eggs. At first glance there seemed to be no change but on closer inspection she noticed a minute hole in each egg. She was over the moon – this was the start; she called for us to come and look and when we saw the tiny holes we were as excited as Mum, but our noise began to worry the Barney Feldy because she came quickly back to the nest calling her chicks who followed behind her like a little golden cloud. Very quickly she nestled them beneath her then sat down. We all gave a disappointed "Ahh".

"Come on," said Mum. "Let's leave her alone now, we mustn't disturb her any more. Besides, tomorrow morning they'll be hatched out, then we can all have a good look."

The next morning was beautiful and sunny and as soon as we were dressed we tore downstairs. Mum and Stanley weren't there so we dashed out into the yard knowing that was the only place they could be. What met our eyes was magic: there, out of the run, on the path between the two sheds were the ten little balls of golden fluff and right in the middle of them two baby ducks of the purest white. The chicks cheeped incessantly, but through it all you could distinctly hear the tiniest of quacks. It was a wonderful sight with the two mums very proudly looking on. Our mum had a big smile of satisfaction and the mother hen proudly strutted around as much as to say, look what I've produced, top that if you can.

It didn't seem all that long before the ducks were fully grown and from the cute little white things with tiny quacks they became big grubby white things with big quacks. Mum very soon had to separate them from the hens as they were much stronger and ate everything in sight. The cockerels were taken from their run and put among the hens, while the ducks took their place.

Dad came in one day from having a stroll around the yard and said to Mum, "Why are those ducks so bloody dirty?"

"I suppose it's because they should be on water really," Mum replied.

"Well let's give 'em some water," he said. "Dig a hole."

"Dig a hole?" she said. "There's hardly enough room to walk between the runs let alone dig a hole."

"Not in the yard, in the run . . . they'll have their own little pond then."

Mum was dubious about this and stood there thinking, because Dad wasn't the handiest of men, in fact he was pretty hopeless when it came to doing jobs around the house. Except for a hammer and a few nails, he didn't own a tool. Yes, Dad was definitely a hammer and nails man; like when the hinges broke on the scullery window, which opened outwards, in place of the hinges he made do with strips of leather, one for the top and one for the bottom. He nailed one end of the strips to the upright and the other end to the window frame. As hinges they were useless, the only purpose they served was that when you opened the window it didn't fall off, and as for shutting it . . . what a performance that was. You had to know the routine, which was to hook your fingers under the cross spar of the window and with the fingers of your other hand under the bottom of the window frame, lift and pull, all in one movement, making sure not to trap your fingers between the bottom of the window and the sill. Many's the time I came in from trying to shut it and showed Mum a dirty great mouse coming up on my finger.

Dad watched her standing there saying nothing. "Well what d'you think?"

"I am thinking," she said.

"Gawd, what is there to think about, you've only got to say yes or no."

But Mum knew from the way he said it that he was hoping for a "yes", and if he didn't get it an argument would develop, so tactfully she said, "It can only be a small hole so I was wondering if it was worth it."

"Of course it'll be worth it, there's quite a bit of space in that run, I'll make it as big as I can."

"How deep will you make it?"

"How deep do you want it?"

"Well you please yourself, but don't make it too deep."

"I'll stop before I get to Australia if that's what you mean."

"Don't be funny, you know what I mean."

"Me being funny, it's you that's being funny . . . 'don't make it too deep' . . . what difference does it make how deep it is for Christ's sake, they're bloody ducks, it's hardly likely they'll drown."

"Well if you're going to be like that about it why ask me for my opinion in the first place?" With that she stamped off.

Dad wasn't deterred, in fact he was determined to make a pond for the ducks in the run.

It was Saturday afternoon when he came in from work with a shovel he'd borrowed from Lucas, his workmate down the street. As soon as he'd had his dinner he got up with an "Ah well" then said to Mum in an expansive manner, "I suppose I'd better make a start on the pond for your ducks."

Hearing this I jumped up saying, "I'll help you, Dad."

"Oh no you won't," he said, "I don't want you getting in my way." With that he spat on each hand, à la navvy, picked up Lucas' shovel, shouldered it and walked out into the yard as though he was going to build Rome.

Mum, sisters Bella and Doris and I were in the kitchen. My younger brother Stanley was out playing football with his mates and Sid was not yet home from work. Mum was in her usual chair next to the kitchen range, sewing, and me and my sisters occupied the kitchen table. Bella was cutting out a dress, Doris was doing the ironing (one of her chores) at the back of the table and I was sitting opposite Bella doing a pencil drawing.

We were so engrossed in what we were doing we forgot all about Dad out there digging. We were soon reminded by the back door crashing open. Our heads shot up with a start and there was Dad standing in the scullery doorway in a frightful mess. His hair was all over the place, half of it straggling across his face which was filthy dirty, and he was covered from head to foot in earth and flakes of whitewash. We were too stunned to speak and when we didn't he fumed, "Are you all deaf or something, didn't any of you hear me?"

"Hear what?" Mum asked.

"Hear what!" he exploded. "I've been screaming my bloody lungs out for nearly an hour." He always exaggerated.

"Why, what happened?"

"What happened! I was at the bottom of the hole digging the last bit out when the bloody shed collapsed on top of me, that's what happened."

"Well we didn't hear anything, did we?" she said turning to us.

"No," we said.

"You don't have to tell me you didn't hear," he stormed. "I know you didn't bloody well hear, that's why I am standing here covered in crap . . . Jesus Christ, I could be out there now buried alive for all you lot care."

At that moment Sid arrived home from work. He hung his jacket up on a peg in the passage and when he came into the kitchen and saw Dad in that shocking mess he just stood there astonished, unable to imagine what had happened to him.

Dad looked at Sid. "Don't stand there gawking at me like that . . . I'm not going to a fancy dress ball as a sweep you know."

"No Dad, it's just that I was trying to imagine what happened to you."

"The bloody chicken shed fell on top of me, that's what happened."

"The chicken shed fell on top of you," he said, finding it hard to believe. "How?"

"How the hell do I know . . . all I know is one minute I was digging away and the next moment there was this terrific thump on my head; it must have stunned me for a moment, because when my head cleared I found myself in complete darkness buried in my own hole; for one terrifying moment I thought the world had come to an end."

"Are you all right, Dad?"

"Well there's no bones broken if that's what you mean . . . mind you I've got this sodding great bump on my head and I'm covered from head to foot in bruises and with all the shouting and hollering

I've been doing for the past hour I'm surprised I haven't got a sore throat as well."

"Before I have my dinner," Sid said, making for the scullery door, "let's see if we can prop the shed back up again." With that we all tramped out to the yard behind Sid.

When we saw the collapsed run it was obvious what had happened. Dad, trying to make the hole as big as he could, overdid it and took far too much earth away from the front, causing it to slide inwards bringing the roof down on top of him.

Sid got me and my sisters to hold up the roof, while he and Dad, with the aid of some old bricks, shored the front up. Sid then shovelled back all the soil that had been taken away from the front, firming it down with his feet. When Mum saw Sid filling the hole in she said, "Thank Gawd for that . . . we don't need a pond anyway."

But Dad was adamant, saying to Mum, "Now look here, you mustn't be put off by one little setback . . . Bogey, you dig a hole, you know how big to make it without affecting the front."

So Sid went back inside the run. The earth having been worked before made it easier to dig, and within about ten minutes he had dug a small hole roughly one foot six in diameter. Dad looked at it saying, "Christ, Bogey, can't you make it bigger than that?"

"No Dad, you can't . . . if I make it any bigger we'll have the same trouble as before."

Mum didn't want it at all. "If it's only going to be that big it's not worth it. Fill it in, Sid."

"No," Dad said, "that'll be big enough for them, at least they'll be on water."

Mum was thoroughly fed up but . . . anything for a quiet life. "Oh all right, please yourselves."

We kids were dying to see the ducks on the water.

"Right," said Dad, "let's fill it up. Reggie, you get the ducks, me and Bogey will get the buckets of water."

Mum, the two girls and I watched Dad and Sid as they filled the hole with water. When they had finished they came out of the run and Dad said, "Reggie, put the ducks on the water." So with a duck under each arm I entered the run and put them on the tiny pond. It was a ridiculous sight really, there sat the ducks on this, the tiniest of ponds, unable to move as much as their legs. They just sat there looking at us and we stood outside looking at them getting lower and lower as the water began gradually to soak away, until eventually they sat at the bottom wallowing in the thick mud, quacking away and loving every minute of it.

After a while they were completely covered in mud and except for the two yellow beaks and four beady little eyes you would have thought they had disappeared. Mum looked at them, their wings so clogged with mud they were unable to move them. "Right," she said, "I'm having no more of this. Reggie, get those ducks out of there, Bella, Doris, go and fill those buckets with water, Sid, fill that hole in!"

Dad said, "Well what do you propose to do now?"

"Clean the ducks up, that's what."

"That's a very good idea, I think I'll do the same," and as he went down the path between the two runs he said over his shoulder to Mum, "If you hadn't said they should be on water, none of this would have happened in the first place."

Mum threw him a withering look then took a duck from me and plunged it into a bucket of water, and I plunged mine into the other bucket.

The only water the ducks got from then on was for drinking.

It was one morning during our summer holidays, not long after this episode with the duck pond, that Stanley as usual dashed out to see his Barney Feldy. It seemed as quickly as he had dashed out he dashed back in, his eyes wide open with panic, words tumbling from his mouth, practically incoherent. Mum said, "Now calm yourself down, if you babble on like that I can't understand what you are saying."

"It's Barney, Mum," he said, slowing down a bit, "she's not well, she's laying down and can't get up, what's wrong with her? Do you think it's cramp?"

Mum was making pastry at the kitchen table and as soon as she heard the news she hurried out, wiping the excess bits of pastry off her fingers with her coarse apron. Me and my sisters followed. When Stanley had dashed in he had left the run door open so when we got out there the other fowls had wandered from the run and were pecking around on the path.

"See, Mum," said Stanley, pointing to his beloved bird lying there. Mum looked, fearing the worst. She stooped down and felt the old hen's breast; she wasn't breathing. Her fears were right . . . she was dead.

"What's wrong with her, Mum? Why can't she get up? Has she got cramp? Perhaps she's got pneumonia like Ethel had, the white leghorn . . . you got her better, let's take her inside and give her your medicine."

Mum didn't answer. She knelt beside the mother hen softly crying, not so much for the bird although she loved it, but more for her boy. This was the moment she had always dreaded but she knew she had to tell him.

He tugged at Mum's shoulder. "Come on, Mum, don't kneel there, let's take her inside. Quick, she'll get worse."

Mum stood up with the Barney Feldy in her arms, its neck hanging limply over her arm. She turned to Stanley, tears falling down her cheeks. "I'm sorry, darling, but your Barney Feldy is dead."

His bottom lip began to tremble and then tears started to pour down his face; he didn't believe what Mum had said, he couldn't. "No, she's not dead, she can't be . . . come on, let's take her inside and give her your medicine."

Mum just shook her head. "It's no good, Stanley, she is really dead."

"She's not, she's not!" he screamed. "You haven't even tried." He was crying uncontrollably now and taking the bird from Mum said, "Give her to me, she's mine, I'll take her inside and give her the medicine, you don't care, you've not even tried." With tears coursing down his face, he didn't want to accept it but now, as he held her, he knew she was really dead. He buried his head in her feathers saying, "Oh my beautiful Barney I love you," and sobbed as though his heart would break.

We watched this poor little boy hugging his treasure to him. He was a pitiful sight but we could do nothing, only stand there and cry for him.

Preparations for Christmas would begin in early December. Mum would start to fatten up the birds for the festive dinner, in this case the ducks. From then on the excitement would build up every day until school broke up, a few days before Christmas.

This particular breaking-up day was no different to those of the past, little being done in the morning, but the afternoon was spent cleaning up. We had to sweep our own little area down to the front of the classroom where the monitor collected up each individual pile and put it in the dustbin. I had always wanted to be the monitor, but after seeing this I thought they could stuff it.

Our next task was to polish our desks with the tiny bit of polish we were given, then remove all the decorations. The paper chains were divided amongst us (with our house already festooned, I didn't want mine so I gave them to the boy sitting next to me) and our paintings were given back to us to bring home. All this was done so that, apart from finding a clean classroom on our return after the Christmas holiday, not the slightest sign of Christmas would remain.

I came out of school clutching my three paintings and suddenly a wonderful feeling of happiness swept over me as I thought about the fortnight's holiday that lay ahead. The lights of Clary's, the corner sweetshop, came on just as I was crossing the road, showing off their Christmas decorations and arched right across the top of the window, in cotton wool stuck on to make it look like snow, was – A MERRY CHRISTMAS. A lot of care had gone into the dressing of the window; rows of bottled sweets of all kinds filled the shelves, and strategically placed were boxes of chocolates with lights flashing off the cellophane that was tightly stretched across the highly decorated lids.

I moved on and when I got to the corner of my road I watched the lamplighter push his pole up through the flap, the light taking the place of the darkness rapidly closing in. As I took all this in another wave of happiness welled up in me, and I thought – Oh! what a lovely time of the year this is.

Mum said that she liked the paintings, but I knew from the way she said it that her mind was on something else. She went on: "Oh by the way, before I forget it, your dad's doing the ducks on Christmas Eve" (that meant killing them) "and he wants you to help pluck them – I'm telling you now in case you have any Christmas shopping to do."

Christmas was only a few days away so I thought I'd better check on my savings, made up of the odd penny and ha'penny given to me over the past few weeks. I took a knife from the kitchen drawer and went upstairs. I had a red pillar-box. It was easy putting the money in but to get it out was a little bit difficult. By putting the knife in the slot and turning the money box upside down you could catch a coin on the blade of the knife and carefully draw it out. Getting the last couple of coins out was a different matter – I've known many a money box of this type to be savagely destroyed in trying to do so.

We kids never told one another what we were buying Mum and Dad for Christmas; it was always a secret. The consequence was that every year Dad used to end up with five bottles of brilliantine and Mum was awash with eau de Cologne. I had bought Mum's eau de Cologne and Dad's brilliantine in the afternoon of Christmas Eve and had just finished wrapping them up when Dad came home from work.

"When are you going to kill the ducks, Dad?" I said.

"Tonight while your mum and sisters are out doing the Christmas shopping."

Mum always bought the meat late on Christmas Eve because when it got round to nine thirty or ten o'clock, the butchers would auction the meat off cheap, not wanting it left in their shops over the Christmas period.

"Can I sharpen your knife, Dad?" (Dad always killed the chickens kosher fashion, by bleeding them.)

"No," he said, "I won't be needing the knife tonight."

Hearing this, Mum's head shot up. "You won't be needing the knife? Well how the hell are you going to kill them?"

"I'm going to wring their necks," he said flippantly.

Mum's face was a picture of astonishment. "You're going to wring their necks?"

"Yes, Charlie said you always wring a duck's neck, you never bleed it." (Charlie was another of Dad's workmates who kept a few fowls.)

"But you've never wrung a bird's neck in your life!"

"I know I haven't, but I know how . . . Charlie showed me."

"Why, did he have a duck in the workshop?"

"No, of course he didn't, he showed me with a broom handle."

"He showed you how to kill a duck with a broom handle?"

"No for Christ's sake, he showed me the special grip you have to use to wring their necks, on the broom handle," and as he was explaining this to Mum he was crooking his fingers up in a most painful-looking way, demonstrating Charlie's grip.

Mum watched the demonstration then said, "Yes but I still think it would be easier for you to stick to the way you know."

"Don't be silly, it's easy when you know how."

"But that's it . . . you don't know how."

Dad, more aggravated than angry, began to raise his voice. "Gawd Almighty, woman, if you don't believe me I'll show you . . . Reggie, go and fetch me the broom from the scullery." Off I toddled and came back with the broom. "Right," he said to me, "now hold the broom out horizontally in front of you while I show your mother the grip and the method."

I held the broom out horizontally, then Dad crooking his fingers up as though they were eaten up with arthritis said to Mum, "Now watch!" With that he put his arthritic fingers round the broom handle and gripped. "Now that is how you grip the duck's neck . . . are you with me so far?"

Mum didn't answer, but, knowing my mum, I could tell what was going through her mind by the expression on her face. (Why is he going to all these lengths to prove to me that he can wring a duck's neck when I know damned well he can't . . . and what's more, never would be able to.)

Not waiting for a reply, Dad carried on: "Now this is the method – a quick twist and a sharp pull." So saying he demonstrated on the broom handle the quick twist and the sharp pull. "There you are. Now if that had been the duck's neck that would have been its lot."

"Yes, well it looks quite easy on the broom handle but I should think it will be a bit more difficult with the real thing. I mean, Reggie was holding the broom handle while you were demonstrating, is he going to hold the duck for you?"

Dad was getting very irritated by Mum's scepticism. "Look, this has gone far enough so let's drop the subject shall we? You go out and do the shopping and leave the ducks to me."

Mum knew better than to take it any further. "Yes, well I suppose you're right," she said. "I'll get your tea."

After this slight bit of aggro I knew the broom wouldn't be wanted any more so I took it back to the scullery and put it where it was always kept, next to the wringer.

It was nearly eight o'clock. Mum and my sisters were already out doing the Christmas Eve shopping and Dad, reading the evening paper, had so far not even mentioned the ducks. I was wondering if he was sulking about the slight contretemps he'd had with Mum during the broom and duck demonstration, when suddenly he put his newspaper down, saying, "Right, Reggie, let's see to these ducks, go out and get them."

"Right-ho, Dad." Feeling very manly I took the torch and went out to fetch the ducks.

Dad was in the scullery practising Charlie's grip when I came back with a duck under each arm.

"Right," he said as he lifted up his arm, "stick a duck under there." I put one duck on the floor and the other one under his arm. The duck started to sway its neck about in front of Dad, just like a snake coming up out of the basket. Dad grabbed its neck then realised he couldn't use his other hand to do the grip because it was occupied holding the body of the duck under his arm. He stood there pondering with the duck under his arm, and the other hand holding the duck's neck. The other duck was waddling about the scullery floor pecking the coconut matting. After a while Dad said, "Well Reggie, I'm in a bit of a pickle here, I can't wring its bloody neck with one hand can I?"

A sudden thought struck me. "Dad, why don't you grip the duck between your knees, you know, like you do when you kill the chickens?"

"What a good idea, now why didn't I think of that?" Straight away he gripped the duck between his knees and putting Charlie's grip on its neck said, "Right, well here goes," and he did the quick twist and a sharp pull. "That's it, I felt it go. Charlie was right, he said I would feel it go," and he put it on the floor. "Give us the other one."

I picked up the other duck and as I did so, the one Dad had just put down on the floor got straight up and waddled about the scullery pecking at the coconut matting, taking over where the other one had left off. I gave Dad the duck, saying, "The other one has got up, Dad, and is walking about."

"Oh that's just its nerves . . . it'll fall over in a minute, you watch," and with Charlie's grip on the neck of the duck I had just given him he did the quick twist and sharp pull routine.

"That's it! I definitely felt it go that time." He put it on the floor, only to see it get straight up and join its mate waddling about pecking the coconut matting.

I sat on the form next to Dad watching the ducks, waiting for them to fall over. They were loving the coconut matting and when they'd nearly polished it off I said to Dad, "When d'you reckon they'll fall over?"

"I'm buggered if I know . . . I must have slipped up somewhere. Let's have a go at the first one again."

"Which one is the first one?" I asked.

"How the bloody hell should I know, they both look alike to me – anyway you should know, you gave it to me."

"I know I did, but they've moved around so much now I don't know which is which."

"Oh give me any one, it doesn't matter which, they're both as fit as bloody fiddles."

This time Dad gave two quick twists and a sharp pull, saying, "Well that's done it this time," and put it on the floor. I picked up the other one and as I did so the one lying down slowly untwisted its neck, got up, walked cross-legged for a few steps, then went hell for leather at the coconut matting again. I drew Dad's attention to this as I handed him the other duck.

"Now that's definitely got to be nerves," he said. "Christ Almighty, I couldn't stand up to what I've just done to that bird," and seeing it still full of life enjoying the rest of the coconut matting he gave the one he'd got three big twists and a long sharp pull and held it in that position for a second or two before placing it on the floor. This time it lay there. Dad, sweating profusely, flopped back on the form, saying, "Die, you bugger, die!"

I sat on the form next to Dad. We didn't speak, just looked at the duck lying on the floor. Suddenly to our amazement it twitched a couple of times, slowly untwisted its neck, got up, fell over, got up again, took a few groggy steps, shook its head, fluffed up its feathers and with a quack-quack joined its friend on the coconut matting.

Dad stood up. "That's it!" He picked up the duck he'd just tried to throttle, stroked its neck as though giving it a massage and said, "Reggie, take these ducks, put them back in their run, then bring me back the two Sussex cockerels."

Mum knew, when she was putting the birds in the oven on Christmas morning, that it was the cockerels he'd dressed and not the ducks, but she didn't say anything until we were all sat down to our Christmas dinner. As she was putting a leg of the chicken on his plate she said, with an arch look, "By the way, what happened to the ducks?"

He said with that well-known twinkle in his eye, "Well they didn't deserve to die, they were too game," and with that he burst out laughing at his own joke . . . and we all laughed. After all, it was Christmas.

12

STARTING WORK

When nearing school-leaving age, which in those days was fourteen, we were taught how to compose a letter to apply for a job. The method used then is still used today – your own address in the top right-hand corner of the page with the date just below it, then the addressee's name and address a little lower on the page, but on the left-hand side, followed by "Dear Sirs," etc. The only difference was that at the end of your letter you always put "Your obedient servant", and signed it, in my case, "Reginald Alfred Varney".

The day I wrote after my first post coincided with the buying of my first pair of long trousers. Mum took me to Woodmansee's, a store in Canning Town which specialised in gents' and boys' outfits only.

I felt very grown up because Dad, although he only had a new suit once in a blue moon, always bought his there. Entering the store was a new experience for me, and as the assistant, with a tape measure around his neck, approached us, I felt very important, knowing that I would be getting all his attention. Also once I had been fitted with my long trousers, I was going to be able to wear them immediately, and the short trousers would be gone for ever.

Imagine my disappointment when, because I was so tiny, being barely four feet tall, even the smallest size of junior long trousers were miles too big for me. The shorts that a moment before I thought had been discarded for ever, had to go back on again. I had been convinced that I would emerge from Woodmansee's a "youth", and was humiliated to realise I had walked in as a schoolboy and was now having to walk *out* as a schoolboy.

When we arrived home I was very depressed, and although Mum had bought the smallest pair of long trousers in the shop, I knew it would take her a few days at least to do the necessary alterations before I could wear them. Until that time I would have to make do with my short trousers. This meant staying indoors, because no way would you get me out of the house to be ridiculed by my school friends, who had already been swanking up and down our street in their long trousers.

That night to help me get over my disappointment, Mum and Dad suggested that, since I had been taught at school how to write after a job, I should sit down and do so now. Moodily I got up and took the pen and ink from the first shelf of the dresser from which hung the cups. Mum had produced a writing pad from somewhere and placed it on the table. I sat down in front of the pad and opened the lid of the inkwell. Just as I was about to dip the jay-nibbed pen into the ink, Dad said, "Just a minute! What are you doing?"

"Writing after a job," I said.

"What bloody job?"

"I don't know."

"Well, there you are then! Now first of all let's sit down and discuss the type of job you would like to do."

Mum said, "Oh there are plenty of jobs he could do."

"Such as?" queried Dad.

"Well, all sorts of jobs."

"All sorts of jobs! Jesus Christ, Mother, use your head, he couldn't do all sorts of jobs; look at him, Woodmansee's couldn't find a pair of trousers small enough for the poor little bugger – so what are you talking about? He could do all sorts of jobs! I can't see him as a navvy, can you?"

Mum and Dad continued to argue the toss about what I could or couldn't do, and in the middle of the argument my brother Sid walked in with his girl friend, Betty. They told Sid and Betty about their discussion and of how difficult the task was because of my size. Betty solved the problem immediately by telling us about her young brother Wally, who had just got a job as a messenger boy in the City of London. I was very interested, and when she said that he wore a nice uniform, that finally convinced me.

I was unable to get a job at the same company as Wally, but I applied for a similar post in the Via Imperial Wireless and Cable Company and was accepted.

On my first day at work I wore my best navy blue suit and while Mum was giving me the once-over, my thoughts of the unknown future filled me with a sort of nervous excitement. I had been told that a senior messenger boy was going to show me the ropes and later in the afternoon I was to receive my uniform.

"You'll do." Mum's voice brought me back to the present as she gave a final adjustment to my tie. "Actually, you look very smart," she added, then gave me a big hug and a kiss. She saw me to the door and as she handed me my sandwiches for lunch, as always wrapped up in Sunday's *News of the World*, she said, "Good Luck." I tucked them under my arm and as I crossed the road, wondered if she was referring to the sandwiches or my first day at work.

STARTING WORK

Although starting out to work was a new and wonderful experience, it had its problems, especially in the rush hours. In those days, when a bus or tram pulled up at a stop, it was every man for himself; each pushing and shoving, forcing his way with brutish determination to get on board. Some men at times showed respect for the women, but that, I suppose, depended on how pretty the girl was, or how late the man was for work.

Barking Road was the main road to London from the east of the city, although once you passed over Canning Town Bridge it ceased to be the Barking Road, and continued on to London, first as the East India Dock Road and then as Commercial Road. Liverpool Road, the road that took me from my home to the Barking Road, and which to me when I was a kid seemed interminable, had to be negotiated first. When I did eventually arrive at the main road on my first morning, the crowds waiting for my bus were staggering.

In the days when Mum had taken me up to London during the morning rush hour to Great Ormond Street Hospital, the crowds, no matter how big, were never a problem. A mother and child were shown the greatest respect by all, being allowed to board first. Now it was a different story . . . without the protection of Mum and short trousers I became just one of the mob. I'd joined the ranks of "every man for himself".

Being good at "every man for himself" was a great art, gained only by a lot of experience. The more experienced, when in a large crowd, had a marvellous trick of continuously tensing and relaxing their muscles, propelling themselves forward in a similar manner to a snake, except that they were perpendicular and the snake moved horizontally.

The young and speedy never joined the waiting crowds anyway. They would walk back in the direction of the oncoming bus or tram, and as it was slowing down, they would run alongside the vehicle, grab the rail and swing themselves on to the platform. It could of course be very dangerous. If they failed to calculate the speed of the bus correctly, they would find that they had swung themselves into the middle of the road, at the mercy of the oncoming traffic.

The more speedy still would go even further back along the road and run behind the bus, so that immediately it began to slow, they would put on a spurt and catch up with the bus, grab the rear hold, and with a mighty pull leap forward and gain the rear end of the platform. This could prove even more dangerous. I recall one particular morning, when a chap renowned for his speed and skill at catching a bus this way started one of his famous runs.

Unfortunately for him, the bus he was after had to stop suddenly to avoid an accident – not having the braking power of the bus, without warning he found his face had joined the back of his head.

It didn't take me long to learn these running and jumping tricks and after a few weeks I became quite expert. I could run very fast indeed and to avoid clashing with the heftier fellows running for the same vehicle I would go back further still to catch the bus. I was thrilled that this worked and thought I'd got it made, until one morning after mounting the bus the conductor said to me, "Where to?"

"Aldgate," I replied, taking out my twopence as usual.

"That'll be threepence," he said.

I was astonished. "Threepence?" I queried. "But it's only twopence from Canning Town station."

He eyed me coldly. "I know it's only twopence from Canning Town station, but from where you have just got on it's threepence." He continued to watch me as I searched for the other penny, and only when I gave the threepence did he speak. "Perhaps now you'll think twice about jumping on a bus between stages." With that he punched the ticket and moved off down the aisle of the bus, with a very nasal "Any more fares, please?" I sat there feeling foolish, and I never did it again.

This was typical of the hostile type of conductor; fortunately they were very rare. Most of them, as I remember, were wonderful characters, possessing a brilliant sense of humour. I recall on another occasion joining the back of the waiting crowd as usual, and as more and more people piled up behind, I became dwarfed in the middle. With everyone towering around me I couldn't see the bus, but I could tell it was approaching, not only by its sound, but by the way everyone started to jockey for position.

The big surge forward told me that the bus was pulling in to the stop . . . I couldn't breathe and was frightened of being crushed by the volume of people behind me pushing forward. There was nothing I could do but go with the crowd, and just as I thought I would die from lack of air, I heard the conductor say, "Right! That's enough," and down came his arm behind me. The rest had to get off.

Those now left on the platform were elbowing their way inside. "No more room inside!" I heard him say. "The rest on top." Then I found myself being ushered up the stairs. Standing wasn't allowed on top of the bus so we were sure of a seat. Halfway down the aisle I spotted an empty seat.

A very smart young woman occupied the seat next to the window. She was wearing a subtle perfume and was dressed in a black suit with a frilly white blouse under the jacket. She wasn't slouched in the seat but sat up correctly, her knees together and with her handbag nestling neatly on her lap. I was pleased that she was reading a novel, as this saved me the embarrassment of her seeing my legs dangling.

I could hear the downstairs passengers laughing at the conductor's funny quips. "Now have your fares ready please, and by the way . . . I don't mind taking farthings, but I won't take jam jars." Their laughter mingling with the constant dinging of his ticket machine created a very happy atmosphere which permeated the bus.

"Now before I go upstairs," I heard him say, "has anybody down here lost their lunch? It's wrapped up in yesterday's *News of the World*." A roar of laughter went up from the passengers. I went cold. Putting my hand to my arm was just an automatic reaction . . . I knew my little *News of the World* parcel wouldn't be there. Getting no response he said, "I'll tell you what I'll do. I'll have a 'butcher's' inside." There was a pause while he opened my lunch. "Whoever owns them comes from a posh family – they've got grease-proof paper round them. Just a minute . . ." There was another slight pause. "Ah, here we are! Two of dripping and two of jam." He waited for the laughter to die down. "No one own it? Right, I'll try on top." Then with a "Get your fares ready please," he mounted the stairs.

"Anyone up here lost their lunch?" were his first words. I was sitting halfway along the bus, and as the sound of his ticket punch and his thank-yous grew closer, I slid down in the seat, shrinking inside myself, dreading the inevitable.

He tried again. "Has anybody up here lost their lunch? It's wrapped up in the *News of the World* . . . two of dripping and two of jam." He eyed the passengers for a sign of the owner, without success. "Gawd Blimey! It must belong to someone, I found it on my platform downstairs."

"I thank you," I heard him say, immediately behind me. "Fares please!" He was standing beside me. I was turned away from him with my arm at right-angles, holding my fare. He took the twopence I offered him, and seeing me squirming with embarrassment trying to make myself inconspicuous, knew immediately that the "two of dripping and two of jam" belonged to me.

"Is this your lunch, son?"

I could feel my neck and face crimson up as I shook my head. I could sense that all the passengers were looking in my direction, wanting to see who the owner of the "two of dripping and two of jam" was.

"You sure it's not yours?"

I nodded, trying to crawl further inside my body.

"I can't understand why you're so shy about it . . . the dripping smells delicious . . . you don't know how lucky you are, all I get from my old woman is cheese."

I was mortified and the laughter from the passengers made me feel worse. Oh why was I so sensitive! . . . why couldn't I say that they were mine? . . . was it because I was ashamed that they were two of dripping and two of jam wrapped up in the *News of the World*? I know the answer now, but then as a fourteen-year-old just starting out to work, I didn't. All I knew was that I wanted to die. The embarrassment and humiliation were too much.

He wrapped the sandwiches up and held them out to me. "There you are, son," he coaxed, "take them."

I had denied owning them too many times to accept them now. Instead I looked at him pleadingly and said, "Please, they are not mine."

This was the first time he had seen my face. He looked at me, saw my agony of embarrassment, and withdrew the hand holding the sandwiches. Stuffing them into his money pouch he said, "I'm sorry, son . . . I can see they're not yours now." He gave me a smile and carried on down the centre aisle with his "Any more fares please?"

The rest of the journey to Aldgate went without mishap and although the conductor never let up on his patter, my sandwiches were not mentioned again.

There was a great exodus of passengers at Aldgate. Once again I was in the middle of a towering crowd, and as we met the crowd from inside, the pushing and shoving started again.

"For Gawd's sake stop pushing me off the bus, I don't want to get off," said the conductor. Then he grabbed my arm. "Come on, son, I'll get you off." He eased me off the bus. I turned to say my thanks but couldn't see him among the crowds still struggling off.

I was standing on the kerb waiting to cross the road when someone tapped me on the shoulder. I turned round to see the very smart young lady with the white frilly blouse. "Be careful – don't lose that!" she said pointing to the side of my jacket. I looked down and there, sticking precariously out of my pocket, was my little *News of the World* parcel. I looked up to thank her, but she was gone.

13

The Perils of Spit and Polish

The head office of the Via Imperial was in Moorgate. The messenger boys' uniform was military style, dark navy blue, and looked very attractive and smart. I spent every spare hour fanatically polishing. The brass cap badge and buttons fairly sparkled, and my boots and leather belt I got to shine like the patent leather peak of my cap. People would remark on my appearance to my parents, and on one occasion a neighbour said to my mother, "I saw your Reggie the other day, going to catch his tram, and by God you needed dark glasses to look at him."

One day not long after I started work I was returning from delivering a cable, and was about to pass through the huge stone arched doorway of the Via Imperial office, when a very distinguished gentleman spoke to me. "Excuse me, sonny," he said. I stopped, fully expecting him to ask if I could direct him to some place in the City. Instead he said, "Would you mind standing there for a few moments while I take a good look at you?" After he had given me a full inspection he said, "How old are you?"

"Fourteen," I replied.

"You look very smart indeed," he said, "and I'm very proud of you – you are a credit to the company."

I thanked him, and feeling twelve feet tall passed along the corridor and into the Despatching Room.

I was sitting on a form awaiting my turn to take another message out, when the gentleman who had just spoken to me came in and spoke to the Head Despatching Clerk. Immediately he left, the Head Despatching Clerk called me over, gave me a transport pass and told me that I was to be the "Kensington boy". This meant that all Kensington deliveries and collections were to be done by me.

Getting this appointment had its attractions. First, at one Embassy you always got a shilling – especially handy in those days when my wages were only twelve and sixpence a week. Secondly, every message took three times as long to deliver, therefore you weren't doing so many foot-slogging local jobs. If for some reason the Kensington boy wasn't there when called upon, after a time the next boy on the form took the message.

One morning as I was walking along the corridor to the Despatching Room, I heard a clerk calling for the Kensington boy. I was just passing the lavatory door when two big messenger boys dived out, lifted me up and whipped me back inside. I was struggling like hell but as I only weighed about four stone the boy holding me did so without any effort. While he held me in a vice-like grip, the other boy removed my cap, undid the top three buttons of my tunic, turned the collar back, and by the little chain inside, hung me up on a coat hook on the lavatory wall. They then dashed out so that one of them could take my job.

Luckily for me, within a few seconds of the two boys running out a despatching clerk came in. When he saw me he stopped dead in his tracks – he couldn't believe his eyes. To him I must have looked like a turkey hanging up in a butcher's shop. Then he pulled himself together and lifted me down.

He looked at me with concern and having convinced himself that I was quite all right and that no damage had been done, he asked me if I knew who had played this bloody dangerous trick. I told him, "No – it all happened too quickly," which was the truth.

Whatever it was he had come in there to do, he didn't do it. We walked out together and as we did so, "It's funny when you come to think of it," he said. "We were calling for you just now. Little did we know that you were hanging up in the closet!"

I was well aware that my spit and polish attracted people's attention. One beautiful August evening when I was coming home from work I caught my tram, went upstairs and made my way to the domed section at the front, known as the balcony. Already seated were three classy-looking girls in their early twenties. Looking at them I guessed they were secretaries or office staff of some sort.

I sat down opposite them, and as the sun, streaming through the windows, caught the highly polished patent leather of my peaked cap and the brass buttons of my uniform, they looked up immediately and couldn't take their eyes off me. This boosted my ego but the thing that embarrassed me, as always, was the way my legs dangled because of my lack of height, and because my feet could not touch the floor I had no control over my body on the heavily swaying tram. I tried to prevent my body from rocking by using the muscles of my bottom, but without much success. Sitting there swaying from side to side with the sun reflecting piercing lights from my buttons, I must have looked to them like a sparkler.

I had certainly made an impression on the three girls, judging by the remarks they were making about my appearance. They didn't attempt to keep their voices down, it was as though they wanted me to hear. I acknowledged their flattering remarks by sweetly smiling at them – they sweetly smiled back. I felt that I had to return their sweet smiles with another sweet smile, which I did, flashing my even white teeth at the same time. They smiled back, showing they had got teeth too. I knew we couldn't sit there grinning at one another for the rest of the journey, but at the same time I was lapping up the smiles and admiring looks. The novelty of the uniform would soon be wearing off, so what else could I do to hold their attention?

One of the messenger boys had not long since introduced me to my first vice – smoking. I had a fag end inside the peak of my cap, so I thought, "I'll have a smoke, that'll impress them." I remembered too that I had a lighter belonging to Dad in my pocket; he never used it because, as he said, "I can never get this damned thing to light." It was rather unusual, made out of a shell case of a bullet from the 1914–18 war. The shell case held the cotton-wool and wick, and soldered to the side was the tiny tube which housed the flint and flint wheel. It was a rather crude effort, but my brother Sid, an electro-plater, had nickel-plated and polished it, making it look a million dollars.

Taking my cap off, with a slightly exaggerated movement, I took the two-inch fag end from its hiding place and stuck it in my mouth. Now came the pièce de résistance – the lighter. I took it out of my pocket with a flourish and once again as the sunshine hit the highly polished nickel, the glinting lights had the desired effect. I now had the attention not only of the girls, but of the other passengers who were sitting in our section.

I knew the lighter wouldn't work because – let's face it – if Dad couldn't get it to light, what chance did I have? Now that I had made such a big thing of producing it, however, I felt some effort on my part had to be made. Everyone in the compartment was looking at me now, eagerly awaiting the finale of this production. I was trapped. It was my conceit that had landed me in this situation. Now I had a choice: either, with a sickly grin, to stuff the lighter back in my pocket, or to brazen it out by trying to light it. I didn't fancy the first choice – not now I was such a success with the girls opposite – so I opted to have a go to light it. Besides, there was always the chance that another passenger might offer me a light before I made my attempt, thereby saving the day for me.

No-one came to my rescue, so I placed my thumb on the flint wheel and pressed – nothing happened. I pressed harder, but still the wheel wouldn't budge – so with a mighty sweep downward with the palm of my hand I struck the flint wheel. A huge flame shot upward with black smoke spiralling from its tip; it was such a shock it made me jump and I nearly dropped it. Everyone laughed. The fag end sticking out of my mouth was now only an inch and a half from my lips, so to light it I had to tilt my head to one side; because the flame was so powerful, I could only make quick stabs with it to the tip of the fag.

When eventually I lit it, I blew the flame out and replaced the lighter in my pocket. I then drew in a mouthful of smoke and very deliberately blew it out. It was a big success, the only thing missing was a chord in "G". I looked across at the girls for their approval – they returned my glance with a smile, then their smiles suddenly turned into a suppressed giggle.

They tried not to look at me, but couldn't resist it, and their giggles turned to laughter. I found this very infectious and started to laugh with them. It made me feel great. There were these three beautiful girls, who to me were several cuts above my station, laughing with me; it was as though they were accepting me as one of them. The more they looked and laughed the more I laughed back, till eventually we were laughing hysterically, with tears rolling down our cheeks. The infectious laughter spread until all the people around us began to laugh and when I looked at them they screamed out laughing which made me laugh all the more. The infection spread throughout the top of the tram, the whole upstairs laughing hysterically.

I got off at my destination and as the people's laughter drifted back to me, I thought, what a wonderful thing – a tram full of people laughing like that, and none of us knowing what we were laughing at. I arrived home in a very happy mood and when I walked into the kitchen Dad was in his armchair reading the newspaper, while Mum was doing some ironing. Dad took one look at me and said, "What the bloody hell have you done to your nose?"

"Nothing," I said.

"Oh no! Well take a look in the mirror."

I walked to the mantelpiece and gazed up into the mirror. I had a dirty great black nose, caused by the smoke from the lighter.

So the lovely girls weren't laughing *with* me, but *at* me. I squirmed at the thought of my vanity on the tram – and as I walked to the scullery to wash my face, I took the lighter out of my pocket and dropped it back into the old coffee pot on the dresser, whence it had come.

14

My Introduction to Show Business

A musical instrument shop stood on the corner of Aldgate and Houndsditch, and every night on my way home from work I used to gaze longingly at the rows and rows of piano accordions they had in the shop window. I had to be content with just looking, because on seeing the prices I knew that no way would I ever be able to afford one – not even the cheapest. The only things I could afford were the catalogues, which I got free.

My fifteenth birthday fell in the middle of the week, so it wasn't until I got home from work, had my dinner and the table was cleared, that my brother Stanley and my sisters Bella and Doris gave me their presents. I opened the last of the presents and thanked them, but still nothing came from Mum and Dad. Hard as I tried I couldn't hide my disappointment. I couldn't believe that they hadn't remembered my birthday. I had to get out of the room before I did something stupid, so I thanked my brother and sisters again and said, "I won't be a moment, I'm just going to pop these upstairs."

As I was about to open the kitchen door, Dad called, "Just a minute, Reggie!" Then turning to Mum he said, "I think we've got something for him, haven't we, Mother?"

"Yes, we have, so stop teasing him and go and get it."

Dad went into the parlour and came back carrying a beautiful black case. I had no idea what was in it, though I could see that it was something heavy by the way he put it down on the table.

"This is from your mother and me," he said proudly.

"Yes, and he'll have to thank Sid, too, when he gets in from work, because after all he helped us to buy it," Mum reminded Dad.

I stood there looking at the case, feeling awkward, not knowing what to say. Finally, I asked in wonder, "What is it?"

"Well, it's yours. Why don't you open it and see?" replied Mum.

Tied to the handle were two keys. I was about to take them off when Dad said, "It's not locked." There was a catch at each end of the case and as I pushed the releasing buttons aside with my thumb, the spring-loaded flaps snapped open. I lifted the lid and there inside was this magnificent accordion. I was stunned; if anyone had asked me what I thought was in the case, never in a million years would I have guessed it to be this. I mean, no one I knew could afford to buy anything so expensive – certainly not my parents.

I was speechless, but most of all I felt guilty, guilty because of my earlier thoughts about their not having bought me a present for my birthday, and there I was staring at something I had looked at every night for months, and never in my wildest dreams thought I would ever possess.

I stood gazing at it for some time, unable to take my eyes off it. Finally I went over to Mum and Dad and thanked them both with a kiss. I was now so overwhelmed by it all I found it difficult to control my emotions. This began to affect the others, and Dad, who could see he would soon have a houseful of howling kids on his hands, saved the situation by quipping, "Gawd! This is supposed to be a birthday, not a funeral."

Learning to play the accordion was at first more difficult than I had thought, but once I had discovered the combination of the base notes, and with the help of the *Accordion Book for Beginners*, I could play passably well within four or five weeks. Up until the age of fourteen I had been a choirboy at Trinity Church, Canning Town, and now that I could play well enough to do so, I used to entertain the family by singing the popular songs of the day to my own accompaniment.

About seven o'clock one Wednesday evening, early in September, we were all sitting around chatting. Dad, who had been home from work sick with pleurisy, was in the middle of telling Mum he would be fit enough to sign off the Panel on Friday, and go back to work on the following Monday, when he was interrupted by a knock on the street door. None of us were expecting visitors so we just sat where we were and looked at one another. A few seconds went by and the knock came again, a little louder. Dad said, "Well, don't all sit there – somebody go and answer the door. Reggie, you go."

I opened the door, and standing there was a man I vaguely remembered having seen a long time ago. He said, "Good evening, sonny, and which one are you?"

"I'm Reggie," I replied.

"Oh so you're Reggie! God, the last time I saw you you were very tiny. Mind you, you're not much bigger now, are you? Your dad's been telling me a lot about you lately. Would you tell him that Mr Bond has called to see him?"

Immediately he said his name I remembered. Mr Bond, or "Bondie" as Dad affectionately called him, was Dad's foreman at work, and a close friend. When I walked back into the kitchen, Dad said, "Who was it?"

"It's Mr Bond, Dad, he's come to see you."

"What!" he exclaimed, and leapt out of his armchair. "Don't tell me you've left him standing on the bloody doorstep."

As he walked to the street door we heard Bondie ask Dad how he was feeling.

"Oh, I'm fine now, I'll be back to work on Monday."

"Well, that's good news."

"What brings you over to this neck of the woods?" asked Dad as they walked up the passage to the kitchen.

"Well I had to come over this way, and I thought I would kill two birds with one stone: see how you were, and bring over your sick money."

At that moment Mum opened the kitchen door and greeted him, dressed in a clean "pinny" she had just slipped on for the occasion.

"Hello, Annie." Bondie kissed her on the cheek, then followed her into the kitchen. After he had said hello to us all, and remarked on how much we had grown and what a long time it was since they, meaning he and Mum and Dad, had all got together, Dad gave us a nod, which was the signal for us kids to make ourselves scarce.

I don't know where the others went, but I disappeared into the parlour to practise a new song that had just come out, "Oh Play to Me, Gypsy". It was perfect for both accordion and voice, but although I knew the tune it still needed a lot of rehearsing.

Mum had made a pot of tea, and later she told me that, just as Mr Bond lifted his cup, I struck up with my new song. The music stopped him in his tracks; he cocked his head towards the parlour, and with cup poised just above the saucer he sat motionless, listening.

When I had finished he sat quietly for a few moments, then turning to Mum and Dad said, "Who's that?"

Dad answered, "It's Reggie."

"The one you've been telling me about?"

"Yes, that's him."

"I just can't believe it," said Bondie rising from his chair.

"Well you had better come and see for yourself, then," said Dad.

I had started the introduction to the number again when the door opened. I stopped and turned round; all three were standing in the doorway. "No, don't stop, Mr Bond would like to hear you sing again." This time, now that I had an audience, I put every ounce of feeling I had into the song, and when I had finished he said to me, "Wonderful! Wonderful! Annie, this boy of yours has a lot of talent, and something should be done about it."

Unable to resist showing me off even more, Mum said, "Oh but you haven't heard him play the piano yet – Reggie, play 'The Tiger Rag' for Mr Bond."

At that time I had been playing the piano for nine years and, for my age, had quite a technique. When I finished "The Tiger Rag" Dad said proudly, "What do you think of that, Bondie?"

"I know you can rattle the keys a bit, Sid, but seeing his fingers fly up and down the keyboard like that – I think he's got the edge on you."

I wondered what Dad's answer to that would be, when he surprised me with, "Edge! He leaves me standing."

After this Mr Bond asked me if I had a good selection of songs and piano numbers. And when I said, "Lots," he went on, "Do you think you could put twenty minutes of entertainment together?"

"Yes, I think so."

He stood for a while with his arms folded, then thoughtfully stroking his chin he said to Mum and Dad, "He should be seen, you know, so if it's all right with you I'll get my Entertainment Secretary to put him on first turn on Saturday night." Then turning to me he added, "Would you like that?"

I said, "Yes," not knowing what I was agreeing to. As Dad had never belonged to any club, the subject of Working Men's Clubs never cropped up in our house – hence my ignorance of club activities and "turns" on a Saturday and Sunday night.

Mr Bond told us to be at the club at six thirty on Saturday night to see how I shaped up in front of an audience. And just as he got to the door, he added, "Reggie, I forgot the most important bit – you get eight and sixpence for your twenty-minute act, and if you should get an encore you get an extra one and sixpence – so have something extra up your sleeve, because you never know!"

Back in the parlour, in answer to my questions, Dad explained that Mr Bond was the Secretary of the Plumstead Radical Club, and as Secretary of the club virtually ran it, which was the reason he had the power to put me on on a Saturday night at such short notice.

We then discussed my début; putting my twenty-minute act together was easy – the problem was, how should I be dressed? Mum suggested "evening dress", thinking that as I was so tiny I would look cute. That was ruled out for two reasons, and both of them were Dad's. As he said to Mum, "If we had the time, which we haven't, Reggie walking on stage in a 'tail suit' would look like a penguin. Besides," and he laughed, "we want the audience to clap him, not throw him fish."

Mum came up with another idea, which Dad and I thought was

brilliant. She said that as I was singing a gypsy song in my act, why not dress me as a gypsy – it would be a colourful costume, and the perfect outfit for an accordionist. My elder sister Bella had become a wonderful dressmaker and Mum suggested that she should make the costume, then we could be sure that it would be made in time.

Bella responded, without being asked, "Just a minute, I'll get my tape measure." Within seconds she was back, and I was being measured for my very first stage costume. The following night I was being fitted, and on the Friday night it was finished. Armed with the patent leather dancing pumps I had bought for three and sixpence (out of my weekly wage), and much to the disappointment of our family, we went into the parlour alone to try everything on. But as Bella said, and she was right, it would be far better if I appeared in front of them fully dressed in the costume than if they saw her dress me bit by bit. Besides, this was her moment – after all she had designed it, cut it out and machined it up, so it was only natural to want everything just right before showing them her skill as a dressmaker.

It was a beautiful costume, and standing there fully dressed in my red bandanna, green satin blouse, black satin godet trousers (the godet being of the same material as the blouse), and not forgetting my patent leather dancing pumps, I felt grand.

Bella looked me up and down. When I saw me, I mean the costume, I didn't exist – only her creation. She fussed around me, her fingers fluffing up the full sleeves, adjusting the bandanna, and untying and retying the red sash about my waist. When she had finished titivating, she said with a satisfied smile, "Come on, let's go and show them."

I let Bella go into the kitchen first, and being the little showman that I have always been, waited outside in the passage to make my grand entrance. The family were already anxious to see me in my finery, and when Bella entered on her own, what little patience they had, left them, especially Dad.

"Well," he said to Bella, "where is he? Jesus Christ, we've been sitting here twiddling our thumbs, waiting to see what he looks like as a 'gyppo' – don't tell me he's gone to show the bloody neighbours first?"

I heard Bella say, "He was with me just now." Then her head poked round the kitchen door and she said, "Why are you standing out there?"

Not bothering to explain my reason, I made my entrance and

stood at the back of the table, which occupied the centre of the room.

The delay had the desired effect: they were stunned. Sister Doris complimented her elder sister, saying to no one in particular, "Why can't I make things like that?"

Bella was thrilled by all the compliments flying about. She had taken only two days to make it (two evenings to be exact, because of course she had been working at the dress factory during the day) and Mum marvelled at her speed; being a dressmaker herself, she knew the enormous amount of work that had been done from the measuring on the Wednesday night to my standing there now, fully clad.

My parents sat either side of the kitchen range, and from that position could see little more than head and shoulders – the rest of me was hidden by the table. Dad said, "Well, come round here and let your mother and me see the rest of you."

I went to the front of the table and posed for them. They looked me up and down, and finally Mum said, "It's lovely, Bella, really lovely." Dad agreed and congratulated her on a marvellous achievement.

For a while, Dad kept looking thoughtfully at me; suddenly he said, "I've got it – I know what's missing!"

Bella looked disappointed at what she thought was going to be a criticism. "What's wrong, Dad?"

"Nothing's wrong. It's what's missing – earrings – all gypsies wear earrings."

Relieved, Bella said, "Oh yes!"

Mum, taking the old coffee pot from the dresser, said, "I think I've got something in here that might do!" She tipped it upside-down spilling its contents on to the table and from among the odd bits of string, rubbers, hairpins and something I hadn't seen for years, the little clown, Mum produced two brass earrings. "Will these be too big?" she asked. Bella, although doubtful, got a reel of cotton and within minutes had hung the two curtain rings on my ears. She stood back for inspection, saying, "There!"

This got an immediate reaction from the family, all agreeing that the curtain rings put the finishing touch to the outfit.

Dad sat there looking very pleased with himself; after all, the earrings had been his idea, and he felt that he had made his contribution to the success of the costume. His eyes twinkled and a broad grin split his face. "Yes, Reggie, you really look the part now, and I'll tell you something else – you look so authentic, even if they don't like your act, you could make a fortune flogging 'em pegs."

Five thirty Saturday night, after the family had wished me luck and Mum had given her last-minute instructions to Dad about bringing me straight home after I had done my show, and not to stay on drinking, we left for the Plumstead Radical Club, and my first public performance.

Mr Bond met us on arrival and introduced us to the Entertainment Secretary, who told me that as I was an extra act to the already arranged bill, I would be going on early, and although the hall would not be full, those that were there I'd find very appreciative. "So if you'd like to follow me," he said, "I'll take you to the men's dressing room."

Dad bent to pick up my accordion, but Mr Bond stopped him, saying, "No, you stay here with me, Sid, the Secretary will look after him; we can watch him from the front."

Neither Dad nor I were expecting this; Dad straightened up from the accordion and we looked at one another. I knew he wanted to be with me to give me his support, and he also knew that that was what I wanted too. There was nothing he could do, however, and in the presence of Mr Bond and the Entertainment Secretary he wished me luck in a matter-of-fact sort of way, but his hand on my shoulder gripped me reassuringly.

The Secretary took my accordion, and with the little attaché case containing my gypsy outfit, I followed him.

To get backstage you had to go through the auditorium, which was a rectangular hall with wall lights all around. The seating capacity was about two hundred and fifty people. The seats (chairs) were arranged in three blocks, with a gangway on either side of the centre block. At the back of each chair was a small rack for holding one's drink.

To the left and right sides of the stage were doors leading backstage and to the dressing rooms. The proscenium arch was fairly large, or so it seemed to me then. As I followed the Secretary down the left-hand gangway, my attention was drawn to the front cloth, ablaze with colour and completely covered with advertisements. The brewery companies took up the larger portion of the cloth, vying with each other, using different words, but saying the same thing – all claiming that their beer was the best.

The Secretary saw me looking around at the handful of people sitting in the auditorium and guessing my thoughts said, "It'll be another twenty minutes before you see any sign of improvement. Most of your audience are in the bar at the moment, and they don't start drifting in until the pianist starts to play the overture."

He opened the door and we went up the few steps and on to the stage. A man with his shirt-sleeves rolled up came over immediately and introduced himself as Ted the stage manager.

He was of medium height and although lean, his arms told me he was very powerful. He picked up my accordion as though the case was empty, and I followed him to the back of the stage and into the small dressing room. It was about ten feet square with a dressing table and mirror running the full length of the left-hand wall; in the corner was a sink and cold water tap and screwed to the wall just beside it was a wooden roller but no towel.

"You've got about half an hour, so while you are changing, if you tell me what numbers you do in your act, I will arrange the lighting to suit them; after that I'll get the pianist up here to go through your 'dots' with you."

I had never heard of "dots" before, but common sense told me that as it was connected with the pianist, the "dots" must mean my music.

"I haven't got any 'dots'," I said. "I play the piano myself."

This was news to Ted. "Oh! So you'll want the piano on stage. They didn't tell me that! I'll have to get a couple of the lads to give me a hand. I can't remember the last time we had a piano act on the bill."

While I was changing into my gypsy outfit, I told Ted all the numbers I did in my act. As he wrote down each item on his pad, he told me what sort of lighting he would give it. "This opening number you sing at the piano, 'Oh How I've Waited for You' – is it a bright song?"

"Yes," I said.

"Good! Then I'll give it a 'full-up' with a white spot on you – yes, that's good," he said without looking up, "always start with a nice lively number, something with some go in it, something that'll make them sit up." He went through my whole act like this: "Red and blue stage; pink spot for this; black out white spot for that"; and although I didn't have a clue as to what he was talking about, when he asked me my opinion I said, "Oh that sounds lovely."

A notice strategically placed above the dressing-table mirror intrigued me. In fair-sized print it said:

MY INTRODUCTION TO SHOW BUSINESS

BLUE MATERIAL WILL NOT BE TOLERATED IN THIS CLUB

I wondered what "blue material" meant; I had read it immediately I had entered the dressing room, but didn't like to ask. Now, as I was changing and it kept catching my eye, my curiosity got the better of me, so I asked Ted, "What is blue material?"

"I'm glad you've noticed it," he said. "It shows it's in the right place. It doesn't apply to you, Reggie-boy, it's put there especially for the comics. Blue material means dirty or suggestive jokes of any kind. The club's very strict about that sort of thing – as a matter of fact only last week we had a comic on the bill, and his material was very near the knuckle, and immediately he had finished the Ent. Sec. came flying round and before he could reach the dressing room he paid him off and told him his act was filthy and he'd never work this club again."

Ted had finished what he called my "lighting plot", and told me he was going to give this to the boys on the "limes", and on his way back he would bring me a lemonade. He left, saying, "Now I won't be long," as though he was afraid to leave me on my own.

Ted was as good as his word. Within five minutes he was back with two hefty fellows, and my lemonade. "The audience are coming in now, and by the look of it you're going to have a fair house to play to." Then taking his watch out of his waistcoat pocket, he added, "You've got about ten minutes before you go on. In the meantime me and the lads will put your piano on the stage."

One of the lads said, "Where's this piano then, Ted?"

"It's up the back here," said Ted.

I could hear the three of them moving about somewhere at the back of the stage. Somebody said, "Is this it underneath this sheet?" Another voice, not Ted's, said, "Well, it's not a sideboard is it!"

Ted said, "I'll take one end – you two take the other, and when I say 'lift' all lift together and move it downstage centre."

Voice: "Why can't we push it on its castors?"

"Because it hasn't got any. Right! Lift!"

All I could hear from then on was a lot of grunting and groaning as they staggered with the heavy piano to the centre of the stage; then one of the two lads gasped, "Christ, this is a heavy bastard – ooh! – I'll make sure I'm not around when you want it put back."

His mate said, "Don't talk – lift the bleeder!"

Finally I heard it put down with a heavy thud on to the stage. Ted thanked the lads. "You'll find us in the bar when you want it put back," said one of them.

Ted returned to me in the dressing room just as the pianist struck up the overture. He took my accordion from me saying, "I'll put it by the side of the piano. It'll dress the stage, and enable you to make a clean entrance.

"Now this is the drill – I am now going to raise the front cloth; the pianist out front times the end of his overture to coincide with the front cloth being fully raised. The Chairman then calls the audience to order, and when he has complete silence he introduces you. He will give you a wonderful introduction, the pianist will then play some bright entrance music for you – and when I say 'OK' you go on. And listen, Reggie, when you walk out there in front of those lights, smile at everyone – don't show them what you are feeling inside. Don't worry! I know what you are going through."

He was right. Standing there waiting to go on was terrifying. I felt hopelessly alone . . . there was no one to help me now . . . it was all down to me.

The butterflies were playing havoc with my stomach, and my bodily functions were sending me messages I had no time now to answer. I found myself wishing that something would happen to me – nothing fatal, of course, but something like fainting or tripping over a stage weight or spraining an ankle. Anything that would prevent me from going on stage. I didn't realise it then, but this was my first experience of how I would suffer before going on stage for the rest of my life.

The Chairman and the committee sat at a rectangular table in the auditorium immediately below the stage. The Chairman faced the audience with an adjustable mirror in front of him, enabling him to see the show. On the table was a jug of beer, and each committee member in turn would nip out to the bar to refill it as it became empty, but never while an act was on.

When the applause for the pianist had died down, the Chairman stood up, banged his gavel on the table and with great authority said, "ORDER!" The noise ceased immediately. Acknowledging their obedience he continued, "Thank you, ladies and gentlemen." He paused. "Now the reason for our early start this evening is that our first turn is an extra. He is a young lad, only fifteen years of age, and this is his first appearance on any stage. I am told he is quite talented, but I am also told he is very nervous, so let's give a warm welcome, and show him what a great audience we, at the Plumstead Radical, can be. Ladies and gentlemen" – and bang went the gavel on the table – "REG VARNEY!"

The pianist played something very fast and double forte, and

94

after a few bars, Ted tapped me on the shoulder: "OK, Reggie. Good luck!"

I moved forward, my heart pounding away, and as the spotlight picked me up, a big round of applause greeted me. The limelight momentarily blinded me, but I kept walking; my eyes quickly adjusted to the light, and as I made my way to the piano the applause seemed to be coming from a big black hole.

The piano was a big old upright, and when I sat down I realised that the angle at which they had placed it was wrong. For me, the keyboard should have been angled towards the audience, not the way they had placed it. No way was I going to get my songs over from this position – it had to be moved. The applause had died away by now, so I stood up and looked towards where Ted should be, but I couldn't see him. I was so preoccupied with what had to be done I'd forgotten about my nervousness. I peered into the wings again, but still could see no sign of Ted. There was no other way but to try to do the job myself, so I went to the front end of the piano – the end I wanted to move – and tried to shift it.

Three hefty blokes had nearly ruptured themselves trying to move it, so what chance did I have? The audience, having no clue as to what kind of act I did, must have thought that what I was trying to do now was my part of the show – a small gypsy trying to move a piano.

Luckily for me Ted eventually came to my rescue, and after a couple of tries got it as I wanted it. Ted got a big cheer as he walked off, and I received another round of applause as I sat down. The clapping I was getting for doing nothing was worrying me – I was beginning to wonder if my act would come up to my piano-moving routine.

"Oh How I've Waited for You", an old Leyton and Johnson number, was the opening of my act. My arrangement of it was one chorus vocal, one chorus piano solo, and the last chorus back to vocal. The reception it got took me completely by surprise – it was terrific. At first I was very excited, then I began to wonder: was this applause just relief that my performance was proving to be something more than moving a piano about all over the stage? I would have to wait and see.

My second number at the piano was a ballad called "Unless" and as I struck up the introduction to it, the whole stage changed from a bright full-up and white spot, to a red and blue stage with a mellow amber spot tight on me. This transformation was very dramatic and had a tremendous effect on me and my rendering of the song. Suddenly I seemed to have more understanding of the lyrics, and I found myself putting light and shade into the ballad where I had never put it before, and my accompaniment automatically followed the same mood.

As I sang, not a sound came from the auditorium – not a cough or a chink of a glass, nothing – but from this silence I could feel the tremendous atmosphere being transmitted from the audience to me.

I had learned early on that to really sell a song, no matter how well you sang it, it meant nothing to an audience without a dynamic finish. "Unless" had such a finish – the last four words were "to make you mine". I was coming to them now and sensing the audience were on my side, I was really going to sell it. I dropped my voice on "to make" – paused – then belted out "you" . . . and at the precise moment I hit the top note of "mine" Ted snapped the stage into a full-up.

It was perfect timing – the audience erupted. This swept away the doubts I had after my first number. Standing there receiving this wonderful ovation, I knew there and then this was what I had to do – this was my reason for being.

Announcing any of my items had never entered my head, and yet when I found myself saying, "Ladies and gentlemen, I am now going to play you my arrangement of 'The Tiger Rag'," I wasn't at all surprised, it seemed the natural thing to do.

I first heard "The Tiger Rag" on the wireless – as it was always referred to in those days. Harry Roy, a famous band leader, had a programme every Saturday afternoon, and on one occasion I happened to hear him announce that his two pianists, Ivor Morton and Dave Kaye, would be playing "The Tiger Rag" – four hands on one piano. They were brilliant, and their technique, to me, out of this world. I vowed then that I wouldn't be satisfied until I could play it like them. I bought their ten-inch 78 rpm recording and practised for hours on end, trying to get my two hands to sound like four. To achieve this effect meant hands and fingers flying over the keyboard at a tremendous rate; it also called for a considerable amount of bodywork. It was of course impossible to copy their exact arrangement but eventually I got it as near to theirs as I could.

"The Tiger Rag" was a piece that started at a fair lick and as it progressed it gradually gathered speed to the end, finishing with a grand flourish. I wasn't reckoning on my earrings taking part, because on my last two numbers they had been very quiet, but now as the movement of my head and body got under way and grew faster, so did my earrings. I could feel them flying round my head thumping against my neck and the sides of my face, and as the music increased in speed they got completely out of control; as I finished, with a gliss from bottom to top of the piano and a showman-like fling of my head, the right-hand curtain ring, having no resistance against such a force, flew off and across the stage into the footlights. The left-hand earring did its best to hang on but finally gave up and limply dropped with a clang on to the piano keys.

"The Tiger Rag" was a knockout; they stamped and cheered and kept calling for more. I would have loved to play it again for them, but after the physical efforts of a moment ago, resulting in the loss of my earrings, my bandanna was none too secure either – it was only will power that was keeping it on – so I thought I had better not risk it.

Instead I put on my accordion and walked to the front of the stage. I doubted if I could top what I had just done – I thought the accordion would be an anti-climax – but I was wrong; had I sat down at the piano again after "The Tiger Rag" then it would have been, but the accordion was in complete contrast.

"Dinah", my opening song on the accordion, was quite a novelty because of all the "scat" singing I did in the second chorus. I was one of the first to do it in this country (if not *the* first). They had never heard it at the Plumstead Radical Club, that's for sure; it went like a bomb. The ballad "Song of Songs" followed, then a piano accordion solo, a march my dad often played – "Under the Double Eagle".

It was at the end of the march (another showy piece calling for a great deal of hard work and energy) that the bandanna got the better of my will power, and with a final toss of my head, joined the earring already in the footlights. The little gypsy was gradually disintegrating in front of the audience's eyes. Now, with the accordion hiding the rest of my costume, I sang my final song, "Oh Play to Me, Gypsy" – the song for which my costume had originally been designed – looking nothing like one. This didn't make any difference to their reaction to the song, because it went as well as everything else I had performed. I took several bows and walked off.

Ted and the Secretary stood in the wings waiting for me. They were just as excited as I was, and above the noise of the cheering the Secretary said, "Have you got another song you can do?"

I said, "Yes."

"Well go out and give them an encore," he said.

I sang a song called "Over the Hill" which referred to the Workhouse, and which was then still the fate of some elderly people, less fortunate than others. It was a real tear-jerker, as you can tell from the following lyrics:

> Over the hill, over the hill,
> Why should they be there, over the hill;
> Where are the ones they cherished when small,
> For whom they provided and gave them their all?
> What have they done for such a fate –
> I know that it isn't God's will.
> In a palace of gold, they should live when they're old,
> Instead of over the hill.

This really tugged at their heartstrings, and who knows, it might have gone home to some of them.

The ovation for this surpassed anything I had received before, and I realised then, if I'd had another song, which I hadn't, I would never be able to top "Over the Hill". From then on I kept it as my closing number.

I took my bow and came off to find Dad, Mr Bond and the Entertainment Secretary waiting for me. The act who should have gone on first was standing with Ted in the wings waiting for the Chairman to announce him. A small trilby hat that had been ironed flat was balancing on his head, and his check suit was too small for him. I could see that he was a bundle of nerves because he was fiddling with his bow tie and kept trying to clear something from his throat that wasn't there. I couldn't help wondering if he had read the warning notice to comics about blue material. Dad and Mr Bond walked with me into the dressing room, and just as we were entering I heard the Chairman announce, "Our next turn is a very funny man – " The door closed. He didn't look very funny to me when I saw him standing on the side of the stage.

Little did I realise then that in years to come I was going to be standing on the side of the stage, a comic just like him, with my guts tearing me apart, and trying to clear something from my throat that wasn't there.

Coming home on the tram, sitting next to Dad, I was waiting for him to say how well I'd done. After a few minutes when nothing came, I could wait no longer. I gave a little cough to signal that I was going to speak, then I said, keeping my voice as matter-of-fact as I could, "I was ever so surprised at the way my opening went." Since it was not a question, he didn't have to answer, but I left a little pause hoping he would. Getting no response, I quickly went on, "'Song of Songs' too . . . and what about 'The Tiger Rag' . . . and the songs with the accordion, especially 'Over the Hill' " – I was beginning to lose all control of myself, so I stopped abruptly.

Fighting back the hurt, I was thinking, Oh God, why can't he say what I so desperately want to hear: "I thought you were wonderful tonight, Reggie," or if that was perhaps a little too elaborate, any small words of praise would have done. Coming from him they would have meant more to me than all the adulation I had just received at the club. Was it his pride that wouldn't allow him to praise? It was my pride that wouldn't allow me to ask!

As I sat there, with my legs dangling, and rocking from side to side with the motion of the tram, I felt thoroughly dejected, and just when I had given up hope of Dad saying anything at all, he suddenly said, "Yes, Reggie, 'The Tiger Rag'." With those few words I was back to my original high. "Well, to tell you the truth, Reggie, I wouldn't know how well it went; I was so mesmerised by those curtain rings flying around your head, it was a relief to see them fly off your lugs into the footlights."

In situations like this he always used his sense of humour to defend his emotions.

I started to laugh, and the more I thought about it the more I could see the funny side of it, especially from his point of view, sitting there with Bondie. It was this thought that really set me going, and as he saw the tears rolling down my cheeks, he said, "It's all right for you to laugh, how do you think I felt . . . the way bits kept dropping off you. I said to Bondie, 'Thank Christ he's got his accordion on, at least he'll walk off wearing something!' "

When we arrived home Mum and the rest of the family couldn't wait to hear how I got on. Between us we told them everything in detail. I showed them the ten-shilling note I had received, and told them I had been booked again for the following Saturday night. Dad had them in fits of laughter, telling them how all the bits kept falling off me: "Yes, Reggie, something will have to be done about those earrings."

The following day, thinking it over, it suddenly struck me that if instead of using thread, we made the loops over the ears of elastic, they would grip more tightly. Bella gave me some round elastic and I made the loops. After trial and error, I got the loops to grip firmly round my ears and tested them by shaking my head vigorously from side to side. This problem solved, Bella decided to rim the bandanna with elastic too, and this also was a great improvement.

Although I was still working as a messenger boy during the day, every night after I had had my tea I would go into the parlour and rehearse each item over and over again, knocking off all the rough edges I knew existed. As the act grew more polished the more confident I became, and now that the problem of the earrings and the bandanna had been solved, the waiting for Saturday night to arrive seemed interminable.

Travelling on the tram to the Plumstead Radical, I was so absorbed with thoughts about my act that I didn't hear a word Dad was saying to me. The butterflies in my stomach had started up again, and the more I brooded about the show ahead, the worse they got. I tried deep breathing exercises to control them but they were a complete waste of time.

I was suddenly brought back to this world by a nudge from Dad. "Come on, this is it!" he said.

It was the music coming from upstairs and the deserted foyer that made us realise that the show was about to start. The concert hall, in contrast to the foyer, was packed with people, all engrossed in their own private conversations, and this, with the smell of beer and tobacco, the sound of the pianist's overture, clinking glasses and chairs being moved, created for me a most wonderful atmosphere.

As we made our way down the gangway to the dressing room I noticed some people nudging one another and nodding in my direction. The Chairman and his committee were taking their seats at their table in front of the stage just as the front cloth started to rise.

Dad and I entered the door to the side of the stage as Ted, wearing a pair of leather gloves, was heaving on the thick rope of the front cloth. "Hello, Reggie-boy," he grunted, then nodding towards the auditorium he grunted on, "what did I tell you?" He tied off the thick rope. "You've got plenty of time . . . you're on third."

I thanked him and moved towards the dressing room. The man already there, dressed in his dinner suit, was manipulating a pack of cards very expertly; I was fascinated watching him produce cards from out of the air, and when he came over to me and took a card out of my breast pocket I was dumbstruck.

He then checked every pocket of his suit, and when he opened his jacket I was amazed to see rows of cigarettes in clips on either side of it. He never said a word, and all the time I was changing he was practising his skills, and every now and then would check and recheck his pockets.

When I'd got my gypsy outfit on, Dad and I went on to the side of the stage to see what was happening. The show had started. Two girls in sequinned leotards were dancing to the music of a waltz on huge balls; they reminded me of hamsters on their treadmills. It was very clever and every time they performed an intricate move they received a round of applause. After a few minutes the card manipulator joined us and began to light the cigarettes on the inside of his jacket.

The girls' music had changed to a march, "Blaze Away". They were doing a military routine to the music, and as they neared the end Ted said, "Stand by." At that precise moment the pianist thumped out the last few bars of the march double forte, the girls gave the audience an eyes front and, smartly saluting, marched off on the balls.

The chap with the cards and the fags went on next and I was amazed because, quiet as he was off, he was just the opposite on stage. He was a comedian as well as being a master of the art of misdirection with his cards and cigarettes. His patter fitted every trick and had the audience in stitches.

I was enjoying his performance so much that I forgot my own nervousness until Ted came up to me and asked how I was feeling. That started it all over again, although I must confess that even though my butterflies were doing a steady rate of knots, I felt very confident . . . after all, I had worked hard on my act, correcting all the mistakes I'd discovered from last week's performance, including the earrings and bandanna, so really, what had I got to worry about?

There was a small break after the comedy illusionist for Ted to put my piano on stage. Having done this and placed my accordion at the front end of the piano, he came off and said to me, "If the piano is not quite right you'll find it very easy to move now." This I could well believe, seeing how easily he'd moved it without the aid of the two heavies. He looked at me and with a big smile asked, "Right, are you ready?" I nodded. "Good boy," he said, then pressed the bell to tell the Chairman.

The audience began to applaud the moment the Chairman announced my name, making it clear that I was the one they were waiting to see. I made my entrance and immediately the spotlight picked me up the applause doubled; it was a wonderful feeling. I bowed, and with my confidence running high couldn't wait to justify their ovation.

It was when I sat down at the piano that the nightmare started. The keyboard was halfway up my chest. The shock nearly gave me a heart attack. I must, I thought, have been given the wrong chair. It was when I looked down to check that I saw that the piano had been mounted on an iron frame with rather large ball-bearinged wheels. This accounted for the piano being so much higher, giving me the feeling that I was sitting in a hole. It also answered the question of how Ted had moved it so easily.

I needed cushions, but knowing that nothing could be done, I pressed on with playing the introduction to my first number.

"Oh How I've Waited for You," being a lively song, called for a lot of facial expression – now, as soon as I started to sing, and my facial muscles came into operation, so did all the elastic attached to my head. The first thing I felt was the elastic gripping tight to my ears and to my head, and as I progressed through the number, the pressure became vice-like. I could feel the curtain rings gradually lifting up, until finally they were sticking out horizontally from the side of my face.

The elastic round my bandanna, being of a much stronger gauge, had now got a firm hold on my hair and was pulling upward viciously, so much so that it was taking my forehead with it, and as my eyebrows followed suit, my eyes became little slits.

The piano had moved away fractionally, and as the audience became aware of my predicament the titters began to escalate. The more I sang the tighter the elastic gripped and I could feel it desperately breaking its neck to get back to its original position. My head and ears were no match for its power and were gradually giving up the ghost. The curtain ring elastic had long overpowered my lobes and was now in the final stage of screwing up my ears like bits of paper, while the bandanna, also having won its battle, was gripping the top of my head in triumph.

So there, at the end of the number, I sat, with slit eyes and cauliflower ears, looking like a tiny Chinese pugilist with a red cabbage on his head.

Once again the bandanna and the earrings had been my downfall. Last week they had been an embarrassment, this week they had made me a laughing-stock. I couldn't hear the applause, only the laughter – it was the laughter that hurt.

I yanked the bandanna and earrings off my head and viciously threw them into the wings. The audience reacted to this in some way, but how I do not know – I was so bitter and confused. Deep down I wanted to run offstage and get away from this hell, but my upbringing and pride wouldn't allow me, so I ignored as best I could the hilarity and pulled my chair up to the piano to play the introduction to my next number, "Unless". This caught the attention of the majority of the audience, bringing some semblance of order.

I started to sing this beautiful song, but those who found it difficult to control their laughter were brought to a sudden halt by the Chairman's crashing blow with the gavel on the table, followed by a furious shout of "ORDER, PLEASE." The ferocity of his voice frightened the life out of them. He could have been a sergeant-major in the Army. On his word of command everyone froze – including me. He stood there, his eyes blazing, listening to their silence, then after a few seconds, when he was assured of their attention, he slowly turned to me saying gently, "You can carry on now, son."

As I once more began the introduction to "Unless", you could have heard a pin drop. It seemed to me they were too quiet, but my fears were unfounded and the ballad got a marvellous reception. Now, with my faith in myself completely restored, I stood up and announced my arrangement of "The Tiger Rag" and with great confidence sat down and struck the first heavy chords.

I've always been told that lightning doesn't strike twice in the same place – this is not true. That night it did. The moment my hands hit the keys, the piano began to move away from me, and after a few bars my arms were fully stretched. I quickly pulled my chair back to the piano and continued to play; it moved away again, and as its weight got caught up in the rake of the stage, its momentum increased. With me in my chair in hot pursuit it made its way slowly across the stage. It became a battle between me and the piano . . . I was no longer playing it – I was fighting it.

The more I chased it the more the audience laughed, until eventually they were hysterical . . . including the Chairman. Shouts of "Go on, Reggie-boy – hold that tiger" were coming from some of the men, while I was being crucified by this second disaster. Once again I wanted to stop, but like the drunken man who has to keep running, I couldn't. I continued to play and as I came to my final gliss in "The Tiger Rag" the piano slewed round and gently came to rest in the footlights.

The whole place erupted. They went wild, clapping, cheering, whistling, stamping their feet, with shouts of "Bravo" and "More".

I got up and ran off, my face awash with tears . . . heartbroken.

Dad was standing in the wings of the stage. I went to him and buried my head in his little fat belly and sobbed my heart out. He didn't say a word; just held the back of my head and pressed it to him.

After a while he took his handkerchief from his top pocket and passed it down to me. Wiping my eyes I looked up at him and said, "Let's go home, Dad, I can't take any more."

I wanted to leave there and then, but as Dad pointed out, my accordion was still on stage. Ted had moved the piano off, but had left my accordion on, and there it sat, in the middle of an empty stage, looking very lonely. The audience were still going wild and after a few minutes when I didn't appear, the Entertainment Secretary came bursting through the door, wanting to know what had gone wrong. Turning to Dad he said, "Why isn't he going back on?"

"He can't go back on like this," Dad answered, defensively. "Just look at the state he's in."

"But, Mr Varney, they love him," the Secretary said, "they adore him, and as for the laughing – they weren't laughing at him in the way he thinks, they were admiring his courage for battling through his adversity."

"You understand that. I understand that. But he's just a kid – he doesn't!"

The Secretary came over to me and bending down to my height said, "Listen, son, if you don't go back out there now, you'll never want to go on a stage again, and that would be criminal, because you're a natural performer." He paused and then he said coaxingly, "Now you go back on and I promise you that when you come off you will thank me."

I looked at Dad for his advice.

"No, Reggie, I'm not going to advise you one way or the other, this is your decision."

It was the tone of his voice that as good as told me he didn't want me to quit. I stared at the floor for a few moments, then without saying a word I turned my back on them and walking briskly on to the stage, picked up my accordion and put it on. I went to the front of the stage amid the applause and cheers, and even to some calls of "Come on, Reggie, my son," but the moment I played the first chord there was complete silence, and from then on they cheered everything I did.

After I had done my encore, "Over the Hill", they were still shouting, "More! More!" "Have you got another song you can give them?" the Secretary asked. I told him that I hadn't. "Well go out and give them 'Over the Hill' again," he said. I did – and earned myself another one and sixpence.

Hardly had I got back into the dressing room when it became packed with men. I soon discovered that they were Entertainment Secretaries from other Working Men's Clubs who, at the request of our Secretary, had come along to see my act. After congratulating me on my performance they asked me if I'd got my book. Fortunately the previous week, on the advice of Mr Bond, I had bought myself an engagement book, so it was with great pride that I took it from my pocket. Between them, in a very short time, they had booked my Saturdays and Sundays for the next month.

When they had gone the Secretary produced a sheet of paper for me to sign for my money. "I was right, wasn't I?" he said, handing me his pen for my signature. Before I could reply he went on, "I think you understand now why I was so anxious for you to go back on." I agreed with him and thanked him for his valuable advice.

As Dad and I walked towards Ted and shook hands in farewell Ted drew my attention to my bandanna and earrings on his little table, saying, "I don't suppose you'll be wanting these any more?"

I just shook my head.

"I didn't think you would," he said.

It was plain that the secretaries who'd seen me perform on that Saturday night were responsible for the amount of mail I received the following week, mostly postcards from other affiliated clubs – clubs I'd never heard of, or, come to that, the districts they were in either. All were enquiring if I was available on such-and-such a date, at such-and-such a time.

The more I performed, the more these cards kept rolling in. Eventually it became possible, if the times could be arranged and the clubs were not too far apart, to do eight shows over a weekend – four on Saturday night and four on Sunday night. To do this you had to open the first half at the first club, then dash by bus or tram to the second club, and close the first half; another scramble to the third club to open their second half, and finally on to close the second half at the fourth club. It was hard work, but with the encore money I could earn four pounds for a weekend's work.

The first time I accomplished this feat and told my dad, he said, "Jesus Christ! That's nearly twice as much as I earn all the week."

It was not long after this that Mum could see that doing a daytime job and doing club work as a sideline was affecting my health. She suggested I should make up my mind, and of course I chose show business – what else?

15

I Learn my First Big Lesson

There is a golden rule in show business: never give your audience too much, always leave them wanting. I had strictly kept to this since my first date at the Plumstead Radical Club, with the exception of one evening show at the Horns, Kennington, where I had been booked to perform at a Buffaloes dinner. The following is an account of events which to this day, whenever I think of them, can cause me a slight blush.

From the very beginning, as we have seen, I always closed my act with "Over the Hill". It never failed. It's what's known in show business as a show-stopper. But no matter how well it was received by the audience, I never broke the golden rule.

For a few days before my date at the Horns, I had been working on a new song called "Chapel in the Moonlight" and on the night in question, "Over the Hill" went exceptionally well. In fact the Buffaloes gave it a standing ovation. Now don't ask me why, but instead of coming off after my final bow as usual, like a fool I fell for this tremendous reception and went back on. This was a great opportunity (or so I thought) for me to introduce the new song into the act.

I was brimming with self-confidence when I started the announcement of "Chapel in the Moonlight" but nearing the end an uneasy feeling crept over me, so much so that on my way back to the piano I could feel my confidence rapidly leaving me. I sat at the piano for a moment or two before playing the introduction, trying to pull myself together, but what little nerve I still had deserted me the moment I began to sing and realised just how under-rehearsed I was.

I sang the first verse without any meaning or feeling whatsoever, so much was I concentrating on the words. I even managed to remember the first line of the chorus, "How I love to hear the choir in the chapel in the moonlight . . ." Then my mind went completely blank. I wanted to stop but I couldn't. It was as though a hidden force within wouldn't allow me to. So there I was, singing anything that came into my head, just words, trying desperately but failing miserably to give the words some sense of what the song was all about. The end result was a disaster. I could feel my face go scarlet beneath my make-up and it seemed an eternity before I heard myself singing the last few words of the song, "Forever be mine," the only ones I remembered.

The silence that greeted the end was eerie; it was something I had never experienced. Before, when I'd heard other performers say they had literally died, I didn't know what they meant – now I did. I have never felt so dreadful in all my life; now I wanted to die physically.

I jumped up from the piano stool, tore off the stage and into the tiny dressing room. I ripped off my stage clothes in disgust, hating myself for my stupidity, and as I was stuffing them into my small case, Dad came awkwardly into the dressing room and put the accordion into its case. I hurriedly finished dressing and without taking my make-up off, I slid my little case off the table, went over and picked up my accordion. Dad stopped me. "All right," he said, "I'll take that." They were the first words to be spoken since I came off.

"No, I want to carry it myself," I said childishly, without looking at him.

"Now come on, give it to me, you know I always carry it."

"I know you do, but I want to carry it myself."

This sort of attitude Dad never tolerated and firmly taking the accordion away from me he said in a tone you didn't argue with, "Now pull yourself together and stop being bloody silly. I know what you're going through and carrying this damned thing's not going to cure it." He stood looking at me, knowing full well there was nothing he could say to ease my misery, then near to a whisper he said, "Come on, let's go."

It was a wretched night to have to walk the considerable distance from the Horns to the tram stop and the cold blustery wind blowing the drizzle into my face seemed to be in keeping with my misery.

Usually Dad made for the top of the tram so that he could have a smoke, but tonight he didn't. He put the accordion in the recess under the stairs and we sat inside. It seemed we were the only two on the tram but that was to be expected, especially as it was in the middle of the week, late at night, and a foul one at that.

We sat there in silence but through my despair I faintly recall the tram going at a hell of a lick, causing us to sway vigorously from side to side. It was as though the driver wanted to get back to the depot and out of this appalling night.

As I sat there, the humiliation and shame I had just brought upon myself kept tormenting me. What had made me do such a thing? Well, it was plain to me now that I'd listened to and believed all the flattery that had been showered upon me over the past few months, making me self-opinionated, smug, cocky and swollen-headed. I thought perhaps this attack of self-criticism might help to ease the pain I was feeling, but it didn't.

I was about to continue the assault when Dad suddenly said, "What a bloody awful night for the middle of July." Immediately he said that I knew he was trying to get my mind off recent events and although it was a statement and didn't need a reply, I said with a deep sigh, "Yes."

Knowing what the deep sigh meant, he came back at me quickly with, "Now look here, what happened to you tonight is not the end of the world, you know! So why do you keep on torturing yourself so?"

There and then I poured out to him all that had just gone through my mind, and when I came to what I thought I had become, I spat the words out viciously. I had to stop at this point and blow my nose. Emotion of any sort always played havoc with my sinuses!

Dad waited for me to put the hanky away, then before I could say any more he came straight in with, "Now I've let you have your say; now let me have mine. Firstly, let me say this. All the things you have just accused yourself of being are not true. If they had been I'd have slapped you down months ago, and you know I would. Secondly, you're blowing this thing up out of all proportion." He paused. "You've barely been a professional for a year and you're carrying on like this. You've got to learn to get things in their right perspective. Tonight you got a little over-confident and put a new song in when you shouldn't have done, that's all. It was a mistake, not the major disaster you're making it out to be. If you only knew it, you have learned a valuable lesson tonight. It's a mistake you'll never make again." Saying this, he put his arm around my shoulder and giving it a little squeeze said, "Come on, Reggie, try to forget it."

He never did mention to me the hash I'd made of "Chapel in the Moonlight", although much later I do recall him having Mum in fits of laughter telling her about it. "Of course," he said to Mum, "I knew immediately he had finished singing the first line of the chorus he'd dried."

"How did you know?"

"Because he started to come out with a load of rubbish, didn't he? Nothing rhymed. He couldn't even think of eyes and skies. I tell you he didn't know what the hell he was singing about. Gawd Blimey! Nobody knew what he was singing about. I knew it was to do with some judy in a chapel, other than that I couldn't make head nor tail of the song. First he had her standing in the moonlight, then he had her standing by the window, next he had her standing in the doorway. By the time he had finished there wasn't a part of the chapel left he hadn't stood her in. It wouldn't have surprised me if someone from the audience had handed him a chair so's the poor little cow could have a sit-down."

I fell about laughing when I heard his version and I marvelled at his gift for turning what for me was a disaster into a hilarious anecdote. I also realised that this was the first time Mum had heard about the incident.

The day after the Horns fiasco, I was in the parlour trying to learn the words of "Chapel in the Moonlight" but with little success. Each time I tried to concentrate I found myself staring blankly at the Landseer print of the Highlands which hung on the wall above the piano, still thinking about and suffering from the catastrophe of the previous evening. Finally, knowing it was hopeless to keep trying, I swung round on the spiral piano stool, looked past the aspidistra which stood in the window, through the starched lace curtains to the depressing rainy street outside and vowed there and then to give up show business for ever.

"Didn't you hear someone knocking at the door?"

It was Mum. She had had to push the parlour door open with her elbows, as her hands were covered with flour and bits of pastry. It took me a moment or two to adjust my thoughts.

"Well don't sit there daydreaming, the Hooper girl is on the doorstep waiting to speak to you."

Iris Hooper was standing in the porch holding a small umbrella over her head with the rain dripping from its points. "You're wanted on the phone, Reggie!" she said urgently as soon as she saw me come from the parlour. Shopkeepers were the only people in those days to possess phones, and Iris Hooper's parents, who owned the corner sweetshop, had kindly given me permission to use their phone number when needed, which was very rare, as ninety-nine per cent of my work was arranged by post.

"Who is it?" I asked as I was getting an old mac off the peg in the passage.

"It was a man. He didn't give his name, but he did mention something about a date in Southend for a week. Anyway he wants to speak to you personally." She hunched her shoulders up into her neck as she said this, shielding herself against the cold wind. (Dad was right, it was awful weather for the middle of July.)

With the news of a week at Southend my spirits rose again. With the old mac draped over my head, I dashed across the road with Iris to the waiting mystery phone caller, all thoughts of giving up show business completely erased from my mind.

16

The Southend Job

The Hoopers' telephone was on the wall at the bottom of a flight of stairs which led up to their bedrooms. Mr Hooper, a very tall man, had the telephone adjusted to his height, so for me to reach it I had to go up three steps. Unfortunately, the stairs leading up to the bedrooms were going away from the phone, so although I was now the correct height I was too far away. Whenever I had a call the Hoopers always left the receiver on a small shelf next to the phone, and to get to it I had to fall forward, stopping myself with the palms of my hands on the wall. To pick up the receiver I had to transfer all my weight on to one hand, leaving my other hand free.

It was a very hazardous task, because, as you can imagine, so many things could go wrong. I mean, should my feet slip or my timing be the slightest bit out while falling forward, then I had no alternative but to rely on my face smashing into the mouthpiece to stop my brains from being spattered all over the Hoopers' wall.

I found this tricky little manoeuvre difficult at first, but after a few calls I became quite adept. In fact I could dash through the Hoopers' side door, run up the three steps, fall forward, transfer my weight and pick up the receiver all in one movement . . . the whole operation, including the writing down of the message, taking only a matter of seconds.

This time it was different. Both Iris and I dived through the side door, Iris disappearing into the sweetshop to the right of the passage while I zipped up the three steps and went into my falling on the wall routine. After the usual preliminaries, this unidentified voice asked what I did. His manner was very brusque and straight to the point. My explanation came out in a strangled sort of voice . . . leaning over at this impossible angle tended to make it sound like that.

"I was just checking up on what my friend said about you, that's all. Right! Now let's get down to business. Are you free next week, that is to say from this coming Sunday through to the following Saturday?"

I couldn't believe my luck – a whole week's work! I did my best not to slide off the wall with elation.

"Good, now if you've got a pencil and paper handy I'll give you the details."

I knew the Hoopers always kept a pad and pencil on the little shelf next to the phone, but getting to them in this precarious position was the problem.

"Just a minute," I stalled.

It was while I was trying to fathom a way of executing this very complicated move, that it happened . . . Never before had I had to lean on the wall for such a long time as this – my arm began to tire. First it trembled, then it suddenly gave way completely, and with a crash, bang, wallop, I landed in a heap at the bottom of the stairs.

"Hello, hello, are you there? What's happened, have we been cut off?" The voice was screaming from the receiver swinging just above my head.

The noise of my fall brought the Hoopers scampering through the door. I picked myself up and assured them that no harm had been done, to the accompaniment of cries of "Hello, hello, are you there?" coming still from the swinging receiver. I asked Iris to take down the details as I dictated them. With my arm recovered I dashed up the three stairs and did my falling on the wall bit again. "Hello," I said, to the voice still bawling his lungs out at the other end.

"What the hell happened . . . were we cut off?" he said rattily.

"No, I dropped my pencil but I've got it now."

"That was a hell of a noise for a pencil. How big was it for Christ's sake?"

"That wasn't the pencil, that was me, I fell off the wall." As soon as I had said it I could have kicked myself for my stupidity – he might want to know what I was doing standing on a wall answering a phone.

Luckily for me, he didn't. "Well take this down. I want you to be at the Queen's Hotel, Southend, on Sunday no later than six thirty, to go on by seven o'clock . . ."

As he was giving me these details I was repeating them out loud for Iris' benefit, at the same time giving him the impression that I was confirming what he said. When I heard him say "the Queen's Hotel", my heart skipped a beat and I was lucky not to fall off the wall again with excitement. I couldn't believe it. I was going to perform at a hotel for a whole week. Wait till I tell Mum and Dad, I thought. The Queen's Hotel, Southend . . .

"Have you got all that down?" I heard him say, and without

waiting for my reply, he continued, "Now for the money!" He paused like he was making up his mind. "I can give you three quid."

After such breathtaking news, what a let-down . . . three quid for the whole week! I could earn more than that over a good weekend round the clubs. Not wanting Iris to know we were discussing money, I said, "Three!" There was no hiding the disappointment in my voice.

"All right," he said, "I'll make it three and a half, and before you jump the gun, let me add that with gratuities for requests you can easily make your money up to six or even seven quid."

That sounded a lot better; anyway I wasn't working next week, and even without the gratuities, three and a half quid was better than nothing. Besides, as I had already found out, there was a limit to the length of time I could lean on the Hoopers' wall at this ridiculous angle.

Iris mouthed to me, "Is that all?" I nodded and with that she replaced the pencil and pad on the little shelf and returned to the sweetshop.

"Well?" he said. "What do you say?"

"I accept," I said, without any great enthusiasm.

"Good! Now I won't have time to send you a contract so we'll have to make this a verbal one." He didn't ask if I agreed, as far as he was concerned the deal was done. He carried straight on: "Right, I'll see you six thirty Sunday night sharp."

Suddenly I remembered he hadn't mentioned whereabouts in Southend the Queen's Hotel was, so I hurriedly asked him before he rang off.

"It's near the Kursaal, if you can't find it ask anybody, they'll tell you where it is . . . everyone knows the Queen's Hotel," he said, rather bumptiously I thought, before ringing off as abruptly as he had started. My arm was beginning to tremble again, so I was glad. Besides I didn't like him, he was what my Dad would have called a "pig of a man".

Mum and Dad were thrilled with the news. I never mentioned that the money was only three and a half quid. I told them I was getting a fiver . . . I was sure to get at least thirty bob doing requests. Strangely enough they made no comment about the money – it was the prestige of performing at the Queen's Hotel that impressed them more than anything.

This would be my second visit to Southend – the first had nearly ended in tragedy. Mum had just come out of hospital following an operation. We kids – that is to say, Stanley and I – didn't know why she had to have the operation, or what it was for. Stanley was too young to care anyway, but I was twelve, an inquisitive age, so I asked Dad one day when we were on top of a double-decker bus, on our way to visit her in hospital.

"What's Mum got to have an operation for?"

"Never you mind," was his sharp retort. "It's something little boys shouldn't be asking about; besides it's got nothing to do with you."

His reply made me even more curious, but much as I surreptitiously tried to find out at that time, I never did. It wasn't until many years later that my elder sister, Bella, told me. She explained that it was a complaint common to many women, a prolapsed womb, nearly always caused by childbearing. It struck me then that Dad had been wrong all those years ago, on top of the bus, when he'd said that it had nothing to do with me. It had . . . well, twenty per cent of it had.

After Mum had convalesced at home for about a week Dad said that although she was getting stronger, he thought what she needed now was a breath of sea air. He saw no reason why, just because he couldn't go with her, she shouldn't have a day by the sea; especially as the three eldest children were off her hands and out to work. Only when he accepted that as Stanley and I were off school for the summer holidays, we could go along too, did she finally agree. That settled, they decided that as it was to be only a day trip, Southend was the best bet. Not only was it the nearest seaside resort, but with three fares to find, it was the cheapest.

The night before our trip, Dad took me aside. "Now look here, Reggie, I am relying on you to look after your mother tomorrow . . . I want you to make sure she does nothing, d'you hear me – nothing! Anything to be carried – you carry it. All I want your mother to do is sit on the bench, get the sun, and breathe in the sea air. Now have you got that?"

Feeling very proud and important at being given such a responsibility I replied, "Don't worry, Dad, I will" – and I meant every word.

We awoke the next day to brilliant sunshine and even before he was dressed Stanley said he was going across the road to Mrs Way to see if he could borrow his friend Ronnie's bucket and spade.

"Don't you dare!" snapped Mum. Her pride was such that the last thing she wanted was Stanley going cap-in-hand to one of her neighbours for a sixpenny bucket and spade. "I'll get you one when we get there," she said, busily preparing the lunch to take with us.

None of us had ever possessed a bucket and spade, simply because none of us had ever been to the seaside for a holiday. Dad's firm never gave paid holidays and even if they had, on what Dad earned he and Mum could never have afforded to go away themselves, let alone with five kids.

Our picnic lunch that Mum had just finished making up consisted of cheese and corned beef sandwiches, half a dozen of her fairy cakes, and an apple each. The couple of bottles of homemade lemonade and the cups were wrapped up in the two small towels we would be using for drying our feet after paddling.

I had been taught to swim by the school, but I wouldn't be doing so at Southend, because I didn't own a costume. At Balham Street swimming baths, where I had been taught, they had supplied all the kids with briefs of a sort. They were a one-piece effort with tapes at either end; you put your legs through the holes provided, and tied the tapes together at the side; and just in case anyone should get the bright idea of walking off with them, woven into the bluey-grey material for all to see was "Balham Street Baths". They were all one size, favouring the bigger boys, so I had the utmost job keeping them on. It puzzles me to this day, how I managed to learn to swim at all – I spent most of the time retrieving my briefs from the bottom of the pool.

One day I had a brilliant idea. I had seen in a St John's Ambulance first aid book, a diagram showing how to make a tourniquet with the aid of a small stick, by twisting it round to tighten the bandage. I thought, why not use the same method to tighten my briefs to stop them from coming off? I pared down a small stick of firewood and took it with me on my next visit to the swimming baths.

I was right – it worked. I tied my briefs at the side then put the small stick through the tapes and twisted it round until my briefs were nice and tight.

What a joy it was to be able to dive in and out of the pool without them coming off all the time. I was having a wonderful time, swimming and splashing about on top of the water for a change, when after a while I felt my legs beginning to go numb. Not understanding what was happening, I dismissed it as nothing and carried on splashing about with my arms and legs, until eventually I was only splashing about with my arms . . . not for pleasure, but for survival. The more I splashed about to keep afloat, the more it gave the other kids the impression that not only was I playing but inviting them to join in. They obliged, of course, and had great fun pushing me under, even more so when they discovered I wasn't putting up much of a fight.

The attendant finally dragged me out and removed the tourniquet, allowing the blood to flow back into my legs. He severely reprimanded me, saying, "Never let me catch you doing such a stupid thing again." After that scare, who wanted to? I was quite happy to go back to searching for my briefs at the bottom of Balham Street Baths.

We alighted from the train at Southend at around 11 a.m. and as we walked down the platform, with Mum holding Stanley's hand and me carrying the rexine shopping bag containing our precious goodies, the slamming of carriage doors, the smell of steam from the engine and the noises from the excited children clanging their buckets and spades together were a new experience for me, and I found it difficult to contain my happiness.

Stanley kept pestering Mum about his bucket and spade. "Be quiet! I'll get you one as soon as I can," she scolded, giving our tickets to the ticket collector. He tore them in half, and gave Mum back the return halves. As we emerged from the shaded station the sudden bright sunshine made us blink, and it took us a few moments to get used to it.

It was a glorious day, and we could feel the sun hot on our heads. Mum had removed her wide-brimmed hat when she got on the train, but now, for protection, she had to put it on.

"Look, Mum, there's a shop over there with buckets and spades!" Stanley cried with glee.

"There!" she said as she was paying for the bucket and spade. "I hope that keeps you quiet for a little while – and don't lose it."

As we made our way to the front, passing all the houses advertising "Full Board" or "Bed and Breakfast", I could see Mum was beginning to tire, so I was relieved when we turned a corner at the bottom of the road, to find the beach with the sea beyond stretching out to the horizon. It was a long beach – well, it seemed so to me then – with breakwaters dividing it up into sections. It was crowded with people.

I was anxious to get Mum settled, so I didn't have time to admire what I hadn't seen before. Plenty of time for that when Mum was sitting down and off her feet. I ran down the slope to the beach, which was more stony than sandy, and was lucky enough to find a spot for Mum to sit, next to a woman of about Mum's age. It didn't take long for the two women to introduce themselves. The other woman then introduced us to her son Edward.

"Everyone wants to call him 'Ted' or 'Teddy'," she moaned, "but I don't encourage it." Mum wholeheartedly agreed and immediately introduced me as "Reggie" and Stanley as "Stan".

Edward saw me and Stan taking off our shoes and socks. "Are you coming in to paddle then?"

"Yes," I answered, still a little shy.

As I stood up Mum beckoned to me to come closer and when I bent down she said quietly, "Keep your eye on him and don't let him go out too far." She was, of course, referring to Stanley. I assured her I would and with that I dashed after Stanley and Edward to the water's edge.

The sea was packed with kids, screeching and chasing one another, making a cacophony of noise and playing "He". At first sight, with all that teeming mass I couldn't see how we would be able to get in, but determined to do so and with a shout of "I'm He!" I raced splashing into the water with Edward and Stanley tearing after me in hot pursuit, Stanley aping Edward's every move, wanting to be one of the big boys.

I had never been so happy, this to me was heaven . . . Time had no meaning, and when I looked back to Mum on the beach to let her see what a wonderful time we were having, she was signalling to me with a cup in one hand and a sandwich in the other. It was time for lunch.

Mum had removed her large-brimmed hat when we had arrived on the beach as there was a cool breeze blowing off the sea, but now I noticed that she had put it back on, and I could see why: her face had caught the sun, making her look quite healthy. This would please Dad, I thought.

"There you are," she said handing us our rations. We were so ravenous we attacked the food like hungry wolves, you would have thought we hadn't eaten for months. It didn't take us long to scoff it, but in that short space of time the tide had gone way out. Stanley and I were very disappointed, now there was nothing to splash about in. Edward, seeing our crestfallen faces, produced a highly coloured ball, shouting out, "Come on! Up the 'ammers," and without giving our digestion a chance we raced on to the now large expanse of hard mud to play football, showing off to one another our skill with the ball.

When I say "our", I mean Edward and me, Stanley being that much younger was no match for us. Feeling neglected at not getting his fair share of the ball, my little brother said to me sulkily, "This ain't fair, now you've got him you don't care about me any more." He started to snivel. "All I've been doing is run around after you two, I ain't had a kick of the ball yet," and before I could console him he'd turned on his heels and was making his way back up the beach.

"Where are you going?" I called out after him. His voice was fading as he drew further away, but it was still loud enough for me to hear him say, "Back to Mum."

I stood there watching him grow smaller in the distance feeling very guilty because what he had said was true, I had neglected him. But now that he was returning to Mum I didn't worry too much, and carried on playing football.

It was while Edward was chasing a long ball that I noticed how all round us the other kids were stooped over intently peering at the mud. Being of a very curious nature, when Edward returned with the ball, I asked him what they were doing. "Cockling," was his reply.

"Cockling?" I said, mystified, "what's 'cockling'?"

"Looking for cockles."

"Looking for cockles?" I was still puzzled, but was more determined than ever now to find out. "How d'you do that then?" I pestered.

"You look for a spurt of water and when you see one you know there's a cockle underneath."

He was revelling in having this knowledge over me, but I didn't care, I was too intrigued by his information. "Can we do that?" I asked, anxiously.

"Of course we can."

"Well, why don't we?"

"Yeah!" he said, having had enough of football. "Why not?"

So we joined the others searching the mud for the telltale spurts of water. I was fascinated, my eyes darting around in a small circle like a couple of goldfish in a bowl.

I had no idea how long we'd been there – it was Edward who drew my attention to our two mothers frantically waving for us to come in. We had nothing in which to carry our cockles so we shared them out to those nearest to us, and made our way back.

A chill breeze was blowing in from the far-off sea, and I mentioned this to Edward. "Yeah! Well, that's because the tide's started to come in," he said cockily.

I was rapidly going off him. It seemed that now our few hours of friendship were coming to an end, a bit of "familiarity breeds contempt" was creeping in, on his part. I had detected it while we were playing football – he was becoming slightly bossy and arrogant then, and markedly so with his superior knowledge about the cockles and now the tide.

Don't get me wrong, it isn't that I don't like being told – in fact I thirst for knowledge; it was his patronising way of telling me that I couldn't stick. Anyway I wouldn't be seeing him any more after today, so what did it matter! After all, except for this last bit of irritation, for me it had been a smashing day, so not wanting to spoil what was left of it, I quickly brushed my chip aside and raced him up the beach.

As we neared Mum I could see that most of the day trippers had packed up and left to catch their trains home. The debris lay scattered about the beach: paper fluttering across the stones; empty lemonade bottles, some broken; flotsam retrieved from the sea by some youngsters, and left; early morning newspapers read and discarded, with one or two pages blown open by the breeze; and big holes dug by little spades with elongated impressions left in the sand where kiddies had been trying to bury their fathers, and crude attempts at unfinished castles. It was difficult to recognise it as the place of a few hours ago. Then it had been packed with people full of camaraderie and the air filled with screeching sounds of happiness. Now it looked as though a pitched battle had taken place.

We came up the beach to our mothers, with me "oohing and aahing" over the sharp stones. Edward's mother was getting very agitated: "For goodness' sake, Edward, get a move on. We've been trying to attract your attention for over half an hour." Then handing him a towel she continued, "Here, dry your feet and put your socks and shoes on, and look sharp about it otherwise we'll miss our train."

"Yes, and I suppose we had better start doing the same," Mum agreed, handing me a towel. "Stanley can use that one too, I'll use this other one for wrapping up the empty bottles and . . ." She stopped. I was digging the grains of sand out from between my toes, and when I didn't hear her say "cups" I automatically looked up. She was staring at me with her eyes full of worry, "Where is Stanley?"

My heart sank. I thought, Oh God, don't tell me we've lost him again! Stanley had, since his "overall" stage, developed a gift for getting lost. This caused great anxiety for all the family every time it happened, especially Mum. Disappearing in one's own district was bad enough, but here in this strange place, with thousands of people milling about . . . just the thought of it made my blood run cold.

"I thought he was with you," I said apprehensively.

"How can he be with me?" Mum expostulated. "The last time I saw him was when he dashed off with you to play football, and that was over two hours ago." She paused, trying to control herself. "What made you think he was with me?"

"When we were playing on the beach he got fed up with playing football with us and said he was coming back to you – didn't he?" I looked at Edward for support.

"Yes," he confirmed.

"He can't be far, Mum," I said consolingly, although I had the feeling that things weren't going to be that easy. "He's probably playing with his bucket and spade somewhere." I stood up to scan the beach for him.

"How can he be playing with his bucket and spade when I've got them here in my shopping bag?" She was beside herself with worry now. She couldn't keep still, kept fidgeting, putting things in the shopping bag then taking them out again, looking from side to side not knowing what to do next. Finally she gave way, buried her head in her hands and said, "Oh my God!"

I knelt down beside her and put my arm round her shoulder. "Don't worry, Mum, I'll find him . . . he might be on one of the other beaches playing. Now you stay here in case he finds his way back."

With that I dashed across the stones unaware of their sharpness now, and leapt over the nearest breakwater on to the beach on the other side. I searched every piece of beach as far as I could go, asking people if they had seen a little boy in a green jersey and brown short trousers. But to no avail. Unable to go any further I leapt up on to the promenade and started to wend my way back through the throng to where Mum was, scrutinising every little boy bearing the slightest resemblance to Stanley.

Mum was the only one left on the beach now – Edward and his mother had obviously left for home. As I looked at this pathetic little figure sitting there gazing into the distance, my heart went out to her. I knew the agonies she must be suffering, because Mum was a naturally energetic woman, and now, because of her recent operation, she was unable to take any active part in the search.

I dropped on to the beach and ran to her calling, "Mum, I'm

back." Hearing my voice she turned eagerly towards me, and seeing me alone her anticipation turned to disappointment.

There were still a fair number of people far out searching for cockles. I told Mum about this. "He might be among that lot, I'll go and see." So off I went again, with her worried voice in my ears, "Do be careful."

The cocklers were in small groups stretched over a wide area, and I noticed that although they were still intent on what they were doing, they were steadily making their way back to the beach. It was only after I had explored a few of the groups that I became aware that the mud was becoming very gooey, in fact it was up to my ankles.

Giving a description of Stanley I asked everybody who was out there if they had seen him, but they all answered, without looking up, that they hadn't. It was stupid of me to ask really – they wouldn't be looking for little brothers, only cockles.

I stood there scanning the horizon and saw what seemed to be a small figure stooping down. Making my way towards it as fast as I could, on coming closer I saw that it was a buoy, but not the one I was hoping to find.

There was nothing I could do now but make my way back. The sea was beginning to reach my calves so I made a hasty retreat. As I walked away from the incoming tide the mud was becoming softer and softer, and suddenly I realised that it was almost up to my knees, making it difficult for me to drag my legs squelchingly from it. The closer I got to the beach the deeper the mud became, till eventually it was almost to my thighs.

Mum, seeing that I was in difficulties, was standing up hysterically waving her arms about. I couldn't hear her but judging by the number of people gathered around her, she must have been screaming something. I could imagine what was going through her mind: she had already lost one of her boys, and now she could only see half of the other one.

My progress was becoming slower now and I was getting frightened. It was more of a struggle to drag my legs from the dense sticky mud and the effort was sapping my strength. My heart was pounding with fear, not for myself, but fear that if the mud got any deeper I wasn't going to make it back, and then who was going to look for her Stanley?

I rested a few seconds charging my batteries for my last attempt. When I thought I had recovered enough, I took a deep breath and with great determination I dragged one leg from the squelching mud and placed it as far in front of me as I could. I could feel the sweat trickling down my neck and into my shirt, and as I pushed my leg down through the warm mud, I was wondering whether this time it would cover my "coms". To my immense relief it didn't, so with renewed hope I pulled out the other leg and pushed it through the mud, to find that the last step had not been a fluke, it definitely was not as deep. So with my strength rapidly returning I slowly squelch-squelched my way back, running the last few yards up the beach to Mum, where I collapsed beside her, exhausted.

When I recovered, which didn't take long, Mum, sick with worry, began wiping the thick mud off my legs. When she had got most of it off, she said, "Oh Reggie! I don't think I can take any more."

I took Stanley's bucket to the water, washed the rest of the mud from my legs and dried them, and as I was putting my socks and shoes on I was telling her my theory. "Well, Mum, I know he's not out there, so he can't be drowned. He must be somewhere in Southend." I looked at her, hoping it would have some effect, but her eyes were vacant and I knew she had not heard a word I had said. So I gathered up all our belongings and took Mum up to a seat on the promenade, to plan our next move.

An elderly lady sat at the other end of the seat. She was a classy-looking woman, beautifully dressed, and she wore a lovely hat, with material with printed roses round the crown. It reminded me of our parlour wallpaper. She must have overheard our conversation about finding Stanley, and seeing Mum's distress came to sit next to her.

"Excuse me!" she said, in a rather cultured voice, "but I couldn't help overhearing your conversation and as you seem so worried I wondered if I could be of any help. I live in Southend."

After she had listened to Mum's tearful story, she turned to me and asked if I had tried the Kursaal. "They have a section there for lost children." She told me where the Kursaal was and I dashed off, leaving her patting Mum's hand comfortingly.

As I raced along the front, my shoes felt tight on my feet after so many hours of freedom, but I didn't let that deter me from getting to the Kursaal as quickly as possible. I found it difficult to thread my way through the crowds of day trippers making tracks to the station, and the holiday-makers sauntering back to their digs for high tea.

"Hold on, son!" said the commissionaire at the Kursaal and disappeared into a small office at the side. The Kursaal was a huge funfair area, and as I looked down the road leading to all the side-shows I could hear screams coming from the thrilling rides of the Big Dipper, the Water Chute, the Whip and the other breathtaking rides that were beyond my mum's pocket. As I was looking longingly down the road, listening to the barkers' cries of "Come on, try your luck, three balls for a penny," and "You look a big lad, ring the bell and win this lovely Teddy for your girl friend," the commissionaire came out of the little office and said, "I'm sorry, son, but they've got no-one there fitting your little brother's description." My spirits sank. I'd had high hopes of the Kursaal. "Listen," he continued, "have you tried the police station?"

Immediately he mentioned "police station" I could have kicked myself. Hadn't we repeatedly told Stanley, whenever he got lost, to go straight to a policeman? That's most probably what he's done this time, I thought. I was so excited I couldn't stop thanking the commissionaire. I gave him another "thank-you" and "wait till I tell Mum", then turned on my heels and was off again back to give her the good news.

On my way back I passed the cockle and whelk stalls with about half a dozen or more people around each stall scoffing from very small saucers. Every now and then they would take a vinegar bottle and give their cockles or whelks a squirt. All the men seemed to be in the same uniform of open-necked shirts, grey flannels and white plimsoll shoes, while their women partners wore flimsy cotton printed frocks through which could be seen their bloomers reaching down to just above the knees. I hadn't seen any of this on my way to the Kursaal, but that was understandable as I was in no state to notice anything at that time.

I could spot Mum in the distance because of the lady with the rose-coloured hat sitting next to her. As I approached them I saw a policeman coming towards me. He was just the man I wanted to see, so I quickened my pace to get to him in case he decided to cross the road or something.

"Excuse me, sir," I said, a little out of breath.

"And what can I do for you?" he asked.

He towered over me and when I looked up at him I had to shield my eyes from the sun with my hand. I told him our situation and pointing to where Mum was sitting said, "That's my mum over there, with the lady with the roses round her hat."

Peering down at me and looking very impressive in his uniform, he asked, "What is your name, son?"

"Varney, sir," I replied, on the point of grovelling so in awe of him was I.

"Right, and what's your Christian name?" he smiled.

I dropped my head and mumbled, "Reggie" – I always became embarrassed whenever I had to say my Christian name.

He took my hand saying, "Well let's get your mum and we'll go round to the main police station and see what we can do, shall we?"

We went over to Mum, and I excitedly told her that in spite of the fact that I had no luck at the Kursaal this policeman was going to take us to the main police station to see what they could do; reminding her at the same time of our instructions to Stanley whenever he got lost.

She glanced up at the officer for confirmation, and when he nodded to her that it was true, a glimmer of light showed in her eyes that was the first I had seen for quite some time.

Mum got up and as the wallpaper-hatted lady wished us good luck we marched off, giving the impression, to all who didn't know, that a tall policeman was taking two midgets into custody.

Stanley wasn't at the police station but Mum was greatly relieved that the law had taken control. Feeling more herself now, she gave all the details of Stanley to the police sergeant behind the desk. The sergeant, a huge rotund man with a jovial rubicund face, the obvious result of many a pint, said to Mum as he took the telephone receiver off its hook, "Thank you, Mrs Varney, if you would like to take a seat I'll make a few enquiries."

Mum thanked him and seeing me inquisitively eyeing the room on the other side of the counter, and fearing that my curiosity might distract the sergeant said, "Reggie, stop annoying the officer and come and sit by me." Perhaps she thought a bit of flattery might make him try harder. Her reprimand immediately stripped me of the authority I had been enjoying in a strange sort of way, and relegated me to being a boy again.

I sat down beside her, and although I felt deflated, knowing the agonies she had suffered for this last part of the day, I bore her no grudge; besides we still had a crisis on our hands.

"Hello Bert, Jack here," said the desk sergeant, glancing at Mum to let her see that things were on the move. "Listen, Bert, have you had any kids brought in to you today? . . . You have! . . . Give us his description." He listened for a few seconds, then we heard, "Mm . . . mm, green jersey . . . brown shorts, eh! . . . little eyes, mm . . . fair, no socks or shoes . . . yeah, that's him! Well look, Bert, you hang on to him, I'll get Bob to bring his mum and brother round to collect him . . . eh, what do you mean he won't be going anywhere? I wouldn't be too sure about that – it seems he's a dab hand at getting lost," and with a laugh, and "Thanks, Bert – see you later," he rang off.

As the sergeant was repeating Bert's description of the boy he had at his end, Mum's gradual change of expression had been magic. When the sergeant said, "That's him!" she leapt up from the bench and rushed over to him showering him with her gratitude, saying, "Thank you, thank you – oh God bless you, it's so kind of you to go to all this trouble, I can't thank you enough."

The sergeant was lapping up Mum's praise, but not wanting to show it, said modestly, "Now, now, Mrs Varney, you don't have to thank me, I am only too pleased it has turned out a happy ending for you."

"Oh but I do." She was clasping his hands now, pressing home her gratefulness. "If only I could repay you in some way – I mean, do I owe you anything?"

He gently took his hands out of Mum's and reversed the order, so that now he was holding hers. "Mrs Varney," he spoke softly, "I want you to know that in assisting you I was only doing my duty, and you owe me nothing." On reflection, he probably wouldn't have said no to a pint.

Bob, the tall attractive PC who had brought us in, rescued the sergeant from Mum's praises, and escorted us to the other police station. When we arrived, it was as though we were standing outside the one we had just left. It had the same frontage with the blue lamp outside advertising that it was the Law; it was weird – even the layout inside was the same, with the door to the left of the corridor opening on to the sergeant's desk. Even more weird was the sergeant himself sitting there, a replica of Jack, the sergeant at the other station . . . portly and with a similar rubicund, jovial face. He had to be Jack's drinking partner.

"You must be Mrs Varney," he said as Mum approached the desk.

"Yes, that's right."

"You've come to collect your boy I take it?"

"Yes, that's right," she repeated with a nod and a smile.

"Well if you would like to come this way" – he lifted the flap for us to pass through – "I'll take you to him."

We entered a room of medium size with a row of filing cabinets covering one wall to our right. Two uniformed men were combing through the drawers and a third was at a table in the centre of the room sifting through a batch of papers. Facing us was a large fireplace with built-in cupboards about three feet high on either side of the chimney breast, and seated cross-legged on the table-top to the right was Stanley, holding a glass of milk and an arrowroot biscuit nearly the size of his head, and looking as though he hadn't a care in the world.

The moment Mum spotted him her relief took the form of anger, a natural enough reaction. "So we've found you at last!" she scolded. Then shaking her head from side to side as though at a loss for words, she continued, "Do you realise the pain and worry you have caused? Your brother here has been everywhere looking for you – what's more, he nearly got sucked under searching for you out on the mud." Then taking her hanky out of her handbag in anticipation she cried, "Oh Stanley, you are a naughty boy . . . I've been out of my mind worrying about you." Then dropping on to the empty chair by the table she quietly sobbed into her hanky.

Stanley put down his milk and biscuit, threw his legs over the edge of the table, and slid to the floor. He stood there for a moment or two not knowing what to say, then suddenly as though he had made up his mind, he ran to her and flung his arms around her, and with his head nestling on her chest said, "I'm sorry, Mum, I didn't mean to get lost, honest . . . I came up the wrong side of the breakwater, and when I couldn't find you I went straight to a policeman . . . just like you've always told me to do." He glanced up and as her tears began to affect him he blubbered, "Please don't cry, Mum, I'm sorry, honest I am," and they cried together. The ordeal was over.

When we boarded the train Mum sat between us, and when we were settled and the train got under way, she said to me in a whisper, not wanting Stanley to hear, "Don't tell your father and the others about 'you know who' getting lost." She dreaded an inquisition by all and sundry.

I understood her sentiments exactly, because once Dad got his teeth stuck into something he'd just go on and on, driving everybody mad. "Don't you worry about that, Mum," I assured her.

Satisfied that our little secret would be kept, she rested her head wearily on the back of the seat, and closed her eyes.

Dad and the rest of the family were anxiously awaiting our return, eager for news of our day out; and being impatient to know, they fired questions at us from all angles. It was difficult to know who was asking what, so we threw in a "Yes, it was marvellous", every now and again which seemed to satisfy them.

Then Dad, seeing Mum's face had caught the sun, said expansively, "Well Mother, it looks as though it's done you good, and I'm pleased . . . well, I mean, that was the whole idea of the exercise, wasn't it?"

"Yes," was her reply, "mind you, I feel a bit tired now."

"You're bound to . . . let's face it, this is your first day out since your operation . . . you're bound to feel a bit tired, but apart from that I can see you've had a nice relaxing day in the sun."

Mum threw me a knowing look, as Dad continued, ". . . and breathing in all that sea air will have done you the power of good. You'll feel the benefit of it tomorrow, you see!"

"I'm sure I will," she answered, but not with a great deal of confidence.

"Well, Reggie?" he asked. "Did you enjoy yourself?"

"Yes, Dad," I replied and told him about Edward and our game of football on the hard mud, and how exciting it was looking for the spurts of water where the cockles were. "Yes, Dad, I had a smashing time."

"And how about you, young 'un?" He always addressed Stanley as "young 'un". "Did you have a good time?"

"Yes, Dad," said Stanley, and with a huge grin spreading across his face he carried on, "I was having a lovely time, then guess what, Dad . . . I got lost."

17

The Date at the Queen's Hotel, Southend

In contrast to the dreadful weather of the past week, much to my delight, this Sunday morning was bathed in brilliant sunshine. Within a few hours I would be setting off for my big date at the Queen's Hotel in Southend. Right now, I was sitting at the kitchen table eating my breakfast of streaky bacon and gyppo with my brothers and sisters. Dad invariably got the Sunday morning meal and this was his speciality. To this day none of us knows why he called it "gyppo", or where the word came from, but we all agreed it was delicious. Simple to make and cheap, it consisted of about two pounds of plum tomatoes (they could be bought for about a penny a pound in those days) cut up and dropped into hot dripping. Once tender they were mashed up, and a little water, salt and pepper added; another five minutes of cooking would evaporate most of the water leaving a sort of thick tomato purée. We could get through two or three slices of bread soaking it up, even to scraping up the last of it with a piece of dry bread, leaving the plates as clean as if they had been washed.

Mum came into the room to the sound of knives and forks on plates as we busily got stuck into Dad's gorgeous concoction. She said to me, "Reggie, I've been thinking: you had better put your stage clothes and make-up in with the accordion and use your smaller case for the other things you'll be needing and these –" she nodded to the clean shirts and underwear she was carrying. "Now listen, you'll find a clean pair of coms and a shirt on your bed for going away in and here's another two pairs of clean coms and a couple of shirts to take with you, so you should be all right for the week."

Hearing this, Dad dropped his knife and fork on the plate: "What," he exclaimed in disbelief, "two extra pairs of coms and shirts? We only change once a week ever. He's only going away for a week, he's not emigrating."

"That's not the point," she argued. "I mean, suppose he gets . . ."

"Knocked over," said Dad, finishing off the sentence for her. "I knew that was coming . . . how many times are you expecting him to get knocked over, for Christ's sake? He can only get knocked over once, unless of course he's a glutton for punishment."

Dad knew Mum's feelings about me going away for the first

time, and this chaffing, as we all knew, was to soften the blow.

As nothing had been mentioned to me over the phone about accommodation for Southend I took it that I was expected to find my own. I had looked up the times of the trains and decided on one that would get me down there by about 2.30 p.m. I could drop off my accordion and small case at the hotel and have plenty of time in which to look for some nice but cheap digs.

The whole family wanted to come and see me off at the station, but I wouldn't hear of it. I visualised what it would be . . . Mum checking and rechecking, making sure I hadn't forgotten anything; the others straining themselves to keep the conversation going, hoping the guard would soon blow his whistle sending the train on its way, relieving them of their awkwardness. No, I made up my mind to say my au revoirs at the street door. I kissed my sisters and young Stanley, but I felt a trifle embarrassed when it came to saying goodbye to my elder brother Sid.

Mum tearfully gave me a big hug and kiss, saying, "Now look after yourself won't you? I shall miss you . . ."

"I shall miss you too, Mum." Feeling a lump come into my throat I quickly added, "And you too, Dad."

To break the tension he nodded towards the accordion, saying, "If it's only for carrying that rotten thing." We all gave a forced sort of laugh and with that I picked up my gear and crossed the road, feeling their eyes on me until I disappeared round the corner.

I came out of the shadows of Southend station with the sun hitting my eyes exactly as it had done three years before when I came here with Mum and Stanley. I stood there for a few moments acclimatising myself to the brightness, at the same time thinking what my next move would be. I didn't want to be aimlessly wandering about looking for the Queen's Hotel, especially with this heavy accordion, so I made up my mind to do what the man on the phone had said – ask: "Everybody knows where the Queen's Hotel is," that's what he'd said. There certainly wasn't a shortage of people so I approached the man nearest to me. He was the typical holiday-maker wearing an open-necked shirt, grey flannels and white plimsoll shoes. "Excuse me, sir," I said politely, "could you tell me where the Queen's Hotel is?"

He looked me up and down for quite a few seconds before he answered. "You sure you want the Queen's, son?"

"No, not the Queen's . . . the Queen's Hotel," I replied.

"Yeah, that's it, the Queen's. It's the same place . . . everyone calls it the Queen's."

A street party outside No. 7 Addington Road, celebrating the end of the First World War. Our Mum, one of the organisers, is standing to the far left of the photo. My sister Doris and me, aged two, are standing in front of the boy in the top hat. Brother Sid is sitting at the table sucking his thumb, and sister Bella stands between him and Doris.

1924. The only existing snap-shot of the whole family. From left to right. *Top*: Sid, Dad and Mum; *middle*: Bella and Doris; *bottom*: Stanley and myself.

1920. Watching the dickie-bird in our Sunday best. A photograph taken for the family album. Doris . . . Sid . . . Bella, and yours truly in the centre. Stanley had not yet arrived on the scene.

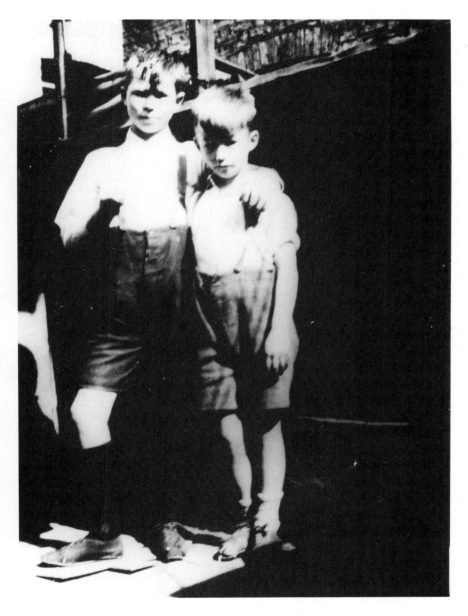

1927. Reminders of the "Ragged Boys' School Outing" days, and of Stanley getting lost in Southend.

A photo taken with my Dad when ten years old. To give you some idea of how small I was, the tiny tricycle belonged to the toddler in the background!

From left to right. Uncle Jack, Aunt Grace and Mum and Dad
on one of their rare outings. It was this Uncle Jack who always
used to call out to Mum at our parties, "Come on Annie, give us
'Indian Queen'". One of Mum's favourite songs.

This was the drawing I was doing when the chicken shed collapsed
on top of Dad.

1930. Posing next to the chicken-run in my very first gypsy outfit, made by my sister Bella from remnants of satin bought in Rathbone Street Market, Canning Town. The complete outfit, including my shiny dancing pumps, cost only seven shillings and sixpence.

1933. Appearing at the Melrose Restaurant in
Weston-Super-Mare. One of my classier dates.

Sunday 1st October 1939. A typical studio photograph from those days, taken of Lily and me and our families after our wedding ceremony at St Bartholomew's Church, Barking Road, East Ham. From left to right: Mum and Dad, my brother Sid (best man), myself and Lily, Lily's sister Ruby (bridesmaid) and Lily's Dad and Mum. "I look awful! Don't tell me you're going to put this photograph in the book?" was Ruby's remark when she saw me writing this caption.

So the man on the phone was right, everybody did know the Queen's Hotel . . . it must be a famous place, I thought.

"Well, it's a bit complicated to tell you from here so I suggest you go down that road over there, which is going in the right direction, and when you get to the bottom ask again."

I enquired three more times after that, each person eyeing me up and down and asking near enough the same question: was I sure it was the Queen's I wanted? It was as if they had all been programmed, with the last of them saying, "Well if you're sure that's the one you want, that's it over there."

I put my accordion down on the pavement and looked across the road at the dirtiest, grottiest pub I had ever seen. I was appalled. This couldn't be it! No, there must be some mistake, so I described the hotel of my imagination to him.

"No, son," he said sympathetically, "I'm sorry to have to disappoint you, but whoever gave you that impression was leading you up the garden path . . . there's only one Queen's Hotel and that's it."

He left me staring at the barely readable gold words of the "Queen's Hotel" above its frontage. The heavily engraved windows were grimed with dirt, as was the glazed brickwork beneath, giving no clue as to its true colour. A drinking glass had been broken and left outside as well as the usual tell-tale signs of those who had piggishly filled themselves up too much and spewed their hard-earned wages down the walls and in the gutter. As I stood looking at this disgusting pub I automatically put my hand in my pocket and fingered the comforting return half of my train ticket. I was wondering what time the next train for home would be when a tall slender chap, whom I took to be in his late thirties, came and stood next to me. I could see he was a musician by the black oblong case he was carrying.

Smartly dressed in beige slacks, nice shirt and tie, with a sports jacket casually slung over his shoulder, he had a warm-looking face, something like my brother Sid's. He rested his black case on the pavement, stood up and surveyed the Queen's. He was silent for a good minute then he tipped his brown trilby to the back of his head and said, "Well kid, I've seen some shithouses in my time but this takes the cake." He loosened his tie with his free hand and asked, "Who booked you here then?"

I was amazed. "How did you know I was booked here?"

"I take it that's an accordion?" He nodded towards it.

"Yeah," I replied.

"Well it speaks for itself, don't it." He clucked his teeth. "Have you got a contract?"

"No, I did the booking over the phone."

"Me too," he answered, still staring at the pub.

"I'm not working in that place," I said. "I shall be catching the next train home."

He didn't answer immediately then he stroked his chin. "Mm, that was my first reaction," he said, "but I've had second thoughts . . . let's not be hasty. Now that we're here we might just as well try it for one night, you never know, it might be all right. If not we can always get a train back tomorrow." He watched me as I pondered. "Well, what do you say?"

"My dad would have a fit if he thought I was going to play in a place like this," was my excuse.

Actually I was scared and he could see it. "Look, there's no need to be scared." He gave me a big smile. "No harm will come to you, I'll see to that."

"Well," I said, still doubtful.

"Come on, kid," he said cheerfully, "we can stick it for one night."

I looked at his reassuring smile and said, "OK, let's try it."

"Good lad." He offered me his hand. "My name's Ron Deeks, but I prefer to be called Deeks . . . what's your name?" I told him. "OK, Reggie." I could have put my money on him calling me that – everybody did. "Let's dump our gear in the pub and go and find a B & B." With that we picked up our cases and crossed the road to the pub.

We banged on the heavy old door that hadn't seen a coat of paint for years and waited. When we got no response we banged again, longer and louder this time. At the third lot of banging a man started yelling at the top of his voice, "All right, all right . . . don't knock the bleedin' door down . . . I'm coming."

Deeks remarked, "I'd know that voice anywhere."

"Me, too," I agreed . . . there was no mistaking that one.

We could hear him moaning and cussing, and although we couldn't make out his words, it was clear he wasn't paying us any compliments. We heard him slide the chain off, then he pulled the bolt back, its noise echoing through the empty pub. As he opened up, a mixture of stale beer and smoke exploded into our faces as though it had been building up behind the door waiting to be let out.

"What the bleedin' hell do you two want at this time of the day?"

"You booked us over the phone to play here . . . d'you remember?" Deeks said calmly.

"Don't be so bloody sarky," he snapped. "Of course I bleedin' well remember . . . I also remember saying I didn't want you here till six o'clock, so piss off."

He scared the daylights out of me but not Deeks, who eased his way past the bully, saying, "There's no need to bust a gut, all we want to do is to leave our gear here ready for tonight while we go and find some digs."

He could see that Deeks was not only determined but looked fitter than him too, so he hissed, "All right, come in and stick your gear up on the stage there, next to the kit of drums, and be bleedin' quick about it."

He was fat, his eyes were bleary with booze and his nicotine breath reeked of it too; in fact his whole appearance matched his piggish manner perfectly. He wore an Oxford shirt with the stud still in the collar band and you could see he had dressed hurriedly to open the door because his braces were looped down at his side and his flies were still open.

The bar of the Queen's Hotel was huge, with the bar itself to the left running the whole length of the room. Against the wall, immediately opposite the bar, were bentwood benches with their plywood seats decoratively perforated. Each bench seated four people. This was obvious from the four highly polished areas where over the years bums had rubbed the original varnish away, leaving the untouched parts of the benches jet black.

Round marble-topped tables with ornate cast-iron legs and stretchers filled the centre of the room. The chairs to go with them had perforated seats to match the benches. Most of these chairs were strewn haphazardly round the room, with those that had been knocked over just left where they'd fallen. The beer that had been slopped on to the marble tops during the lunchtime session still remained, although some spills were beginning to congeal round the edges. The blackened parquet floor was barely discernible for litter, paper wrappings of all sorts and fag ends; some of the fag ends had been stubbed out on the marble tops then brushed to the floor, but most of them had been simply dropped on to the parquet and twisted out by the sole of a boot.

The atmosphere was even more powerful than at the door, my first intake nearly making me sick. We shuffled our way round the tables and upturned chairs trying not to breathe in too much of the polluted air. We dumped our gear next to the pathetic set of drums on the stage and as we were making our way back to the door, I looked around at this state of dirt and disorder and thought ironically . . . and Mum gave me two extra pairs of clean coms for this.

Fatso was standing by the door and as we approached he said, "Right, satisfied?" Without waiting for us to thank him he carried on, "Now piss off and don't come back till six thirty." We walked past him into the street with him slamming the door behind us in temper, and as we strode smartly away, gulping in lungfuls of fresh air, we heard the chain being pulled across followed by the bolt slamming into position.

It was coming to the height of the season and finding accommodation was difficult. As neither of us had eaten since breakfast we were famished, so we were hoping to find somewhere soon, but every terraced house we tried with a B & B card in its window was full. Then success: the little old lady who opened the door to Deeks' knock was spotless; the white cuffs on her dress complemented the pure white starched apron she was wearing. Her hair was pulled back into a bun which nestled in the nape of her neck, and her rosy cheeks shone as though they had been buffed up ready for a Lifebuoy advert.

She told Deeks the only room she had left was a single at the top of the house, but it was big enough to fit a small camp bed in for me if that would suit us. Deeks accepted immediately, paid her in advance and then we hurried off to fill our bellies.

Between mouthfuls of pie and mash, Deeks satisfied my curiosity as to how he had been booked to play at the Queen's. Two years before, doctors had found a shadow on his lung which had put paid to his playing the saxophone. On being given the all clear a couple of months ago, he found that he had lost all his old contacts and now had to take anything that came along.

We finished our meal and after a second cup of tea Deeks looked at his watch. "Well, we've got just over an hour to kill, so I suggest we find a seat on the front and fill our lungs with as much sea air as we can to fortify ourselves for the evening's work in the fug."

When we crossed the road to the pub we could see that the broken glass had been swept up and by the look of it a couple of buckets of water had been sluiced down outside. The pub door was wide open and when we entered we were agreeably surprised. It was the same rough pub but it had had a wash and brush-up. The bar counter had been cleaned down, with batches of about fifteen to twenty pint glasses placed at intervals along the length of the bar ready for the evening rush. There was no litter on the floor now, that too had been swept clean, and the marble table-tops had been washed down and the chairs placed evenly round them. A door at the back of the pub somewhere had been left open, allowing a flow of fresh air to sweep right through the bar and out of the door we had just entered. Four men stood at the bar, three or more feet apart. You got the idea that they had come in together, had an argument, then separated. Apart from the drummer fitting up his set of drums on the stage the rest of the pub was empty. When I say stage, I really mean platform, because that's all it was – about eight foot square and roughly four feet high with a set of wooden steps for clambering on to it.

Deeks and I were making our way to the platform when one of the four chaps at the bar came over and met us. He was an enormous size, but not in height. He had bulging eyes and a bulbous nose, one that had brushed the top off many a pint, and his bloated face holding up a large double chin was in keeping with his brewer's goitre. Yet with all his size he didn't appear to be any older than Deeks.

"You must be the two new blokes?" he said.

"That's right," answered Deeks. "Are you the guvnor?"

"No, it's the guvnor's night off; he's left me in charge." He thrust a podgy hand out to Deeks: "I'm Tubby the band leader . . . I play the banjo."

He finished wringing Deeks' hand and then without bothering to shake mine said, "Hiya kid, you must be the one who does a bit of everything." He said it like a comic uses a throwaway line. Getting no response from me, only a glassy stare, he gave a little embarrassed cough. "Yes, well, let's go on the stage and I'll introduce you to my drummer."

The drummer was sitting at his miserable set of drums and having trouble with his snare drum stand. He was as thin as Tubby was fat. His beady little eyes made his big ears, which stood out like two small kites, look larger than they really were. The sunken cheeks accentuated his long narrow nose and with his two front teeth protruding beyond his top lip, he looked just like a rat.

"Well, gentlemen," said Tubby turning to us, "this is my drummer, Rats." I nearly fell over. I turned to Deeks and saw that he was just as stunned. Rats grunted an acknowledgment and carried on trying to fix the stand for the snare drum, grumbling the whole time. The thread of the wing screw which kept the collapsible legs of the stand in position had stripped and would no longer tighten on to the centre stem. He finally gave up trying and, still moaning, began to rummage through a tatty old box containing some special effects gadgets.

I noticed, among a load of other rubbish, a ratchet, an old motor horn, and a few whistles of various types. He eventually found what he had been looking for and holding up two rubber bands to us he moaned again, "Bleeding workmanship of today is not worth a light . . . it comes to something when you've got to hold the bloody lot together with these." With that he twisted the rubber bands round the centre stem as tight as he could, then adjusting the collapsible legs to the height he wanted he pushed the tight rubber bands up to keep them in position. He moaned on incessantly and I wondered if this was another reason for calling him Rats.

After being introduced to the drummer, Deeks turned to Tubby: "What time is the rest of the band arriving?"

"The rest of the band! What rest of the band? We are the band." I could see he was getting ruffled with Deeks.

"Surely you mean group?" said Deeks.

Tubby turned scarlet and lost his temper. "Don't be so bleedin' high and mighty, call it what you bleedin' well like, just you remember one thing, when we're up on this stage I'm the boss and if I want to call it a bleedin' band I will." He eyed Deeks. "And let me straighten you out on another point. Unless you're asked, only me an' Rats do the bottling." Turning to me he continued, "And you kid" – he spat "kid" out – "unless you want to go for a piss you keep playing . . . have you got that?" He went to turn away, but having second thoughts he spun round and hissed, "And we don't read bleedin' music, so if you don't know our numbers you'll be playing on your own." With that he stamped off to the bar.

His rage certainly brought to the front his true colours. Deeks and I watched him dip his big fat nose into the froth of another pint, before Deeks turned to Rats and said, "He's got a vicious temper hasn't he? What was all that in aid of?"

"Because you pulled him up about us being a group and not a band."

"But it's the truth," said Deeks, "anyway as a musician I thought he would have known that."

"It's probably the first time he's ever heard the word. If there's more than one person playing, to him that's a band . . . and as far as him being a musician" – he gave a little snort – "that's a laugh. He only knows three chords, as you'll soon find out." Rats gave his snare drum a tap with his stick, testing its tension. "Oh yes." Rats put a penny in the slot of a tension screw and gave it a twist. "He's got plenty of mouth up here, but you should hear him when he's at the bar with the guvnor, it's 'Oh yes, Guvnor' and 'Oh no, Guvnor . . . leave it to me, Guvnor . . . have another pint, Guvnor.' He's a right crawler. And I can always tell when the guvnor's had a go at him because he comes straight back and has it out on me." He gave the skin of the snare drum another tap. "Oh yes, he's brave enough up here."

I suddenly felt very sorry for him and I knew Deeks did too by the tone of his voice as he asked, "How the hell do you stick him, Rats?"

He rested his drumsticks on the top of the bass drum: "Because he gave me this job when I needed it and by Christ he never lets me forget it . . . you see he's my brother-in-law."

At seven thirty sharp Tubby came on to the platform with the flush of a few pints beginning to show on his face. He took his banjo from its case and without attempting to see if it was in tune with the piano he said, offensively, to me and Deeks, "Right, you two follow me" and immediately struck up with "Yes Sir, That's My Baby" followed by "Ain't She Sweet" and "Robert-E.-Lee". Rats was right – he did only know three chords; to me and Deeks it jarred, but all the customers seemed to be enjoying it so what did it matter?

By eight o'clock the pub was getting into full swing, some of the customers singing along with Tubby's old favourites. The last of this medley was a number called "The Shores of Wai-Ki-Ki", obviously a showpiece of Tubby's because when we came to the second chorus he speeded it to double time with his plectrum hand becoming a blur and the regulars encouraging him with shouts of "Go on, Tubby boy, let it go." The more the crowd encouraged him, the faster he played. Perspiration was pouring down his face, his hair had fallen forward and was sticking to the sweat on his forehead and where his shirt touched the skin dark patches began to appear. He ended the number with a great flourish and jumping up from his chair he tossed his banjo high into the air, letting it spin two or three times before catching it to a shout of "YEAH!" The customers, admiring his showmanship, went wild, and when the applause subsided he looked at me and Deeks and said sarcastically, "Who's the boss now?"

He mopped his face with his handkerchief before turning to me. "Right-oh, kid, I've warmed 'em up for you, now it's your turn. Give us a couple of songs." With venom in his voice he added, "Let's see what you can do!" He mopped his face once more then walked over to Rats. "OK, Rats," he said, "give us the bottling box." Bottling box, I thought, what the hell is a bottling box, I'd never heard of such a thing. Rats handed him a large well-worn wooden money box with a handle attached. So this was a bottling box . . . I'd learned something. He took it without thanking him and as he was going down the wooden steps he called back to us, "And you lot keep playing. I want to hear music all the time."

It was obvious that Tubby's showpiece, "Wai-Ki-Ki", was the cue for the bar staff to get his refreshment ready, because above the heads crowding the bar I could see a barman's hand hoisted high holding a frothy pint and signalling to Tubby.

For my first number, I chose the ballad "Song of Songs", a good song to sing with the accordion. It went tremendously well, with Deeks extemporising around the melody beautifully without getting in the way. From then on requests were shouted from all parts of the pub and I've got to admit that, without Tubby, Deeks and I were enjoying ourselves. Tubby too! He was having a field day with his bottling box and came backstage to empty it several times to my knowledge, but into what I do not know. Deeks and I were kept at it all night and whenever Tubby wanted a drink he got Rats to do the bottling. The crowd were very nice to us, supplying me with lemonade and Deeks with an occasional beer.

As the night wore on the pub became packed with people making the atmosphere heavy with smoke. It began to attack my eyes, also my throat, so I was very pleased when I heard the shouts of "Time, gentlemen, please" and "Come on now, let's have your glasses."

Deeks and I put our instruments away and were waiting for the pub to clear to get our share of the bottling money. "I'll tell you what, he's taken some money tonight," said Rats, referring, of course, to Tubby who was still at the bar drinking.

Deeks took me aside quietly. "It could be worth our while staying the week . . . what d'you think?"

"Not half," I agreed.

After about ten minutes we saw Tubby finish his pint and come jauntily back to where we were standing by the piano. "Well I've been through our take. I've changed it into silver over the bar and this is your share," giving Deeks his money, "and this is yours," he said handing me mine.

When I looked at the measly three and sixpence in my hand I nearly cried. There was a bit of a scuffle – I looked round to see Deeks trying to throttle Tubby over the piano and calling him "a twisting bastard". I saw two big fellows come from behind the bar and quickly make their way towards us. Sensing trouble, I became very frightened and brought Deeks' attention to the two heavies now mounting the steps to the stage.

One of them said, "Having trouble, Tubby?"

Seeing that we were in a hopeless position, Deeks quickly said; "No, it's all right, fellers, just a little misunderstanding, that's all. We're leaving now."

"You sure you're all right, Tubby?" the other one said.

"Nothing I can't handle," answered Tubby. The two heavies went back to the bar. Deeks and I picked up our gear, bid good night to Rats and as we passed Tubby, Deeks said, "Tell your guvnor you'll be playing on your own for the rest of the week."

On our way back to the digs we called in for a snack at the same café we had been in earlier. Deeks bit into his sausage sandwich. "D'you know, Reggie, we made a lot of money tonight and apart from a paltry three and a tanner we saw none of it, so I've been thinking – why don't we do it for ourselves?"

"What, find another pub?"

"No, on the beach."

"What! On the beach . . . you mean busking?'

"Well it's no more than we've been doing tonight is it?"

I agreed with Deeks, but I told him I was worried about being recognised by an East Ender, and if Dad got to hear about it there would be hell to pay. Dad looked upon busking as degrading and he'd been horrified when, not so long ago, I told him I had been offered ten pounds a week by the lead of the famous busking act the Lunar Boys to play piano for them and sing a few numbers with the accordion. "I don't care what they have offered you . . . no kid of mine is going busking on the streets and that's final" were his words. But Deeks talked about dark glasses to try and disguise myself and that sparked off a memory of how, purely for the amusement of the family, I used to impersonate Al Jolson by blacking up and singing his songs from his first talking pictures, "Mammy" and "Sonny Boy". We settled for this idea and jauntily walked back to our landlady with the Lifebuoy cheeks to tell her we would be staying the week.

The next morning I bought a stick of black grease paint from the chemist, found the nearest gents' toilet and made it my dressing room. I needed the mirror to make up in so I had to pay the attendant the twopence required for a wash and brush-up; he took the money and returned to polishing the copper pipes of the row of stalls immediately behind me. I stood in front of the mirror, took out my stick of black grease paint and within a couple of minutes had transformed myself into a very young Al Jolson.

I washed the grease off my hands and as I threw the towel into the used towel bin the attendant looked up. Startled at seeing this black kid grinning at him, he exclaimed, "Jesus Christ!"

"No, Al Jolson," I was dying to say; instead I showed him more white teeth and left.

When Deeks saw me he said it was a great disguise, although he reckoned that I must be the only black kid with blond hair.

By now, it was going on for ten o'clock and turning into a beautiful day with the sun beginning to warm up; the sections of the beach between the breakwaters were becoming very crowded. The general hum of voices and noise of screeching children wafted up to us, and as we watched the parents dress their tiny claim of beach with towels, unpack and strip off their offspring ready for the scorching day, Deeks thought it best to wait another half hour to give the late-comers time to settle.

As we slowly strolled along the prom, deciding which section to start from, I felt that the whole of Southend was staring at my black face, and as ten thirty approached I began to make all sorts of excuses, dreading the start. Seeing that I was stalling, Deeks took the plunge and dropped lightly on to the beach knowing that I was too conscious of my disguise to stay on the prom by myself.

The incoming tide was squeezing people into the top half of the beach, which suited our purpose perfectly because the previous evening we had planned to split each section between the breakwaters into three pitches . . . two ends and a middle. We had also mapped out a programme to avoid a hold-up once we had donned our instruments.

We chose to start with a medley of toe-tapping numbers well known to the public, followed by me accompanying Deeks playing a piece specially written for the saxophone, called "Vanity Waltz". Then came a ballad by me, of my choosing, with Deeks extemporising round the melody as he had done the night before in the pub. We had worked it out that by now we would have given them about twelve minutes' entertainment and it would be time for Deeks to start the bottling, while I sang another ballad.

It wasn't until we were standing in front of the crowd that we understood the gigantic task that lay ahead of us. First of all they didn't send for us, we were there of our own choosing, and therefore our being there, to them, was an intrusion, an annoyance. Secondly, we had to compete with all the other extraneous noises and distractions: screeching kids in the sea trying to get away from those chasing them; the occasional nudge from a child running about the beach not looking where it was going; mothers hollering, "How many more times am I going to tell you . . . stop throwing sand about!"; dogs vigorously shaking sea water from their sodden fur over those closest, bringing cries of "Get away" and "Who does this bloody dog belong to?"

We looked at one another knowing that now we were here we would have to stay and battle it out, and at the same time endeavour to win them over.

Deeks tuned his sax to the "A" I had given him on my accordion, by adjusting the mouthpiece, then after a couple of sucks on the reed he gave me four in and away we went with our medley. Our music split the air, startling those nearest to us, at the same time halting some of the other noises, but only momentarily, because after a few bars everything went back to normal. However, I did notice a few smiling faces indicating that they were enjoying it, which was encouraging. The medley received polite applause, but Deeks' solo went extremely well and with it went my self-consciousness. For my first song I had decided to sing "Oh Play to Me, Gypsy". It wasn't until well into the introduction that I suddenly realised how ridiculous it would be to sing a gypsy song blacked up like a coon, so I quickly changed the introduction to Al Jolson's "Mammy".

Deeks was an excellent sax player and his extemporising round the melody to my vocal rendering gave the song a touch of class. I could sense that we were now beginning to capture our audience, not only from the people on the beach, but from the crowds on the prom who were gathering to listen. The end of "Mammy" brought shouts of delight and Deeks, hearing this reception, picked up his trilby and immediately started the bottling. As he did so I went into "Sonny Boy". The timing was perfect; money was coming at Deeks from all directions, he couldn't collect it fast enough. People on the prom were throwing money down and, amazingly, the money that Deeks missed was picked up by those on the beach and dropped into his hat.

Halfway through "Sonny Boy" it occurred to me that I didn't know any more Jolson numbers; luckily I was rescued from my dilemma by someone at the end of the song shouting out, "Give us 'Mammy' again." We had won.

After the success of the first pitch I could sing what I liked; being black didn't matter to them so long as I was singing. Deeks realised this too, so from then on, after playing his solo he left the entertaining to me, while he concentrated on the bottling. When he had finished working the second pitch the pockets of Deeks' jacket and trousers were bursting at the seams with money; in fact the weight of it was such that he had great difficulty in walking . . . actually he didn't walk, he waddled and on getting started he found it just as difficult to stop because when he did the money didn't; the sheer weight of the coins swinging from side to side made him stagger forward a few extra paces. He was slowly tottering his way to working the third pitch when what I had feared happened. It was the slightest of trips, that was all, but it was enough for the swinging money to do the rest and bring him crashing down on to the beach. I tried several times, with his help, to rock him back up on to his feet, but with no success; the carrying of that colossal weight had sapped so much of his strength there was no way he was going to make it. The crowd must have taken it as the comedy routine of our act because nobody came to help us, all they did was laugh and the more I tried to rock Deeks up the more hysterical they became. I was reluctant to keep rocking him backwards and forwards in case the steady rhythm made him drop off. We finally solved the problem by transferring the money into his saxophone case.

Deeks waved his trilby to the crowd as he stood up and we continued to the final pitch. "Blimey, that was a frightening experience . . . for one horrifying moment I thought I was never going to get up and visualised someone sending for the vet to have me shot." I liked Deeks, especially his sense of humour.

It was past midday by the time we had finished our third performance. The sun was really belting down now; women had donned sun hats to protect them from its rays while most of the men had stretched handkerchiefs, tied at each corner, over their domes. Perspiration was seeping from every pore in my body. My coms clung clammily to my skin as did the trousers to my legs. It pumped freely from my forehead down into my eyes; it seemed the more I wiped it off the faster it flowed. My handkerchief became absolutely saturated with sweat and the thick black grease paint.

Sitting on a bench overlooking the sea, trying to cool off, the conversation turned to the mistakes made on our début as buskers. As far as I was concerned, tomorrow my coms would be left in the digs, along with my two extra clean pairs, which would remain clean, at least until my journey home on Sunday. We both acknowledged that a change of shirts and a supply of drinks was essential, the drinks especially as this was the first time I had sung in the open air and the strain was beginning to tell on my voice.

Having agreed on all these points Deeks suggested that while he changed the money at the bank I should go for a wash and brush-up. As he said this he looked at me and burst out laughing. "What's so funny?" I asked, fully expecting him to refer to our predicament on the beach. Instead he said, "You look as though you are melting and need topping up."

Over lunch Deeks took the money he had changed out of his pocket and gave it to me to count. The notes had a rubber band round them and the small change was in a paper bag. There were nine pounds in notes and just under ten shillings in silver. It was hard to believe; I couldn't stop looking at it and counting it, and when finally I gave it back to him he said, with a huge grin, "Not bad, is it? And we've only just begun."

After the success of the morning period the afternoon session was disastrous. For one thing the huge crowds of the morning weren't there and then the low tide enabled those that were to spread themselves, giving the beach a deserted look. Deeks reckoned that most of the morning throng were now screaming their heads off at the Kursaal.

We busked for about an hour to the small groups dotted around, and apart from being very embarrassed playing to so few people, we barely took ten shillings which was hardly worth the effort. We decided to call it a day, both concluding that when the tide was out, busking was out; which meant, with the tides as they were that week, every afternoon.

Our reputation had clearly got around because, although we worked a different section of beach each day, we recognised a fair number of familiar faces. I also knew we were among old friends by the songs they called out for me to sing again. This of course made everything a lot easier and much more enjoyable. Likewise, Deeks was becoming quite expert at the art of bottling . . . he was learning fast how to cajole people who were reluctant to cough up with a penny or two, to do so. All this helped to swell our morning take. Tuesday's bettered Monday's and Wednesday's was up on Tuesday's, but only by a pound or two.

This was all very exciting except that at the end of Wednesday morning's session, in spite of the lemonade I'd been pouring down my neck, my voice had all but gone and when I awoke on Thursday morning I had no voice left. Deeks was convinced it would be at least a week before I would be able to sing again, so he proposed there and then that we should pack up and go home. I pointed out to him, in a whisper, that for me to go home in the middle of the week would bring a lot of awkward questions from Mum and Dad; for them there had to be a reason for everything. I couldn't tell them I'd been busking and I was hopeless at lying; actually it wasn't so much that I was hopeless at lying but that they were so much better at interrogating. It was natural they would want to know why, after being booked for a week, I was home now . . . had I been paid off because my act wasn't suitable, or had I been guilty of some misdemeanour? The questions would go on and on and all my answers would be countered by "Oh I see, then why . . ." or "If that's the case, why . . .?" and "But just now you said . . . so why did you have to . . .?" The whys would go on and on until they finally got to the truth. Whereas if I went home on Sunday, when I was expected, none of these prying questions would be asked and no one would be the wiser. Instead all the family would be anxious to hear how I got on and Mum would be thrilled with her fiver.

Thursday and Friday were spent like any other holiday-makers, only perhaps enjoying ourselves more because we had the money and Deeks being the Chancellor of the Exchequer insisted upon the best of everything. Come Friday night my voice had greatly improved and on Saturday morning, much to our surprise, it had completely recovered. There and then we decided to go out and do a final busking session. The tide was later coming in and as it was changeover day the beaches weren't so crowded. Nevertheless we took about six quid, which we had to take back to the digs because the banks did not open on Saturdays. Deeks said not to worry, he would change it Monday morning at a bank where he lived.

Deeks had kept an account of our expenses so on Saturday night, in our bedroom and armed with pencil and paper, he got to work on how much our take-home pay would be. I guessed he had come to a final figure, but it wasn't until he had checked and rechecked, to make sure his deductions were correct, that he looked up. "Well, Reggie my son, we have netted thirty-six pounds and I insist that since you were the attraction you should have twenty pounds and I'll take the rest."

I was deeply touched by his generosity but wouldn't hear of such a thing, reminding him that if he had not intervened last Sunday I would have been on the train home with nothing. Besides, hadn't he looked after me and protected me all week? Well, now it was my turn to insist that we share the profit equally. He tried to reason with me but I was adamant I would have none of it. He eventually gave in saying, "All right, you win, I'll put your half in this little envelope and give it to you tomorrow morning before we leave." That settled, I was happy.

During our week together we'd always found plenty to chat and laugh about, but now on the Sunday morning as we stood on the platform waiting for our respective trains to depart, we were both very subdued; even when we did speak our conversation was so painfully artificial that it was a relief when the guard for my train blew his whistle and shouted, "All aboard!"

"Well Reggie, this is it." It was the way Deeks said "This is it" that made it final. I boarded the train and as I put my cases on the luggage rack, Deeks slammed the carriage door shut. I leant out of the open window and as we shook hands he said, "It was a great week, kid, I'll keep in touch."

"Yes, don't forget," I replied, but as the train pulled out I knew I would never see Deeks again. It was when I put my hand in my pocket to check that my return ticket was still there that I found my wage packet. I opened it to take out Mum's money and found four fivers. Deeks had had his way after all.

18

THE AUDITION

In 1932 I was sixteen and had been steadily performing in Working Men's Clubs for two years. One morning I was in the parlour polishing up one or two numbers when my attention was attracted by the sound of something being pushed through the letter box. I dashed up the passage to see what it was. Letters coming through the door always gave me a thrill, as did finding eggs in our chicken run. To this day I still get a kick out of finding letters on the mat.

This time it was a card from the Entertainment Secretary of the Shoreditch Working Men's Club enquiring about my availability for the coming Sunday night at nine thirty . . . if "Yes", would I confirm by phone? I already had two club dates in my book for that evening but luckily they were local and the times of appearance were early: two Working Men's Clubs – East Ham first followed closely by its opposite number in West Ham. I would have finished by eight thirty and by keeping on my costume and make-up could make Shoreditch comfortably within the hour. Satisfied that this was so I nipped round to Hooper's, did my falling on the wall bit by the phone and confirmed.

I arrived at the Shoreditch Club in comfortable time and as I made my way through the packed auditorium to the dressing room the Chairman rose to announce the next act.

"Now let's have a bit of order," he bawled, as he banged his gavel on the table. He looked round, glowering at the audience, waiting for the noise to subside. "Thank you, and now the next act is a very fine siffleur . . . to you lot a whistler. His bird impressions are lifelike . . . Ladies and gentlemen" – and with another mighty swipe on the table with his gavel, he announced, as though introducing a boxer – "Eddie Sharpe!" With that the pianist thumped out Eddie's play-on music and the highly coloured front cloth crammed full of adverts rolled jerkily upwards to the tempo of the unoiled wheels. The moment the squeaking ceased, Eddie, resplendent in white tie and tails, made his entrance. I had been on the bill with Eddie once or twice before and of all the siffleurs doing the rounds I considered him the best.

Eddie started his act with a great variety of English birds, naming each one in turn. I hadn't even heard of the birds, let alone what their calls to their mates were like. The white-throated warbler, the red-spotted bluethroat and the gold something-or-other all sounded alike to me, as I suspect they did to the audience. Each impression received just a smattering of applause, denoting they were a tough lot. I never knew if those who did applaud did it out of politeness or mere snobbery. It certainly wasn't their knowledge of birds – I mean, practically all of them, like me, were born and bred in the poor districts surrounding London, where the houses were blackened from the smoke belching out of the factory stacks, to say nothing of that pouring from the chimney pots of the terraced houses. For three-quarters of the year the sun was rarely seen and even in summer it was hazy, struggling through the polluted atmosphere. It took us human beings all our time to keep healthy (a good proportion suffering from chronic bronchitis, emphysema or asthma), let alone exotic birds. The only bird that survived round our way was the cockney sparrow, and even that had a struggle at times, not from the pollution, but in the search for grub.

It struck me at the time that this being the case, how did Eddie, and all the other bird impressionists, know what these exotic birds sounded like? It mattered not – the point was that Eddie was an excellent entertainer and his patter to go with his act quite brilliant. He concluded his performance, as did most siffleurs, with his pièce de résistance . . . the nightingale. In this case, even if the audience had never heard a nightingale, at least they had heard *of* it. Following the impression he did the nightingale singing to the piano accompaniment of "In a Monastery Garden". The nightingale seemed to be a combination of all his other bird impressions, but whatever, it was performed superbly. The delicate movement of his fingers and hands in front of his mouth was a work of art and the emotion shown in his eyes something to see. He would let them float to the top of his head then close them in ecstasy. At the end of the first chorus, while the pianist was playing a few bars solo, with great showmanship – letting the audience see that something special was to come – he filled his lungs with a mighty intake of air and at a certain bar in the music gave a prolonged trill of the nightingale all through the melody of "In a Monastery Garden". This trill he kept going until the applause came. This night, the audience was exceptionally tough; and the continuous trill didn't bring the applause as quickly as he had hoped. Nevertheless, he would not give up. I watched him as his ballooned cheeks grew redder and redder. It was now becoming a battle between him and them as to who was going to break first. Watching Eddie's face change from red to purple I had my doubts. He used every trick in the book to egg them on but they weren't having any. His face was now a deep purple and his eyes were bulging from his head like organ stops. He began to shake from effort and lack of oxygen and just as I thought he was on the point of flaking out, one of the sadists started the clapping which grew to quite a respectful round of applause; not for his brilliant impression of the nightingale but for his sheer guts in being prepared to kill himself for them. Had they hung on a few seconds longer Eddie, I am sure, would have done just that.

Standing in the wings watching Eddie suffer I could now understand why the Shoreditch WMC was renowned for its tough audience. As for me, standing there waiting to go on (this being my first visit to the club), I was wishing I hadn't accepted the date.

Bang went the Chairman's gavel on the table: "And now, ladies and gentlemen, although the next artiste is a first-timer to this club, I am assured by the Entertainment Secretary that he is quite a talented young lad. Well, let's see . . . ladies and gentlemen," and bang went the gavel, "Reg Varney." It was as if the Chairman was out to destroy me before I started, but this appalling introduction had the reverse effect; as soon as he announced me I walked out to this hostile lot keyed up and determined to show them. My entrance was greeted with a few polite claps, which had ceased long before I had reached the piano; nevertheless I acknowledged this pitiful applause with a sweet smile and a bow, then sat down at the piano and worked my first number as I had never worked it before. Not expecting any fireworks for the first number, imagine my surprise when it received a good solid round of applause. From then on the act went from strength to strength and that night I got three encores, making my money up to thirteen shillings, the first time I had achieved this since starting on the clubs.

When you are successful everyone wants to know you, everyone wants to talk to you, everyone wants to congratulate you . . . life is wonderful . . . you fall over your words with excitement when talking to people . . . oh yes, it's a terrific feeling and show business is the greatest business in the world. But when you are not successful it's the reverse. You are ostracised, banished from society. You don't fall over your words because there is no-one to talk to. Life is not worth living, it is hell. Show business is not the greatest, it is the worst. You wonder how you ever got into it in the first place and you make a vow there and then never to tread another board, a vow which, of course, you never keep.

This night was my night and when I came off half a dozen people were waiting to offer me their congratulations. The first to do so was a short fattish man who eagerly thrust out his hand and grabbed hold of mine before I had time to lift it up. "I'm the Entertainment Secretary," he said. He didn't notice me wince as he vigorously shook my hand in his vice-like grip. "You certainly paralysed them tonight, Reggie-boy . . . I haven't heard a reception like that at this club for a long, long time." I was in agony now as his continued pumping up and down crushed every bone in my hand. Oblivious of my pain he carried on, "And I'll tell you something else, if you can go well here you can go well anywhere!" Then turning to the others he said, "You'll vouch for that, won't you?" If they answered him I didn't hear it. This wasn't a handshake, this was torture.

Imagine my relief when I heard a voice say, "Well done, Reggie, that was a great show you put on tonight." It was Eddie. His call distracted the Ent. Sec. sufficiently to make him loosen his grip. Thank God, I thought, as I snatched my hand away and made straight for the dressing room. I dumped my accordion on the floor, dashed to the sink and let the cold water from the tap run over my mangled hand.

The Entertainment Secretary followed me into the dressing room and after a few more complimentary remarks, offered me a choice of dates for a return booking. I selected a date, flexed my fingers several times to get the circulation going again, then entered it into my book. He gave me his paper to sign for the thirteen shillings, which I did, and petrified of another crippling handshake on his departure stuck my fingers into my pot of removing cream. "Well Reggie-boy," he said taking the sheet of paper I'd just signed, "I'll say good night," and as his hand came up for the shake, with an apologetic look I showed him my gunged-up fingers. "That's all right, Reggie-boy, not to worry," and agonisingly gripped my shoulder instead.

I was still ugh-ughing from the pain when Eddie came into the room. "Do you know, Reggie," he said as I exercised my crippled shoulder, "I watched you work tonight, and do you know something – you should be on the professional circuit. Have you ever thought about it?"

"Of course I have," I replied, "but I don't know how to go about it because I haven't got an agent."

"Now I'll tell you what you do . . . write to a Miss Stephanie Anderson, care of the Carlton Cinema, Islington, and ask her for an audition." All the time he was telling me this he was writing it in the back of my date book. "When you write you can mention my name as I've worked for her quite a few times and know her pretty well. In the meantime I'll give her a ring saying I've seen you work."

I couldn't thank him enough.

"Don't thank me yet," he said. "Wait until you pass the audition."

We left the club together and walked to the tram stop. "By the way, take my advice – never lose contact with the club circuit because, believe me, as sure as eggs are eggs there'll come a time when you'll need them." He paused. "That's why I was working there tonight." Later in my career I discovered how true Eddie's words would prove to be.

First thing Monday morning, with very little optimism, I wrote to Stephanie Anderson mentioning Eddie's name and requesting an audition. I posted it straight away, and then, with the experience of so many past disappointments, dismissed it from my mind.

Two days later, having spent the morning doing the rounds of all the music publishers, picking up professional copies of the latest songs, I returned home about two o'clock to be greeted by Mum shouting down from upstairs, "What's the ABC?"

"The ABC?" I repeated. "I don't know, I've never heard of it . . . why do you want to know?"

"I don't want to know anything – it's a letter that arrived for you by the midday post and it's got 'ABC' on the top left-hand corner of the envelope . . . you'll find it on the mantelpiece." I walked into the kitchen mystified, racking my brains for an answer as to what this ABC letter could be. I took it from the mantelpiece and looked at the bold ABC capitals, wondering what they stood for, but my mind drew a blank. It wasn't until I caught the small print underneath saying " . . . Cinemas Ltd" that I knew at once what it was.

These were the days when all the big number-one cinemas put a variety show in between two feature films, and there I was with a letter from Miss Stephanie Anderson the booker. My heart shifted up a couple of gears, making my adrenaline flow. I put my thumb behind the flap to open it, then stopped, wondering if it would be good news or bad news? I pondered this for a moment or two, then convinced myself . . . it had to be good news, otherwise why such a quick reply?

I ripped open the envelope and with slightly shaking hands

took out the letter and read it. Sure enough, here was Stephanie Anderson asking me if I would be prepared to come to the Carlton Cinema, Islington, for an audition on the following Monday morning at 10 a.m. If so would I confirm by return of post?

My excitement was such that I could hardly contain myself. I had to read it several times to make sure I had got it right before dashing to the bottom of the stairs and yelling the good news to Mum.

Our stationery consisted of odd sheets of paper and grubby man-handled buff-coloured envelopes stuffed into one of the drawers of the dresser. Miss Anderson's letter to me was written on high quality company-headed paper. I couldn't be a cheapskate and reply on the Varney stationery, as I had done when writing off for the audition; no, this good-news letter deserved better than that, so I nipped round to Hooper's, who apart from sweets sold practically everything, and splashed out on a Basildon Bond pad and envelopes. I came back and in my best handwriting promptly confirmed the audition and posted it off.

The rest of the week was agony waiting for the Monday to come round. When it finally arrived my nerves started to play me up making me wish that I hadn't got to go, but of course I was committed now so there was no turning back.

The journey from Canning Town to Islington was an awkward one, calling for three tram changes, so to make sure I'd be there in plenty of time for my ten o'clock audition I left home at 8 a.m.

I arrived at nine fifteen, much too early. The stage doorkeeper let me leave my accordion in his little office. I thanked him and went in search of a café.

I took the cup of tea and slice of dripping toast I'd ordered and sat down in a seat by the window. I knew the nerves of my stomach wouldn't allow me to eat the dripping toast, or drink the tea come to that. I had only ordered them so I could sit there and while away the time instead of having to walk the streets. All aspects of the audition kept worrying me, so to take my mind off it I cleaned a space on the steamed-up window with the palm of my hand and watched the activities of the Essex Road.

A brewer's dray laden with hogsheads of ale, drawn by two magnificent shires resplendent in their highly polished brasses, drew up outside the pub opposite with its regular Monday morning delivery. I watched as three portly draymen alighted from the dray, removed their half bowlers and went into action. Number one disappeared into the pub while number two, the driver, took hold of the shires' bridles and with a rattling of chains and a slipping and sliding of their hooves on the cobblestones, expertly backed the heavy dray to the exact position he wanted it. At the same time as this was going on the third drayman opened the street flaps to the pub's cellar and when the dray was in its correct position unhooked four chocks from it, placed one under each wheel, then hopped back up on to the dray. The driver, having put the nosebags on his horses, came round to the back and fixed to the dray a small skid, which rested on the pavement. Drayman number three upended a hogshead of ale, manoeuvred it to the skid and slid it the short distance to the pavement. The driver then rolled it to the edge of the cellar, roped it in a certain way, looped the rope over a hook at the back of the dray and lowered it down the cellar skid to the waiting drayman below. When the last barrel had been delivered, number three closed the cellar flaps, number two removed the horses' nosebags and then both went into the pub for their traditional pint; seconds later the publican came out with two iron pails of water . . . one for each shire.

Although the unloading of brewers' drays was a common sight in those days, because of my situation, this was the first time I had seen an unloading operation properly. I was completely absorbed watching the way they accomplished their task with such precision, but what impressed me most of all was the way they manoeuvred the heavy hogsheads of ale; each one of them must have weighed 5 cwt and yet they handled them just as though they were toys.

I came to with a start thinking, God, what's the time? A glance at the clock on the wall behind the counter told me it was 9.50 a.m. I jumped up immediately and left, and as I passed the window of the café I noticed that the untouched cold tea and dripping toast had already been cleared from my table.

The kindly old stage door keeper peered over the top of his glasses at me, then looked at the little clock on his office wall. It was now nearly ten o'clock.

"Well cock, you've timed it just right haven't you?" I nodded my reply and with that he picked up my accordion saying, "Right, this way."

His stiff white collar with its black tie was attached to his Oxford shirt. He wasn't wearing his jacket and as I followed behind him I looked at his braces and wondered why he was wearing a belt as well. My churning stomach, that had been subdued by my engrossment in the pub delivery, returned with a vengeance the moment we stepped through the door marked "STAGE". Every

muscle in my body was alive and my racing blood began to affect
the capillaries in my face, making it burn.

"Harry, this lad here says he's got an audition with Miss
Stephanie Anderson." Then he turned to me: "This is Mr Driver,
the stage manager, you'll be all right with him."

The stage manager was seated at a small desk studying some
papers in the prompt corner (although I didn't know it was called
that then). On the wall facing him was a telephone level with his
head and next to it on an adjustable arm was an electric light with
a shade covering just the top half of the bulb. He reached for
another paper, put it on top of the ones he had just been studying,
looked at it and then, without turning, said, "What's your name,
son?"

"Reg Varney," I said, finding it very difficult to control my voice.

"OK. I was just checking, that's all! Miss Anderson is going to
be a few minutes late, but rest assured she will be here, so if you'd
like to take a seat . . ." He pointed to a chair. "I'll let you know
when she arrives."

On the wall at the back of where I was sitting was a line of stout
ropes, all counter-weighted, for hoisting the heavy curtains and
scenery. I looked up to see where they finished but they disappeared
into the darkness giving the impression that they went on for ever;
it was awesome. This was my very first audition and I was scared.
I could not keep a limb still and sitting down made it worse so I
got up, went over and took my accordion out of its case. I was
shutting the empty case when the phone rang. "Hello," I heard the
stage manager say, then a moment's silence – "Yes he is." There
was another pause. "Very well, Miss Anderson, I'll send him on."

I was crouched down shutting the case and at this moment I
nearly did a "Seymore". I'll never be able to stand up, I thought.
The stage manager came round to me and, seeing the state I was
in, gently helped me up saying, "Now come on, son, you'll be all
right – you've got nothing to worry about – she's a very nice lady
and will give you all the time you need, so come on now, pull
yourself together – just you go out there and show her what you
can do." With that he ushered me on to the stage.

I held the accordion by its straps as I walked on to this dimly lit
stage; I had hardly taken a few steps when a woman's voice called
out from somewhere in the darkness, "Give me some lights would
you, Harry." Bang went the switch and simultaneously the whole
stage was flooded in blinding light, stopping me in my tracks.

"Come on, son," a voice from nowhere said, "don't be scared."

I shielded my eyes and made my way to the centre of this vast space.

"What do you do?" she said kindly when I reached the centre. The gentleness of her voice calmed me down considerably.

"I play the piano first," I replied as I rested my accordion on the stage.

"How lovely, well carry on."

I looked round for the piano but couldn't see one. I peered into this huge cavern of blackness and judging the direction the voice was coming from asked, very feebly, "Excuse me but where is the piano?"

She didn't answer for a moment, then apologetically she said, "I'm terribly sorry but I had completely forgotten the stage has been set up for Jan Ralfini's Band . . . the piano is on one of the rostrums at the back of you . . . d'you think you could manage?"

I'd been too scared to notice anything when I had entered but now when I looked round and saw this enormous staircase of rostrums going way up in the shape of a pyramid, already set with chairs and music stands for the musicians, I was flabbergasted, especially when I saw what rostrum the piano was on. I looked up at it, and although it wasn't on the top rostrum, from where I was standing it might just as well have been. It was on the one immediately below, the fifth up from stage level. I surveyed the situation and knowing there was no way out looked back into the black void, gave a slight shrug of "Well, here goes," and prepared myself for the climb.

Each tread was eighteen inches high, so there was no way of walking up them gracefully; in fact, with me being so small, I couldn't walk up them at all; no, for me it had to be knee-up and over, crawl . . . knee-up and over, crawl . . . all the way to the top, thinking as I did so – what a humiliating way to start an audition! I reached the top without mishap and with what little wind I had left breathed a sigh of relief.

Now you don't have to be an Einstein to work out how high up I was . . . five rostrums, each with an eighteen-inch tread, add to that my height of three feet six inches (as it was then when sitting at the piano) and you will see I was eleven feet up above the stage. Suddenly a limelight flashed on; I could feel its heat on my legs and body, but that was all, my head was still up in the cold.

"Carry on," she said. "You'll have to cheat yourself into the spotlight I'm afraid."

She was so far away I could hardly hear her. Sitting up there, nearly in the flies, with the stage lighting doing me no favours and the spotlight a complete waste of time, to say I was at a disadvantage was a gross understatement. Nevertheless I did as she suggested and ducked my head into the spotlight. With my nose barely two inches above the keys it must have looked as if I was smelling it to see if it was a good one!

I struck up with my showpiece "The Tiger Rag", difficult enough in itself, with its flashy runs and tricky arpeggios, without having to play it bent over like the Hunchback of Notre-Dame. It goes without saying that I was making an awful hash of it and although I tried to smile through my adversity it was a fiasco. I didn't hear Miss Anderson screaming her lungs out for me to pack it in . . . it was the stage manager frantically waving his arms from below that brought me to a halt. I looked at him gratefully and before I could speak he said, "Miss Anderson realises you can't work up there so would you do something for her on the accordion?"

Back at stage level I gave her my vocal scat-singing arrangement of "Dinah", followed by a number just out called "I'll String Along with You".

"Thank you, that'll be enough." When I heard that after my dreadful start I fully expected her to carry on, "I'll let you know," or "Don't ring me, I'll ring you." Instead she said, "Do you have a stage costume?"

"Yes," I replied into the darkness, unable to believe my ears.

"Well, I like what you've done on the accordion, so go home and get it. Get back here by two o'clock and I will introduce you to Jan Ralfini."

I thanked her profusely and with my head in the clouds went home and excitedly told Mum.

Miss Stephanie Anderson, a very smart, good-looking woman, was in Jan Ralfini's tiny dressing room when I returned. "I've told Mr Ralfini all about you and he would like to hear the numbers you are going to do to see if it's possible to arrange for some sort of backing. All right?"

"Yes," I said meekly.

"There's a good lad; well, now that that's settled I'll leave you in the capable hands of Mr Ralfini." Then, wishing me good luck, she left.

This was the age of the big bands and although Jan Ralfini wasn't a Jack Hylton or an Ambrose, nevertheless his was a name to be reckoned with.

I stood with my accordion on, looking at him in awe waiting for him to tell me to go ahead, but first he asked me my age and how I had started. "Miss Anderson tells me you have an unusual version of 'Dinah'?"

I just smiled and shrugged my shoulders.

"Don't be so modest, kid . . . come on, let me hear it."

I unclipped the bellows, gave myself an F seventh chord and went straight into the scat-singing introduction to "Dinah". I had a big voice for such a little fellow and the accordion, a naturally loud instrument, in this confined space was deafening; as for me, I ignored the noise and carried on giving it everything I'd got. Halfway through the song I glanced at him searching for some sign of approval, but with his hands clamped over his ears and his face screwed up as if in pain, it was hard to tell. He started to open and shut his mouth, but as I couldn't hear what he was trying to say I continued belting it out. It was only when he jumped up and wrestled with me, stopping me from operating the bellows, that I realised what he'd been yelling at me to do.

"Thank God," he muttered into the silence, then let the peace and quietness of the room waft over him. "Well kid," he said when fully recovered, "with a pair of lungs like you've got you won't be needing a microphone, that's for sure."

I stood in the wings waiting to go on dressed in the new costume my sister Bella had recently made me. It was a green satin Russian-style blouse with full puffed sleeves and satin trousers. I'd got my accordion ready to slip on just as the band number I was to follow came to an end. Jan Ralfini walked to the front and as arranged looked in my direction, which was my cue to stand by for his announcement. Expecting me to be in my street clothes, he was obviously surprised, although I must say by his expression agreeably so, to see me in my Russian outfit. He had given me a rough idea of what he was going to say, but it was clear that when he saw me dressed in green he suddenly changed his mind and decided to switch his original introduction for a more dramatic one.

He acknowledged the applause for the number the band had just played and then said, "Ladies and gentlemen . . . I am now going to introduce you to a tiny lad I saw last night singing, with his accordion, in the streets of Dublin . . ." I couldn't believe my ears – what a load of rubbish, I thought. He went on: "I think he's fantastic and I am sure when you hear him you will think so too, so here he is, ladies and gentlemen, all the way from Ireland, the tiny lad with the big voice . . . Reg Varney!" With that he raised his arm for me to take the stage.

All the time I'd been standing there waiting to go on my stomach had been churning over, but now the moment I walked on and heard the applause that stopped.

Jan Ralfini was centre stage waiting to greet me and as I walked towards his outstretched hand I remember thinking to myself – I'm in the big time now so it's up to me to prove I'm worthy of Miss Anderson's faith. The tremendous applause both songs received thrilled me beyond belief, and even more so when after taking several calls in acknowledgment I came offstage to find a beaming Stephanie Anderson waiting to congratulate me.

As a result she kept me on for the rest of the week and also booked me nearer home for the following week at the Carlton Cinema, Upton Park, West Ham, again with Jan Ralfini. His introduction about finding me singing in the streets of Dublin had gone down exceptionally well at Islington and it was plain he enjoyed doing it. Unfortunately, at Upton Park, much to his surprise, the same introduction was met with a certain amount of derision, with catcalls coming from different parts of the house. He couldn't understand why, especially as the reception I got on entering was even bigger than at Islington. Unlike the vast majority of his audience he didn't know that I had been born in the district, and that everyone in West Ham knew Reg Varney.

At the same time as I was with Jan Ralfini, Richard Hales, a boy soprano, was being introduced at the London Palladium by Bud Flanagan and Chesney Allan as the singing Palladium Page Boy. Although he wore the uniform and made his entrance from the stalls, the whole thing was a gimmick. It so happened that the end of his run at the Palladium coincided with the end of my fortnight with Jan Ralfini and Miss Anderson, always on the lookout for new acts for her ABC circuit, thought it would be quite a novelty, as we were both so very young, to put us together as a double act in harmony.

I was introduced to Richard at the Carlton, Upton Park, where we were to rehearse. Although about the same height, he was plump and I was slim. There was a slight difference in age too. I was just turned sixteen and he was not quite fifteen. Nevertheless he was a nice little chap and we hit it off right from the start.

Three chairs had been placed on the stage in such a way that when we sat down for our discussion with Miss Anderson she was facing us. She first of all chatted to both of us about how she had hit upon the idea of a double act, but when the conversation turned to the point of the meeting, the act itself, she addressed herself to me; the reason being, I assumed, not only my age but my additional experience. When she'd finished telling me what she had in mind for the act, she handed me the songs she thought would suit and said, "I'll leave you to work out the harmonies." She looked at us for a moment before dropping the bombshell: "I've booked you to open on the circuit in a fortnight's time." She let that sink in, then as though reading our thoughts continued: "Yes, you won't have a great deal of time for pleasure will you?" And to me she added, "And Reggie, when you think it's in good enough shape for me to see, give me a ring." She rose from her chair and with her best wishes to us both the meeting was closed.

We worked extremely hard, not only at the cinema but in my home, and at the end of ten days we had, I thought, a polished close harmony act. After seeing it Miss Anderson was quite complimentary, saying the act had great charm, although in her opinion it was still a bit raw. She had no doubt that given a few live performances it would be excellent and extremely bookable.

"I've given a great deal of thought as to how you should both be dressed," she said, "and out of several ideas I have decided on grey flannels, brown and white shoes with a maroon pullover over a white open-necked shirt . . . à la American college boy. This outfit will be perfect for the name I have chosen for the act." Well, she was the boss, so we went out and bought the clothes of her choice to go with the name of her choosing . . . "the 'YALE BOYS' in close harmony".

We started the four-week tour at the same time as the ABC introduced the five-shows-a-day schedule – the five shows were split up between two cinemas, three at one and two at the other, the latter usually being the smaller cinema. A coach shuttled the four acts, and the band, between the cinemas, the first show commencing at 2 p.m. and the last at 9 p.m.

Our opening dates were the Prince of Wales, Harrow Road doubling with the Palace, Kensal Rise. Our first performance was marred by nerves and lack of confidence, but Miss Anderson was right and after a few shows we settled down. By the end of the week, having done thirty shows, we had a very polished act which went extremely well, so much so that Miss Anderson booked us for a second run. I recall coming home on the tram that night intoxicated by my good fortune. Eight weeks' work at five pounds a week, coupled with the Sunday club concerts I was still committed to do, would gross me £48 . . . a fortune.

There was another enthralling aspect, which to me was of the utmost importance. I had known for some time now that to get anywhere at all in show business you had to have an agent, and no agent would take you on without first seeing your work and liking what he saw. However, the main hurdle was to persuade an agent to come and see you perform, which in the past was impossible because none would come out to a Working Men's Club. Now it was different . . . I had a tour of first-class dates from which an agent could choose. As every London theatrical agent, big or small, advertised in the *Stage* and the *Performer*, I made my plans and on Monday morning I left home early to start the second week of my tour at the Putney Hippodrome, doubling with a cinema in Wandsworth.

Putney was a hell of a way from Canning Town but brother Sid informed me that a District line train from West Ham station would take me direct to Putney, so although it was a long walk from my home to the station with two cases, especially as one of them was a heavy accordion, it was worth it. From the newsagents adjacent to the station I bought the *Stage* and the *Performer* and armed with my Basildon Bond pad and envelopes, I was ready the moment I got to the theatre to put my plan into operation.

I stood on the platform waiting for the train, my mind crammed to bursting point with thoughts of what the future held for me. As I saw it, nothing could stop me now, the heights I could climb were limitless. New thoughts kept racing through my head, with my spirits rising as each new idea was released until finally I became so jubilant I found it difficult to control myself. It wasn't until a woman's voice interrupted my mental exaltations, saying to some-one what a bitterly cold and depressing day it was, that I suddenly felt the driving sleet stinging my face. Yes – she was right, it was a bitterly cold day, but not a depressing one . . . well, not for me it wasn't.

The Putney Hippodrome had been an old Variety Theatre and standing in the dressing room allotted to us I looked at the scribbled names on the walls of artistes who had played there in the past. Some had little notes written by the side, or underneath their names, and it was plain to see from the comments whether their act had gone well or died a death. Others had their bill matter added. Bill matter was a recognised thing in those days, and is even to this day. For instance my bill matter when I was doing variety was "REG VARNEY" . . . then in smaller print below, "Music and Madness".

It is too long ago now for me to remember all of the bill matter on the wall but two acts remain with me because they were extremely funny. One was called "The 'Brothers Jolly' Beating about the Bush", and right beside it another act had written "The 'Brothers Balls' – The Two Hangers On". It made me laugh a lot, but it wasn't the sort of thing I could tell Mum and Dad.

I stood in the middle of this small but cosy dressing room, letting the atmosphere of what had been waft over me, and when after a few moments I sat at the dressing table and switched on the mirror lights, they revealed more evidence of the past. The bruised table-top with its stains of different coloured grease paints that had been ingrained into the wood over the years was proof that, apart from the names scribbled all over the walls, countless other performers had sat where I was now and made up.

I had changed into my stage clothes and was just putting the finishing touches to my make-up when Richard came in. "Here," I asked eagerly before he had had time to take off his overcoat, "what did your mum and dad think about Miss Anderson booking us for a second run?"

"Great," was all he said, then he gave a couple of croaks as though clearing his throat. I ignored his seeming lack of interest and gave him the sheet of paper with the list of agents' names and addresses I'd jotted down from the *Stage* and the *Performer*; then, bubbling over, I told him of my intention to draft a letter with all the information concerning the tour and send a copy to every agent on the list.

"What d'you think?" I said, my eyes sparkling with enthusiasm. He was in no hurry to speak and when he did he said flatly, "Yeah, great," then handing me back the list he turned away to change, giving a couple of croaks as he did so. I looked at him in disbelief; shocked by his attitude of indifference which had already destroyed my enthusiasm. I went back to the dressing table and sat down, lost for words. His behaviour was beyond my understanding, especially knowing how ecstatic he had been on Saturday night after Miss Anderson gave us the news of our extended tour.

I sat there unconsciously patting my face with the powder puff, racking my brains for an answer. Then suddenly, fearing something disastrous had happened, I asked cautiously but with concern: "Richard . . . is anything wrong at home? I mean, is your mum or dad ill or something?"

"No, of course not," he said sharply. He paused, then turning slowly, added, "I'm sorry but I don't feel too good . . . I think a bad cold is developing." I was just about to reply, "Well, I'm glad to hear it's only a cold," when he beat me to it, saying with a quizzical look: "Well, I hope it's just a cold."

Straight away I knew exactly what he meant . . . he meant he hoped that his voice wasn't breaking.

It was strange but when he came in and started croaking and clearing his throat that thought did cross my mind, but I dismissed it immediately – it couldn't be, he had not long turned fifteen. Now, watching him dress, I began to doubt. I remembered the signs so clearly . . . the croaking and trying to clear your throat, that's exactly how my own voice had started to go. Of course, his could be only a cold coming on, and recalling once again that he was, after all, just turned fifteen, I convinced myself that's what it was. Yet all the time I was doing my best to draft a letter to the agents the doubt kept niggling. Eventually we heard the show start and as we were the second act on I took my accordion out of its case and we both made our way to the side of the stage.

I was worried about Richard's voice and although he didn't say anything I could tell by the concern on his face that he was worried too. The curtain came down on the dancing act and while the band was playing them off and they were acknowledging their applause, we hurried on stage and took up our positions.

The moment the dancers disappeared from view the conductor struck up the introduction of our opening number, "I'll Never Say Never Again Again". As he did so, the curtain rose to reveal me sitting at the piano with Richard standing in the bow. Our introductory music led us straight into our number and as we burst forth I could tell Richard was singing very cautiously, although to me his voice sounded in good shape. Halfway through the song he must have decided that everything was OK because he looked at me and smiled then let it rip; I smiled back letting it rip also, my fears allayed – but, alas, not for long.

His solo – "When Irish Eyes Are Smiling" – he sang without orchestra, just my piano accompaniment, and as I listened to the beautiful bell-like tones of his voice, I wondered why he had been in such a hurry to doubt that it was a cold in the first place, so there and then I put all thoughts of his voice breaking out of my mind. Then, as he was reaching the top register of the song, my ears pricked up . . . was that a slight crack in his voice or was it my imagination? I listened intently and detected nothing more until he reached the very top notes of the song; there it was again, only more pronounced this time. I hadn't imagined it the first time; it was there all right, the familiar cracking sounds I knew so well.

When we came off neither of us spoke until we got into the dressing room, then very dejectedly Richard said, "I think my voice is breaking."

"Let's not be hasty," I replied cheerfully, "it still might only be a cold . . . look, you stay here, keep yourself warm and I'll go round to the chemist and get you a good gargle." I dashed out and within a few minutes I was back with a gargle the chemist had recommended, and a packet of throat lozenges to go with it. He gargled and sucked lozenges all through the break we had before doing our second performance at Wandsworth, but neither gargle nor lozenges made the slightest bit of difference . . . they were no match for nature.

Despite this, he continued the treatment and when after our final show that evening his voice didn't seem to have deteriorated any more I said to him optimistically as we were getting ready to go home, "Your voice hasn't got any worse, perhaps it is just a cold after all." He looked at me for a second or two then slowly shaking his head from side to side said, "I'd like to think you were right, but I'm afraid you're not."

"How d'you know I'm not?" I said, a little vexed. "After all it's only the first day, so how can you be sure?"

"Because it's MY voice," he snapped back. Then regaining his composure he continued, "It's just wishful thinking on your part." Deep down I knew he was right, but I was fighting against the truth. It's all right for him, I thought bitterly, he's got nothing to lose. If not now, sooner or later his voice was going to break, ending his career in show business; in the meantime he'd been making the most of a beautiful voice while it lasted, so for him it was fun. However, for me, although I enjoyed what I was doing very much, it wasn't fun, it was my living, my profession and right now my big chance to get agents to come and see me, with perhaps the luck of one putting me on his books. Yes, of course, my mind screamed, I wanted it to be a cold; of course it was wishful thinking on my part; of course I was clutching at straws.

Richard's voice disturbed my thoughts: "Well, good night, Reg." He sounded cheerful, as though he'd resigned himself to his fate. "See you tomorrow." He was standing in the doorway with his overcoat on.

"Oh yes, good night, Richard," I replied softly, then he closed the door behind him.

Left alone in the room I looked around to see if everything was in order – I always did that out of habit – and I took my overcoat off its peg. Seeing the letter I had composed lying next to the *Stage* and the *Performer* I put it between the two papers and placed them neatly back on the dressing table. I went to the door, put on my overcoat, switched off the lights and forlornly made my way home.

By Wednesday night I'd surrendered to the fact that his voice was breaking. Now it was a terrible struggle for him. Every time he came to the top register I found myself playing louder and putting in flourishes to camouflage his inability to reach the notes, in fact I doubted if he would last out the week. Fortunately he managed to struggle through. It was no surprise to us, however, when on the Saturday night, during one of our evening performances, we were summoned to the Manager's office, I assumed to be told the inevitable.

I remember so clearly standing outside the highly polished mahogany door with its gleaming brass knob. "Come in," a voice said, in answer to our knock. I closed the door behind us. The Manager looked up from his desk and seeing us standing there just inside the door, smiled as he said, "Hello lads, don't stand there – come over here and sit down." We walked across the red plush carpet and sat down on the two chairs already placed in front of his beautifully veneered desk. "I shan't keep you long," he said. "I've only this small matter to attend to then I will be with you." We sat there feeling a little awkward so for the sake of something better to do I watched him as he started to read the half dozen or so lines that were on the paper. I was fascinated by the way that, while still reading, he meticulously put his hand into his breast pocket, withdrew his fountain pen, unscrewed the top, removed it, signed the letter and put it to one side.

"Well that's that," he muttered, more to himself than to us, and although the reading and the signing of the letter were timed to perfection I couldn't help feeling it was just a delaying tactic to enable him to think of the gentlest way to tell us what we already knew. He appeared to have made up his mind, because he put his elbows on the desk, placed his fingertips together, then looked straight at us. "Well, Miss Anderson has asked me to tell you that although she is reluctant to do so, under the circumstances with Richard's voice breaking, she has no alternative but to terminate your contract as from the last performance this evening."

After the Wednesday night Richard and I knew it was a foregone conclusion that we'd be paid off on Saturday night, but hearing it officially, especially with the use of the word "terminate", it sounded like a death sentence. We sat there looking at him not knowing if he had anything more to say and when we didn't move he pushed his chair back and stood up. "I'm sorry, but that's all I have to say."

"Thank you," I replied, standing up, but God knows why – I'd just been given the sack.

The last performance was a dismal affair, with me doing my best to help Richard out by harmonising "When Irish Eyes Are Smiling" with him, covering up the cracks in his voice. In fact it was a relief when the act finished. Any last night is a sad one, but this one especially so, with Richard not knowing what his new singing voice would turn out to be – that's supposing it came back as a singing voice – and me with my hopes dashed of getting into the big time. With this cloud hanging over us conversation in the dressing room was difficult.

"Would you like this?" Richard asked, holding out the make-up he'd bought only a fortnight ago. "You might as well have it, I don't suppose I shall be needing it any more."

"No, don't be silly, of course you will." He didn't speak, just shook his head and put it on the dressing table. I didn't protest again.

As always Richard had finished dressing before I was halfway through packing. I heard him snap down the clips of his case, then out of the corner of my eye I saw him put on his overcoat.

"Well cheerio," I heard him say. I turned round and he said, walking towards me with his hand out, "I'm sorry."

"Sorry," I queried as we shook hands, "what about?"

"Me losing my voice. I know what this tour meant to you."

"Forget it" – I turned away to hide my emotions – "it wasn't your fault. I lost my voice last year and I couldn't do anything about it either." When I turned back he was standing in the doorway with his suitcase in his hand.

"Well cheerio," he said once again, "and let's keep in touch."

"Of course," I called after his retreating figure. But we never did.

I finished packing the outfit that would never be worn on the stage again, clicked shut the case and put on my overcoat.

As usual, before going out I checked the dressing room and seeing the *Stage* and the *Performer* on the table I picked them up for something to read on the train home. As I did so, the letter I'd drafted to the agents fell out. I picked it up, took a brief look at it then screwed it up and tossed it into the wastepaper-basket. Like Richard with his make-up I wouldn't be needing it any more.

In 1975 I was booked for a concert tour in New Zealand as a result of my success in *On the Buses* and my musical *Reg Varney Specials*. Upon arrival in Auckland I was handed a considerable amount of mail. Alone in my hotel room I began sifting through the letters and greetings cards of welcome, the last of which said:

Dear Reg . . .
   Welcome to New Zealand . . . See you when you get to Rotorua.
   By the way – do you remember the Putney Hippodrome?
                                   Richard Hales

19

NEVER COUNT YOUR CHICKENS

With my elbows on the table and hands cupping my chin, I sat gloomily staring at the frying pan on the kitchen range in which Dad was cooking his usual Sunday morning concoction of streaky bacon and gyppo. Normally the smell of it made my taste buds run wild – but not this morning. The disappointment of the past week had dampened my enthusiasm and as I glanced out of the kitchen window, the miserable drizzling day did nothing to relieve my depression.

As a rule (with the general banter among us all and Dad's stories over breakfast), a very happy atmosphere existed. This Sunday morning, however, my despondency was contagious. In fact, apart from Mum, the rest of the family were nowhere to be seen.

"It's no good you sitting there brooding over what might have been." I looked back at Dad as he spoke. He was shaking a little salt and pepper into the pan. Mum sat at the table spreading margarine on two piles of bread; she never interfered when Dad was about to launch into one of his lectures on logic.

"You've had these setbacks before," he said. "I should have thought you'd have got used to them by now." Admittedly, what Dad said was true but I thought (although I wouldn't dare say it) it was easy for him to talk when he wasn't the one whose hopes had just been crushed. "So agents won't come and see you work at the clubs, so what?" He turned to look at me, then pressed his point home. "You've always earned a very good living without agents so I can't for the life of me see why they are so important now. Besides, you wouldn't want to become part of a double act all your life would you?" He waited for my reply and when none came he repeated, "Well, would you?"

"No, of course not," I answered solemnly.

"Well," he emphasised, "supposing you had got the agents to come out to see you, that's exactly what would have happened." He took a plate and started dishing up. "As I see it, Richard losing his voice was a blessing in disguise. Now think carefully about that and you'll see that I'm right."

I didn't have to think about it, I knew he was right from the moment he'd said, "You wouldn't want to be part of a double act all your life." "Anyway, it's taught you one thing," he said, putting the plate in front of me.

"What's that?" I asked.

"Never to count your chickens before they're hatched." And with that old proverb he closed the subject.

He turned back to his dishing up and in answer to his call of "Now come on, let's be having some of you," my brothers and sisters appeared as if by magic from different parts of the house, bringing Sunday morning back to normal.

My decision to forget about big-time show business was the outcome of Dad's few words of wisdom. I spent Monday writing to all my old contacts, giving them a brief reminder that I was back in circulation. The response received for my efforts was so encouraging that before long I was working practically every night.

As the weeks and months rolled by and my act improved, I began to attract a better class of work, such as Masonics and other concerts of quality. By 1936 (without the aid of agents, I might add) I was firmly ensconced in big-time show business, albeit on the lower rungs. If I were asked to recall any specific date that benefited my career more than most, I suppose I would say the twice-nightly concerts I did that year at the Town Hall in the Mile End Road, for which I was paid two guineas a night.

Had the running order remained as originally intended, then I, being second turn on, would never have been spotted by the bookers, who seldom arrived until the show was well under way. As it was, when I turned up on the Thursday for band call, I was told by a very agitated Manager that the double act closing the first half were forced to pull out owing to illness. They had tried all day to find a suitable replacement but, at such short notice, had failed and as time was running out they were compelled to take anyone they could get. This was a stroke of good luck for me, since the only act available to them was a juggler, and as the management considered a juggling act totally unsuitable for closing the first half, I was promoted to take over that spot.

I was thrilled beyond belief with the news, but later, standing on the side of the stage waiting for Dusty, the compère, to announce me, I became unsure of myself and started doubting. With all my experience of show business – from a fourteen-year-old raw recruit, till now, quite a competent performer of twenty – was I really accomplished enough to be given such a responsible job as closing the first half?

"Reg Varney," I heard the compère say. There was no more time for speculating now . . . I was on. The moment I walked into the blaze of lights I knew my fears had been unwarranted. What is

more, this was confirmed, not only by the reception I received at
the end of my act, but by the number of first-class offers that poured
in the following week.

I also have one other particular memory whenever I recall this
date, and that is about the substitute, the juggler who took over
my spot.

Actually I never would have seen him had it not been for Dusty.
I was quietly sitting in my dressing room contemplating my success
when I heard the bar bells faintly ringing, signalling the last five
minutes of the interval. Just then Dusty, with whom I was sharing
the room, hurried in. He had been in the pub across the road for
a drink and had left it a bit late.

Quickly exchanging his outdoor jacket for his stage one, he went
to the dressing table. " 'ere," he said, giving his face a few quick
dabs with the powder puff, "have you copped the juggler yet?"

"No. Why, is he any good?"

"Good! He's unbelievable . . . he's a must . . . do yourself a
favour and watch him second house." He tossed the powder puff
back on to the dressing table and picked up his white trilby, saying
as he made his way to the door, "I tell you what, I'll be watching
him second house, that's for sure!" With that he donned his hat at
a rakish angle then rushed out to open the second half of the show.

After Dusty's enthusiasm, I visualised an immaculately dressed
young man, full of vitality, performing unbelievable tricks. What
I saw was the exact opposite. I found myself looking at a man I
judged to be in his sixties, grey-haired and slightly stooped, but in
spite of this he seemed powerfully built. His old-fashioned dinner
suit had seen better days; it was green with age, and the tell-tale
brown stains down the front of his dress shirt were a dead give-away
to his being a snuff taker.

His props were even tattier than the suit. An old fold-up card
table which held them was covered by a faded cloth with a
moth-eaten fringe. A huge goldfish bowl full of water (it must have
weighed a ton) occupied the centre of the table, with pieces of
carrot floating about to resemble goldfish. The heavier pieces
floundered on the bottom of the bowl, with the lighter bits clinging
to the sides at the top, but when he gave the water a couple of
vigorous twists with his finger, the pieces of carrot sprang to life,
chasing one another round the bowl at a speed any ferret would
have been proud to attain. The real reason for the pieces of carrot
was to show the audience that the bowl was full of water. His other
juggling equipment on the table was a set of Indian clubs, in

desperate need of a coat of white paint; half a dozen balls, and a pack of playing cards.

As Dusty announced him and the curtains began to part, he put his thumb and forefinger into his waistcoat pocket, drew out a large pinch of snuff, sniffed a portion up each nostril and shuffled on, dusting himself down as he did so.

I watched him perform and he was, as Dusty had said, unbelievable. Not good in the sense I'd taken Dusty to mean, but unbelievably bad. His clumsiness and dreadful juggling suggested that he hadn't done his act for many a year and was badly in need of practice.

His first trick with the playing cards was a complete disaster. He showed the pack to the audience, gave the cards a quick flick with his other hand and then, like the expert card manipulators we've all seen at some time, he sprung the cards from one hand to the other, only in his case he completely missed his other hand and the cards scattered all over the floor. As I watched him crawling about on all fours, cursing the cards as he collected them, I couldn't for the life of me understand why, as a juggler, he had opened his act with an illusionist's trick anyway. The effort of gathering the cards together was making him puff and blow and on finally retrieving the last one, with a loud grunt he stood up, letting out an even louder "Ooh" as he straightened his back.

Dusty was screaming with laughter and although I didn't want to, because to me it was very sad, I couldn't help myself joining in, especially when he had another go at the card trick and again sprayed them all over the floor; the last straw for me came when he looked at the cards scattered all over the stage, and unable to face another crawling about job, ignored them and turned back to his card table muttering to himself, "Oh sod 'em." At the table he gave himself a quick fix of snuff, stirred the water in the goldfish bowl round with his finger, then picked up three of the balls and went straight into his juggling act.

He was doing fine with the three balls so I guessed the fix of snuff was what he'd needed. In my opinion he should have left it at that but being encouraged by a few sympathetic claps from the audience, he made the fatal mistake of picking up a fourth. I could tell by the way he was looking at the two balls in each hand that he wasn't sure he'd done the right thing. After a few moments deliberating he went for it. Up went the four balls and down came the four balls, and with neither hand anywhere near a catching position, he once again ended up on all fours cursing to himself,

"The bloody balls" this and "The bloody balls" that, as he chased all four into the footlights.

His juggling with the clubs was an improvement on the balls. In fact, after several cries of "Whoops" when things went wrong, he managed to get five up, until going for the sixth, when with another "Whoops" disaster struck again. The air appeared full of falling clubs as I watched him ducking and diving, shielding his head with his hands and arms as he frantically tried to avoid being clobbered. Looking contemptuously at the clubs strewn all over the floor and with no intention whatsoever of picking them up, he swept them to the back of the stage in disgust.

From the moment he placed the goldfish bowl on top of the pole, I knew what was to come, since only a few weeks before I had seen the same trick performed by another juggler, with one difference; instead of a goldfish bowl, he'd used an art-pot out of which was growing an aspidistra.

The trick, let me explain, was to balance the pole with its object on top on the chin, and when steady whip the pole away, catching the falling object on the back of the neck.

Knowing the terrible hash he'd made of his other tricks, I was horrified at the thought of a man of his age attempting a trick of this calibre, which called for such precision and perfect timing. I know I had laughed, I'm ashamed to say, at his bungling and misfortunes, but right now I felt extreme pity for this old man. Were, I thought, his circumstances such that he was compelled to do it? Whatever the reason, I wished fervently that what he was about to attempt wouldn't end up a disaster like the rest.

I watched with great admiration as the old man knelt down, gripped the pole near the bottom and, with a grunt and a groan, cautiously stood up. I was amazed at his strength and even more so when he tilted his head right back and heaved the pole bearing the weighty goldfish bowl on to his chin. His eyes, glued to the bowl, were so high in his head I could only see the whites; his pupils must have been floating about somewhere up in his forehead.

The pole was steady all the while he had hold of it, but the moment he let go all hell broke loose. His antics to keep the whole lot balanced were hilarious. I nearly had a heart attack when at one time water spilled over the edge of the bowl as it swayed nearly to the point of no return before he miraculously retrieved it.

Thankfully he gradually began to master the situation, and when finally he got it completely under control, he flung his arms out and waited for the applause which never came. I could feel my fingernails biting into the palms of my clenched hands as I waited apprehensively for his next move. With monotonous regularity he put his hand up to pull the pole away, only to check himself each time he did so. The drummer's roll grew louder in anticipation at each of his attempts but after a while, when nothing happened, he gave up and kept the roll at a constant pitch.

It was after the umpteenth time, when I was convinced he would have to abandon the trick, that he suddenly whipped the pole away.

I watched with bated breath as this huge bowl with its pieces of carrot spinning around inside rushed towards his head, and just as it looked as though catastrophe was inevitable, with split-second timing he threw his head forward. At the precise moment when he caught the bowl with a mighty thwack on the back of his neck, through clenched teeth he grunted, "Jesus Christ!" When I heard that I collapsed once more with laughter and thereafter never missed a performance just to hear him say it.

After my final performance on the Saturday night, I was making my way along the corridor to the dressing room when a smart, middle-aged man came towards me. "I watched you work tonight and was very impressed," he said as he warmly shook my hand. I was thrilled and wondered what agency he was from. I was hoping he would ask me if I was represented by anyone, but he didn't. I was trying to think of a way to approach the subject when he said, "I never got a bleedin' titter all week . . . mind you, I knew on Monday night first house when my first trick with the cards didn't get a laugh, I was in for a rough week. Thank Gawd you and the compère were laughing, otherwise I'd have felt very lonely."

I thought I'd hidden my look of incredulity until he said, after we'd shaken hands in farewell, "And I don't take snuff either." I went into my dressing room knowing I'd still got a lot to learn.

By the mid 1930s Cine Variety, as it was known on the big circuits such as the ABC and the Gaumont, became so successful that privately owned cinemas, faced with rapidly dwindling audiences, found that if they were to survive, they would have to do the same. While it was comparatively easy for the top-class main street houses to make the transition, the poverty-stricken back street bug hutches (or flea pits, as referred to by all and sundry), had to make do with what facilities they already had, which was very little.

Although they now ran talkies, most of them still had the piano in the pit which had been used for mood music for the silent films;

also the faded, moth-eaten curtain hanging from the tarnished brass rail that hid it. The stages were very small and the beam from the projection box had to double as the spotlight. The stage was used for maintenance purposes or for any brief announcement from the management should the picture break down. When this happened, which was quite frequently, the behaviour of the paid customers, who didn't think they were getting their tanner's-worth, became very ugly.

By this time I was earning roughly £250–£300 a year, but to achieve it I had to put up with a fair number of these dates. Some weren't too bad but in general they were pretty grim, with audiences to match.

If the stages were too small for a piano, then I did an extended accordion act. When this was the case I applied the same method for my opening that Richard and I had used as the "Yale Boys" – I opened my act behind the curtains, then at a given cue had them raised to reveal me already spotlighted centre stage. It was at a dive such as this that I had an embarrassing and humiliating experience.

The Apollo, being tucked away in one of the back streets of a district foreign to me, was difficult to find. I eventually found the name of the street it was in, wedged between two tin-plate adverts, one for Robin Starch and the other for Veritas Gas Mantles. I enquired at the box-office as to the whereabouts of the stage door. The big-bosomed middle-aged blonde, black at the roots where it was growing out, said, "It's down that side street there." I looked to where she was pointing and thanked her. She nodded in reply and in doing so the ash from her fag dropped on to her knitting. "Oh shit!" I heard her say as I walked away.

A tough-looking individual met me backstage and as it was July he was in his shirt-sleeves, with a wide belt beneath a fat gut holding up his baggy trousers. I judged him to be in his late fifties but couldn't be sure because the brightness outside made the backstage seem very dark.

"And who are you?" he said. When I told him, he merely grunted, "Oh," making no apology for his rudeness. "Well I'm Gus, the stage manager."

"Pleased to meet you," I lied, and as I offered him my hand (which he completely ignored) I realised that the mumbled conversation I could hear was coming from the sound-track of the movie being shown.

"Come on, I'll show you to the dressing room." He took me

down a musty-smelling passage, stopped at a door halfway along, unlocked it and flung it open. The mustiness of the corridor was nothing compared to the smell that hit me from the dressing room.

The room was dark and it was only when Gus switched on the naked electric light bulb dangling from the ceiling, that one understood why. Heaped high against the walls and windows were countless numbers of rotting cinema seats from way back, smothered with flakes of distemper peeling from the damp walls and ceiling. Buckets, mops, brooms and other discarded cleaning utensils littered the floor, while leaning against the wall behind the door in a dreadful state of disrepair was a massive ornate gilt mirror with half its glass missing. I looked round at this decaying heap of junk, puzzled as to why it was kept locked.

For changing and make-up, Gus indicated a dilapidated table with a rickety bentwood chair, and on the table, propped against the wall, a piece of broken mirror, most probably from the monster behind the door. It took me twice as long as usual to make up – owing to the appalling smell, I had to keep nipping out to the musty passage to catch a breath of air.

When the film finished and the house lights came on, the auditorium immediately became a hive of activity. I could hear the usherettes calling out their wares, "Cigarettes, ices, chocolates," as they made their way down the aisles, kids hollering to one another, the banging of seats springing up, and the sound of peanut shells being crushed underfoot.

Above all this noise I tried to explain to Gus about my opening. He didn't get it at first but after I'd repeated it to him he said, "Gotcha." I was putting on my accordion just as the pianist struck up the overture. "Right, this is it. Ted only has time for a couple of tunes so you might as well take up your position ready for the off."

Making my way behind the curtains, I was amazed at the narrowness of the stage; in fact when I faced the front the curtains hung barely six inches in front of my accordion . . . it was like standing on a windowsill. One false move, I thought, and I'll be doing a double act with Ted in the pit. The piano didn't sound all that close though, so I assumed the stage continued a few feet beyond the curtains.

Ted's overture seemed to have no effect on the audience whatsoever. If anything they sounded even more raucous, and standing there waiting for him to finish, I got to wondering what I'd let myself in for. If the blonde in the box-office, Gus, and that vile dressing room were anything to go by, then I was in for a very rough time. The mere thought of it made my bottle go, but as always I managed to control it. It was just as well because at this type of crummy date it went quite frequently.

The piano suddenly stopped, catching me unawares. I froze, but only for a moment or two, although then it seemed like an eternity. I took a couple of deep breaths to steady myself then pulled the bellows hard on to a big E flat seventh chord and burst forth with "Red sails in the sunset, way out on the sea . . ." My stage smile automatically split my face now, ready for the curtains to part on "Oh bring back my loved one . . ." – but when I got to it nothing happened.

The audience began to get restless, stamping their feet to the chant of "Why are we waiting?" I was about to shout for Gus to open the curtains, when a torch light shone on my face. Shouting to be heard above the noise, he said, "Oi, whatcha doing behind those curtains?"

"Waiting for you to open them," I replied angrily.

"They're not the house tabs, you stupid little bugger, they're the curtains for covering up the screen!"

I'd never felt so crushed and to top it all, when I did show my face and struck up with "Red Sails in the Sunset" again, someone yelled out, "Gawd Blimey, is that the only song you know?" I tried to ignore the roars of laughter but the audience was too intent on amusing themselves at my expense and after struggling through another couple of numbers (making sure of my money) I gave it best.

I had had my fair share of rough dates but this one has to go down as the roughest; although I have often questioned myself since . . . would it have been such a debacle had I not been so stupid as to stand behind the wrong curtain? But remembering how sadistically the customers got stuck into me, I very much doubt if it would have made any difference.

By the time I came out of the stage door it was a beautiful summer evening, and as I walked smartly away, thankful to be rid of that dreadful place, a comforting thought struck me; on tonight's showing I knew I'd never be booked back at the Apollo again.

I was about level with the Robin Starch and Veritas Gas Mantle adverts when I noticed approaching me a portly middle-aged man with thinning hair brushed back and wearing steel-rimmed glasses. He had a look of purpose in his face, and I wondered what he wanted. It wasn't my autograph, that was for sure. Panic gripped me as I thought, could he be one of the advance lynching party?

I was racking my brains for a way out when he said, "The name's Ted Boyce, I'm the pianist."

I vigorously shook his offered hand in relief, saying, "Pleased to meet you." Little did he know how much I meant it.

"You don't know me, but I know you and I thought as I live quite near you we could travel home together."

It transpired that Ted had been quite a fan of mine from the first time he'd seen me performing at the West Ham Working Men's Club. He was intrigued with my piano-playing and wanted to know how I had developed such a technique. Naturally I was highly flattered by his compliments, especially as he was a brilliant pianist himself, which I'd noticed while waiting like an idiot behind the wrong curtain.

He was astounded when I told him that I'd never had a music lesson and couldn't read a note, although I would have loved to be able to do so.

"I tell you what!" he said. "You show me how to do some of your runs and I'll teach you how to read."

"You're on," I said, and with that we arranged a meeting for the next day. We had a very pleasant journey home, never once mentioning the Apollo, just talking music.

It was through this chance meeting with Ted that I was invited to the party some time later where I met my future wife Lily and fell in love.

20

The Angel

I had been so shaken by my ghastly experience at the Apollo I vowed I would never again play another back street dive, or, come to that, any privately owned cinema; but in show business you soon learn not to make rash promises because it seems that the moment you do, work dries up . . . With only two dates in my book for the next month, and nothing in the foreseeable future, I regretted ever tempting fate by making such a vow. So it was a great relief when one Monday morning I heard the lovely sound of a letter being popped through the letter box.

It was brief, from the manager of a cinema in Hanwell, asking me whether I was free next week, and if so, would I ring him at my earliest convenience.

I looked at the letter-heading again, and my heart sank when I saw that the cinema was privately owned. But this was no time for personal feelings; it was the work I needed, and beggars can't be choosers, so I dashed round to Hooper's and made the call.

His charm over the phone won me over immediately. He told me he had just taken over as manager and in an effort to build up an audience he thought as an experiment he would try putting in a variety act to separate the supporting film from the main feature.

"So if you are free as from next Monday, and are interested," he went on to say, "I could pay you five pounds for the week." I accepted immediately.

I also learned that prior to taking over as manager, he had been a professional pianist with several of the big bands of the day. As he didn't volunteer their names, I didn't ask. He did say, however, that if I needed accompaniment, he would be delighted to oblige. I told him that I provided my own, but thanked him all the same.

As there was another matter he said he would like to discuss with me, we arranged to meet the following Monday at 11.00 a.m. I was about to replace the receiver when he said, "Oh, by the way, my name's Bob Greaves." Then he rang off.

The following Monday morning I sat staring out of the window on my way to Hanwell, tormented by the thought of what lay ahead. My apprehension about taking on another privately owned cinema was understandable. After all it was not long since my engagement at the Apollo.

When I got off the bus the cinema was immediately across the road. One look told me it was certainly not a back street dive; with its fine façade and the way it presented its forthcoming attractions, one could easily be misled into thinking it was owned by one of the big syndicates.

I was very impressed and feeling much happier I crossed the road, mounted the few steps, and being hampered by my two cases, shouldered open the door, and with my footsteps echoing round the deserted foyer I made straight for the box-office.

I peered through the grill at the very pretty young cashier (a sharp contrast to the blousy blonde at the Apollo) and gave my name.

"Oh, of course! You can go straight up, Mr Greaves is waiting for you in his office, it's up the stairs and the first door on the right along the corridor."

As I walked up the easy-tread staircase with its highly polished brass rail, I casually glanced at the photographs on the wall of Lillian Gish, Ronald Colman, Joan Crawford, Charlie Chaplin, and many other stars of the past and present, and wondered, for the first time since our telephone conversation, what the other matter could be that he wished to discuss with me. Anyway, I thought, as I stood outside his office door, I would soon know.

A voice answered my knock. "Come in!"

More framed pictures of famous stars decorated the oak panelled walls, and beneath one of Mae West was a beautiful mahogany serpentine sideboard. At the far end, in front of a leaded-light window spanning nearly the width of the room, was an antique desk with a tooled leather top. The rest of the furniture consisted of a huge settee with two matching armchairs, one of which was strategically placed in front of the desk.

Bob Greaves, well over six feet tall, and in his early forties (so I guessed), stood in the centre of the red patterned carpet, his hand outstretched in greeting. As I approached an expression of surprise suddenly spread across his face. I was racking my brains for an answer to his "Don't I know you from somewhere?", or some other such remark, when he shocked me with: "Jesus, you're just a kid."

As we shook hands I felt my face redden. Ever since a child, and until I knew better, I was highly sensitive about my "titchiness" and anyone referring to it could easily be the recipient of a vitriolic retort, which of course was way out of character. Luckily, this time I managed to keep myself in check, but couldn't avoid saying, with a slight edge, "Well, I'm twenty you know! And next month I'll be twenty-one."

It sounded so childish, I could have cut my tongue out the moment I'd said it. I might just as well have put my thumb and fingers up to my nose, and completed it with a "So there!"

He made no comment, just shook my hand with a smile and carried on as though I hadn't spoken. I admired the way he so diplomatically ignored my infantile remark.

"I believe you know a very old friend of mine . . . Paul!"

"Paul?"

"Yes, the resident pianist at The Hendon Way."

"Oh Paul! Yes, I've known him quite a while."

We were praising Paul's qualities, not only as a pianist but also as a man, when he said, "Look, if we're going to have a chat we might as well make ourselves comfortable." Then pointing to the armchair beside his desk he went on, "Take a seat, Reg . . . and by the way, do call me Bob."

Until this moment I had been in awe of him, but now that he'd made me his equal, I felt that I should live up to it; so I swaggered over to the massive armchair and drawled, "Thanks Bob," plonked myself down, and immediately disappeared among the feathered cushions. What dignity I had was instantly destroyed. Oh God! I thought, as I struggled to free myself from the suffocating cushions, why *do* I do it?

Trying to be the "sophisticated gent" never failed to cause me great embarrassment. Some months later an old "pro", having witnessed one of my unsuccessful attempts to play the sophisticate, bluntly said to me, "Don't emulate other people, Reggie . . . the public love you for what you are, not for what you are trying to be." Although his directness hurt at the time, it was one of the most valuable pieces of advice I have ever received. I never did it again.

When I had finally extricated myself from the cushions and had wriggled to the front of the chair, Bob reached over the desk for his cigarette case.

"It was Paul who told me what a good pianist you are."

My dignity returned at once as I realised he hadn't seen my predicament. "Oh that was good of him," I replied, accepting one of his cigarettes. I took my lighter from my pocket, but when it refused to light after several attempts I sheepishly accepted a light from him.

Resting his bottom on the edge of the desk he asked, "Are you free next week?"

"Yes," I said, surprised, "but why do you ask?"

"Well, I haven't booked another act for next week, and should this experiment prove to be successful I was wondering if you would be prepared to do another week."

"I'd love to, although I don't really like doing the same act two weeks running."

"That wasn't what I had in mind – no, I thought perhaps we could work out a two-piano act."

"That would be great!"

With this agreed, I followed him out of his office, through the auditorium and on to the stage.

"This is your piano!" he said lifting the lid. "Try it . . . I think you'll like it." I did a few arpeggios, and he was right, it was a lovely piano. I played him a few stride numbers to justify Paul's praise, and when I stood up I could tell he was impressed by the way he said, "Very good!"

To show me his virtuosity as a pianist, he sat down and struck up with a few old "standards". He was excellent and his style not being unlike my own, I sat down and joined him in a duet. And when we'd finished the last number with a great flourish, we both jumped up laughing and shaking hands at the same time, knowing that if today's experiment was a success it would be the simplest of tasks to work out a two-piano act for the following week.

"Come on!" he said, full of enthusiasm, "I'm going to take you out for a nice lunch."

The restaurant, although not large, was tastefully decorated and, when I scanned the menu and saw the prices, it was of a class that I certainly could not afford.

Bob ordered for both of us and within seconds the wine waiter brought a bottle of wine saying, "I believe this is your favourite Mr Greaves?" Bob recognised the label and asked the waiter to open it, turning to me saying, "This is a beautiful wine, you're going to love it!"

"Pop" went the cork, and after wiping the inside of the neck of the bottle with his napkin, the waiter poured a small drop into Bob's glass.

Bob solemnly picked up the glass by its stem, gave the wine a couple of twirls around the bowl, then stuck his nose into the glass and gave it a good sniff. Happy with the bouquet he took a swig and swished it round his mouth (as one would after cleaning one's teeth) then swallowed it. The ritual finished, he nodded his satisfaction to the waiter, who I thought for one dreadful moment was shaping up to say, "Let us pray". Instead he promptly filled my glass, then topped up Bob's before placing the bottle with care on the table.

I watched fascinated as he went through this routine, and as in the past, when I'd seen this identical ceremony performed, I could not fathom the reason for the sniffing, swooshing and tasting; particularly as no matter what their decision, they drank it just the same. I was dying to ask Bob, but daren't for fear of showing my ignorance.

This was going to be my first taste of real wine. The nearest I had ever got to it before was Christmas Eve.

After we (meaning my brothers, sisters and myself), had had our bath in front of the fire, Mum would hand us clean night clothes to put on, then just before going to bed, Dad would give us each a small glass of port wine. At the time we thought it was to celebrate Christmas, but in later years we all came to the conclusion that it was given to us as knock-out drops, to make sure we were fast asleep while the slightly inebriated, but happy, Father Christmas, was falling about in the dark trying to find the bedrail to hang up our Christmas stockings.

"Cheers!" said Bob, lifting his glass. "Here's to a successful week . . . and I sincerely hope, fortnight."

Then, anxious to taste this delicious-looking red wine, I chinked his glass saying "Me too!" and took a big gulp.

I couldn't avoid the loud "Uuggh" of disgust that escaped me. It was the most obnoxious stuff I'd ever drunk. If ever it was my misfortune to have to drink red ink this was how I would expect it to taste.

"Don't you like it?" He looked concerned. I then told him about our Christmas Eves when we were children.

"It's just as well I don't like it," I said, and went on to tell him that I had never touched a drop of alcohol before going on stage since the time when, because of a severe cold, some well-meaning person gave me a brandy and port. Instead of helping me through my act, as was expected, it had the reverse effect, and within a matter of minutes, when it was plain I was in no fit state to perform, I was being helped off the stage.

"You're very wise," he said, taking a swig of wine. "I've seen too many brilliant 'musos' ruin their careers because of this." With that he downed the rest of his glass.

During lunch we jotted down on the back of the menu all the numbers we both knew, and by the end of the meal had roughed out the shape of the act.

It was his enthusiasm when discussing the arrangements of the old standards that told me how badly he must be missing his days as a musician.

I thanked him for a wonderful meal and as we were about to leave he began to chuckle for no apparent reason.

"What are you laughing at?"

"You, in the office this morning. The way you disappeared into the cushions of the big armchair was hilarious!" And with the picture of it still fresh in his mind, he laughed his head off.

I could tell by the hollow sound of Bob's music, as he played the overture, that the cinema was virtually empty. I hated performing to so few, and it was at times like this that I wished I was back in my eight to five job. There's nothing more degrading than having to play to a handful of people who are even more embarrassed for you, than you are for yourself. I always felt that I was intruding on their privacy.

Bob finished his overture with a flourish – to complete silence. A few seconds later came the sound of someone blowing into the microphone to make sure it was on. "And now, ladies and gentlemen, for your entertainment the Management are proud to present a young up-and-coming star. Let's give a warm welcome to . . . Reg Varney."

This announcement received twice as much response as his overture. I began to wonder if there was anybody there at all, and to make the situation more ludicrous Bob played me on with the first eight bars of "I Want to be Happy", and because only one man was operating the heavy house curtains, making them painfully slow in rising, he had to keep repeating the eight bars over and over again, so that by the time they were up high enough for me to enter, the miserable few that were in had been brainwashed into thinking that Reg Varney was a red-nosed comic, instead of a singer of romantic ballads.

It was agony playing to such a pitifully small audience, and I had to call on all my courage and will power to check the urge to tear through my act. To make matters worse, when I eventually came off Bob was nowhere to be seen. I naturally took this to be the thumbs-down sign for next week, and I could visualise him sitting in his office regretting his generosity in buying me such a nice lunch.

I stood in the dressing room wondering what to do with myself until my next performance at 8.30 p.m. A glance at my watch told me that it was barely 3.30 p.m. I toyed with the idea of going home, but remembering that it had taken me near enough two hours to get here, I dismissed the thought immediately.

Normally I would nip through the pass door and see the rest of the programme, but as nobody was around to give me permission that was out, and as it was against all my principles to pay to see the film where I was working, it was a case of having to find another way in which to fill five hours.

It was a baking hot afternoon and as I aimlessly strolled along the main street I could feel the heat from the shimmering pavement penetrating the thin soles of my pumps, the only part of my stage outfit I hadn't bothered to change.

To while away the time I looked in every shop, and although I scrutinised every item nothing registered. My mind was cluttered with the thoughts of the evening performance. When I reached the end of the shopping area I crossed the road, and after I'd repeated the same routine on the way back, was surprised to see by my watch that two hours had passed.

Feeling now in need of a little refreshment, I walked back to a café I'd noticed on my way up and spent another half hour over a cup of tea and two rounds of buttered toast. Had it not been for the owner eyeing me suspiciously for taking more time than was necessary over such a small snack I could have made it last longer.

I arrived back in my dressing room at about 6 p.m. utterly exhausted. The traipsing up and down in the heat, coupled with the continual worry about what was to come, had taken its toll; I suddenly felt very tired and longed for a bed to lie on, but as the only furniture in the room was a Windsor chair, I climbed on to the dressing table, put my head on my folded jacket, and immediately fell into a deep sleep.

Bob hurried in while I was making up for the second performance. "I can't stop now," he said rather breathlessly, "but I thought I'd give you the good news before you went on."

I was looking at Bob through the mirror but when I heard him say that, my head automatically came round.

"Yes," he went on hurriedly, "I've decided to go ahead with the plans for next week, and to save our sanity I am cancelling all matinée performances with the exception of Saturday for the rest of the week." I was so overjoyed with his news that I was practically grovelling with gratitude.

"I thought you would like that," he said. He turned to go, then stopped. "Oh yes, there's something else that you will be pleased to hear . . . you have a very good house to play to."

As he left I turned back to the mirror and with his good tidings still ringing in my ears, I continued to put on my make-up, the misery of the afternoon already forgotten.

We rehearsed the two-piano act every morning and it came so easily to us that by Friday we could have put it on. We did debate whether we should try it out that afternoon, but after thinking about it, resolved to break it in the following Monday afternoon, when it would be fresher in our minds for the evening show.

On Monday morning we had just finished a quick run-through of our act, before the full dress rehearsal, when Jack, the cinema maintenance man, came over and told Bob that although he had worked out the lighting plot, he had hit a snag. He had just realised that with only one spotlight at his disposal, it was impossible, with Bob and myself sitting so far apart, to pick us both up; and as there was now no time to hire another, what should he do?

We talked about the situation at great length, but we found all our suggestions impractical, and had to concede that Jack was right. We were still pondering over the problem when a gruff voice said, "Turn 'em rahnd the uvver way!" All three heads shot round. It was Alf leaning against the proscenium arch putting a wad of tobacco into an AG paper to roll himself a fag.

Alf, a man nearing his sixties with a face more befitting an undertaker, was the projectionist and operator of the one and only spotlight. He lit the end of his fag which flared up like a piece of flash paper, took a deep drag, then repeated, "Turn 'em rahnd the uvver way!"

When we didn't move, obviously puzzled, he sauntered over to the piano nearest him, slewed it completely round, then did the same with the other one. With the keyboards now facing each other, he turned to Bob and me, saying, "Nah! if we shove the piannas as close togevver as we can, leaving of course, enough room for your pianna stools, although you'll be sittin' back to back, this way, by spreading the spotlight I'll be able to cover the two of yer."

With the problem solved, he took another deep lungful of shag, then shuffled off, shouting over his shoulder to Jack, "I'll be up in the box . . . give us a shaht when you're ready."

We marvelled at his perception and as he made his way up the aisle to the projection box, Bob called out, "Thanks, Alf!"

With practically no response coming from the few who were in it was impossible to assess the true value of the act and we had to treat the afternoon performance as another dress rehearsal.

We had planned our show to run twenty-five minutes, but when we came off we were astonished to find, even after allowing for the poor reception, we had only done fifteen minutes. With the cinema's programme being continuous, it was not possible to rehearse other piano numbers so I agreed to put in a couple of vocals on the accordion, with Bob backing me on the piano.

Being short of time did us a favour really, since, now that I'd introduced the two vocals, not only did they make up the time needed, but they gave the act more variety. In fact, though the second house was not full, we knew a good week lay ahead from the reaction shown by those that were there.

With the success of the first night our confidence grew and our performance blossomed; so much so that by the end of the week the ovations we received were tremendous.

"Thanks, Reg," Bob said, wringing my hand after the curtain had fallen on our final performance. "It's been a wonderful week, one I shan't forget." He paused, a little embarrassed as to what to say next. "Anyway, you'll be popping in the office for your money so I'll see you then." With that he hurried off to attend to his managerial duties.

"Ah Reg!" Bob said the moment I entered the office. "I'd like to introduce you to J.J., a musician friend of mine who would like to talk to you."

J.J. was not quite so tall as Bob, but looked just as smart in a beautifully cut navy blue pin-striped suit. We shook hands and after a few pleasantries he said, "I saw your act last week, and I must congratulate you on it, and on Bob's recommendation I was in again tonight."

I was wondering where all this was leading, when he said, "I'll come straight to the point – I am forming a big band show; I have all the other musicians, but I am in need of a good pianist. Your piano playing impressed me quite a lot, so I was wondering if you'd like to take the job on? It's worth five pounds a week."

My pride wouldn't allow me to tell him that I couldn't read music, so instead I thanked him saying, "No, I'm afraid it's not for me."

Taking this to mean that his offer of five pounds wasn't good enough he pondered for a minute or two, then suddenly coming to a decision said, "All right, I'll tell you what I'll do. If you'll consider doing your act in the show as well, I'd be prepared to up it to eight pounds a week."

This of course was a different proposition altogether and far too attractive not to give it some thought. Especially as Lily and I were saving to get married. He had previously told me that it was to be a four months' tour, and that eight weeks of it had been booked already. A quick calculation told me that even if it turned out to be just the eight weeks alone, fifty pounds out of the total could be saved with ease, so with this happy thought in my mind, and without seeming to be too eager, I accepted. The problem of not being a music reader I would face at the ten o'clock rehearsal on the following Monday morning.

I arrived at the hall in good time, and the first thing I noticed was that the chairs and music stands had already been set out. The drummer was still in the process of fitting up his kit and the other musicians who had arrived before me, were tuning up in general, all doing their own thing. One was oiling the slide of his trombone, a couple of trumpet players were doing a few scales getting their embouchures into shape, while a couple of saxophonists, after they'd moistened the reeds and adjusted the mouthpieces, warmed up with a few arpeggios. As more and more musos arrived and began going through the same routine, the din became unbearable, but J.J. who was sitting at a table with the librarian sorting out huge piles of music, was completely unmoved.

So far, not a soul had spoken to me, but it was plain by the way the musicians chatted among themselves, that nearly all were well acquainted with one another.

With my stomach churning over and over, I watched as the sax and trumpet players, along with the rest, began slowly to take their seats. It wouldn't be long now, I thought, before my secret was discovered. I kept asking myself why I was torturing myself in prolonging the agony? Why hadn't I the guts to go over to J.J. now, and tell him I couldn't read music? I knew this was the right thing to do, but instead I found myself wandering over to the piano. I sat down, opened the lid, and ran my fingers over the cigarette-burnt yellow keys. It was a grand piano all right, but only in shape, not in quality.

The librarian giving out the arrangements of the first number, handed me mine which opened out like a concertina to the length of about three feet. I looked at it from one end to the other, the masses of black notes meaning absolutely nothing. They might as well have given me the Rosetta Stone.

J.J. finally stood up from the table, removed his jacket, draped it over the back of the chair, rolled his shirt-sleeves halfway, then took up his position in front of the band.

"Well, gentlemen," he said as he took his baton from the music stand, "I know most of you, but for those of you who are first timers, welcome to the J.J. Band Show."

He let a bit of "rhubarbing" go on, then tapping his baton on the music stand, he went on, "Now that the introductions are over, let's try this one, shall we? 'I'm in a Dancing Mood'." He looked at his arrangement, then smiled before saying, "Well, that's what it says on my copy, I don't know what it says on yours." Everyone laughed far more than the joke was worth, but nevertheless it had the desired effect. The tension was broken.

J.J. allowed the laughter to continue for a few more seconds, then bringing them to order with another couple of taps on the music stand he raised the baton.

"Right, gentlemen!"

He cast his eyes over the band and when he was sure of their full attention, the baton came down; the silence was broken immediately by the ear-splitting noise of the band. The sudden blast shook me momentarily, but I quickly recovered and since I knew the melody of "I'm in a Dancing Mood", I joined in, playing it by ear, or as they say in the profession, busking.

Now a band pianist and a soloist are two entirely different things (although in fairness to myself, I was ignorant of this fact at the time). A band pianist never deviates from what is written, and there was I rattling away, playing it like a solo.

The strings section (of which there were four) had been positioned just in front of me, and as orthodox musicians one can imagine the look of horror on their faces as they listened to my stride-playing version of the piece.

It was so off-putting for them that they were making a terrible hash of their parts. I was concentrating so much on what I was doing, that their seething looks at me went unnoticed. I was totally unaware that anything was amiss, that is, until the little bespectacled fiddle player sitting just in front of me, unable to stand it any longer, suddenly sprang up from his chair and yelled, "Jesus Christ, this is impossible!"

His outburst immediately brought the band to a discordant halt. Staggered by this fit of temper, but more than that, furious that a member of his newly formed orchestra should show such disrespect for his leadership, J.J. threw down his baton, stormed over to the little fiddle player, and with eyes blazing, snarled "Got anything else to say?" Not intimidated by J.J.'s fury, he retorted, "Yes! This kid here's rattling up and down the keyboard like a bleeding lunatic . . . is this supposed to be a band rehearsal or a bleeding busking session?"

J.J. thrust his now aubergine coloured face into the little fiddler's and spat out, "Pack your bloody things and get out! You're FIRED!"

I sat there terribly ashamed, not for being caught out, that was inevitable, but for not speaking up when I should have. Had I done so, then none of this would have happened. Hating myself for my lack of courage, I angrily shoved back the stool and sprang up. My sudden movement made the two men turn round. I looked at their faces still flushed with rage and before either of them could speak I quickly apologised to the little fiddle player, then blurted out to J.J. all that I should have said earlier. In the stunned silence that followed, I swiftly crossed the parquet floor to the exit, feeling the accusing eyes of the orchestra on my back.

Half walking and half running, I made my way towards the end of the street where I knew I could catch a bus or a tram; either would do, so long as it took me as far away as possible from the scene of my shame and humiliation.

I suppose I must have covered half the distance between the hall and the main road, when I heard J.J. hailing me. I didn't stop or look round, if anything I increased my pace. He must have put on a spurt, since the next I knew he had caught hold of my shoulder and stopped me. Standing with my back to him, fully expecting a good dressing-down, I was surprised by his gentle, "Where are you going?"

Being floored by this unexpected question, I didn't know what to say. I turned round to face him, just as he continued, as though he'd read my thoughts, "Look, I know you should have told me, but you didn't and the little bit of aggro it caused is water under the bridge. And, if you're worried about the fiddle player, forget it, he's got his job back."

It was after expressing my relief about this that he reminded me of the other half of our verbal contract, saying, "So if you want to do your act in the show the offer still stands. But," he emphasised, "as I've got to get another pianist in to replace you, I can't, of course, afford to pay you the original eight pounds. If you'd be prepared to do a couple of numbers with the band, I could make it six pounds." He looked at me and without waiting for my reply stuck out his hand saying, "Is it a deal?"

With a big grin splitting my face, I returned his look, and we shook hands on it.

We were about to turn away when he said, "Oh, by the way! As you're no longer the pianist . . . Thank God!" We both laughed at this before he continued, "I shan't be wanting you until Thursday." I thanked him and we parted, still laughing heartily at his remark.

On the Thursday, when I returned to the hall after our mid-morning teabreak for another vocal session with the band, I saw a tall stranger talking to J.J. He was immaculately dressed, and from my position I could just see, hidden behind the lapel of his jacket, the slender silver water holder that kept fresh the red rose he wore in his buttonhole.

"Who's that?" I asked Ray, the librarian.

"Oh, he's the Angel."

"The Angel!" I said, mystified. "What's an Angel?"

"He's the backer," Ray explained. "He finances the show to get it under way, then he takes a percentage, if and when it starts to make a profit."

"Isn't that a bit risky?"

"Yes, but these people have got stacks of money . . . losing a few quid means nothing to them. Besides, apart from all his other interests, he owns, so I'm told, a private nursing home for the mentally disturbed."

I didn't see the Angel again until the start of our tour, at the Heely Green Theatre, Sheffield. Prior to the curtain going up on the first house, he came round to wish us all good luck. And I thought, judging by my morning's reconnoitre of the surrounding district, and the theatre itself, we needed it. And I was right.

With the first house being so poor, and the audience being so tough, the show ran ten minutes early. So to make up the time J.J. asked the elderly comic and myself, being the only two performers who could adjust our performance at such short notice, to lengthen our acts for the second house.

Putting in an extra number for me was a simple task, but my heart went out to the comic, who, knowing his act had just died, said, "OK Guv! I'll do my best, I'll stick in a few more gags."

My act followed his, and while standing in the wings watching him suffer, although it was sad, I laughed a lot when after he'd cracked one joke which was met with stony silence he said, "Ah! So that's how you like 'em, is it?"

Business picked up as the week wore on, but it wasn't until

Thursday that one began to notice any difference. Unfortunately as the audiences grew, so did the rowdiness.

Accompanying myself with songs at the piano and accordion, I had little trouble, and, all things being considered, I went quite well. But on the Friday night, as I made my way to the piano through a fearful din, the aftermath of the comic's reception, I knew a tough time lay ahead. With the theatre, being so small, as I opened my mouth to sing, smoke from countless fags billowed up from the auditorium and caught my throat, causing me to choke. The dryness in my mouth grew worse with each song, and although I continually tried to moisten my mouth and lips, I wasn't having much success. Nevertheless I struggled on.

My last number at the piano, much to my surprise, brought a smattering of applause; so heartened by this I strapped on my accordion. At about this time, America had discovered a new singing star, and since he accompanied himself on the accordion he was dubbed, "The Street Singer". His name was Arthur Tracey. My impression of him singing "Marta", the song he made famous, was a winner, so encouraged by their change of attitude, I went to the front and announced that this was what I was about to do.

I started the song, but now that I was practically standing in the footlights, the smoke, being even more dense, was clawing at my throat, making my voice sound like a rasp; to make matters worse, a couple of louts in caps, with Buster Keaton-like features, were hanging out of the nearest box sadistically drawing noisily on half a lemon each – the sight of which nearly drove me out of my mind.

As if this wasn't cruel enough, a baby started screaming its head off in competition, and even more distressing to me was the fact that it was winning.

I looked down to see where the bawling was coming from and was just in time to see a woman of about fifteen stone, who was occupying a double seat for courting couples, take out an enormous breast and feed it to the infant, whereupon the yelling ceased immediately, as its little cheeks pumped furiously in and out to the rhythm of its sucking.

I had been in show business long enough to know that with such poor attendances for most of the week we weren't going to break even, let alone make a profit; and unless the engagements to come were of a much higher standard, I couldn't see the show ever making a profit.

Right from the start I had felt a little uneasy about the tour, but whenever I thought about the Angel's backing, I dismissed my doubts at once. Yet when the final curtain came down on the second house Saturday night it was a great relief. All that remained to do was to pack up our gear and wait for J.J. to pay us . . . and wait we did. When after an hour had passed and we were still waiting, we knew something must be radically wrong.

At first the band were in a buoyant mood, knowing that they would be rid of the place that night, but as time dragged on, and with no explanation for the delay, they became restless and indignant at the injustice of being ignored. Another half hour passed before J.J. finally put in an appearance and by the expression on his face it was obvious that the news wasn't going to be good. He walked across to a large table at the far end of the musty band room, which was underneath the stage, and pushing aside a couple of instrument cases, squatted on its edge, and waited for the angry rumblings to die down.

His explanation was no surprise to me. He told the band that because business had been so disastrously poor, his 70 per cent share of the gross was only enough to pay for our digs and to get us to our next date, the Hippodrome, Wednesbury.

I was wondering where the Angel came into all this, when I heard J.J. say, "Cecil has caught the night train to London and on Monday will be sending me a Banker's Order to cover the deficit. So, it's just a matter of tightening our belts till then." From this I deduced that Cecil must be the Angel.

Ray, the librarian, who was also the road manager, came in just as J.J. had finished, and took the floor. "Now that J.J. has explained the situation," he said, "I have worked out that, after paying the four acts, which we are legally bound by contract to do, and retaining sufficient for our rail fare to Wednesbury, I can give you all thirty shillings each, which should be enough to pay for your digs and get you out of town." This was met with a number of "Jesus Christ's" and many other expletives, which he cut short, saying, with raised voice to quieten them down, "Now let me finish . . . Monday midday we will muster in the band room at the Hippodrome, where the balance owing to all will be paid in full."

I watched him paying out thirty shillings to each of the members of the orchestra and when the last man had received his, Ray came over and gave me mine. He waited for me to pocket my thirty bob before saying, "Come on, let's go and have her bloody cold salad again."

Walking down the badly lit, dingy, cobbled street to our digs, I said, "What about the Angel?"

"Yeah!" he replied, "what about him!" His voice was so ex-pressionless I didn't know which way to take it. Could it be doubt, I wondered?

Monday, everyone arrived in the band room in good time and good spirits. That is, until once again we found ourselves waiting. As the minutes ticked by, the boys began to argue among themselves to see what the best way was to approach their situation. Some were all for finding J.J. and sorting him out; the more level-headed were, as they said, "against this stupid idea". And as their arguments became more and more heated, each side turned to the neutrals for support. No-one asked for my opinion or support; but that wasn't surprising since I'd been ignored by them from the outset. The conflict between the two sides was beginning to get out of control, and just when I thought a fight might ensue, Ray rushed in, flushed of face and rather agitated. Immediately questions were being flung at him from all round the room. He tried to reason with the boys but his words were lost amid their angry shouts. The scene was becoming more frightening with every second and as the circle round Ray began to close in I panicked. With my popularity among the musicians being practically nil, and before I became involved, I fled up the stone steps, through the stage door and out into the street.

This was only the second time I had been away from home and as I tramped the working-class streets of the Midlands, not knowing a soul, and being surrounded with an accent I could barely under-stand, I felt terribly alone and homesick.

After a while when I realised there was nothing to be gained by aimlessly walking the streets of a place completely foreign to me, I turned and made my way back to the theatre, wondering if I would encounter any toothless or black-eyed musicians along the way. Ray was coming out of the stage door as I arrived.

"Ah, you're just the bloke I've been looking for!" Then thrusting two green pound notes into my hand he said, "That's to be going on with." I looked down at the two pound notes, then up at him, but he was gone before I could say anything. His quick withdrawal made it clear that he was in no mood for answering another lot of awkward questions, and as we weren't "digging" together that week, my chances of unravelling the mystery were slim.

Our band show, including the four acts (which Ray had told me were being booked by a North Country agent), was far too big for the small provincial date, and when I discovered that the seating of the Wednesbury Hippodrome was only six hundred and fifty, I knew that even if we did capacity business, and unless the Angel turned up trumps, the possibility of our taking a weekly wage, let alone that already owed, was negligible.

Ray had told me during the week that the money he had paid us on the Monday had not come from the Angel, but was from money borrowed by J.J. from the theatre. So come Saturday night, even though the business had been a great deal better than the previous week, by the time the theatre had deducted the amount borrowed, we were once again back to square one. And to make matters worse, J.J. was forced to pay out an extra fifty pounds for an additional feature act, insisted upon by the Management, to close the first half.

Now that my earlier doubts were proving to be right, I was determined, after I had paid my digs, to save as much as I could out of the mere pittance I was given, for my train fare back to London. But when we got to the Tivoli, New Brighton, two weeks later, I still, with all the determination in the world, hadn't saved enough for my fare home. Although it hurt my pride to do so, I wrote to my brother Sid and told him of my plight.

On Wednesday morning the stage door keeper handed me a letter. I knew that it was from my brother. It was a single folded sheet, which just said,

"Dear Brother, Sorry to hear your sad news about the show . . . Looking forward to seeing you on Sunday. Your affectionate brother, Sid." There was no mention of the pound note inside that he'd sent for my fare.

It was natural that I should be elated after receiving Sid's letter, but even so I went about my work as usual, not giving the slightest sign of my intentions. Saturday night, second house, I sang my second and final song with the band, "One, Two, Button my Shoe", then, as always, I went to the band room, removed my make-up, packed my stage clothes, and after bidding the stage door keeper goodnight, I slipped quietly away, to the strains of J.J.'s band playing . . . "I'm in a Dancing Mood".

The first train out on Sunday morning from New Brighton was already standing in the station, and as I walked along the platform, I was amazed at the number of people travelling at such an early hour. I eventually found a compartment that was not full. The only other passenger, a man, had his head stuck in a newspaper, studying the sports page. I had put my accordion on the rack above, and was in the process of doing the same with the smaller case when the voice I knew so well said, "Hello Reg, going home for the weekend?"

I was so shocked to hear Ray's voice that for a second or two I froze with my case in mid-air. Now that I had been caught, the excitement of making my escape suddenly left me. I pushed the case on to the rack and when I was sat down Ray, sitting opposite, said with a sheepish grin, "Isn't this nice, I couldn't wish for a better travelling companion."

Feeling now like the mouse that is being played with by the cat, I answered, "No, not for the weekend, but for good." Once I had started, and knowing that without a contract no-one could stop me anyway, I poured out everything that I had wanted to say for the past few weeks. He slowly nodded his head with understanding, then said, "Well, what do you think I'm doing on the train? The same as you. I'm finished, I've had enough!"

After listening sympathetically to his reasons for leaving, I asked him what I had been dying to know since Sheffield. What had happened to the Angel?

"Ah yes!" he said. "The Angel! Well when his cheque didn't arrive J.J. immediately got on the phone to the Private Nursing Home for the Mentally Disturbed, and asked the operator to put him through to the Director, Mr Cecil Bernard. The Matron came to the phone, and she told J.J. that the home was not run by a lone Director, but by a Board of Directors; and although they did have a Mr Bernard there, he wasn't a Director . . . he was one of the inmates."

21

THE WINDMILL

From 1936 to 1939 I continued with my act but although I was earning a steady living I just couldn't seem to get off the bottom rungs of the ladder. The rumblings of war didn't help any, because show business, being a luxury trade, is always among the first to suffer when trouble is brewing. With dates hard to come by, you had to forget about climbing the ladder and concentrate simply on getting work.

It was coming up to the end of May 1939 and with very little in my book for the future I began to get worried, especially as Lily and I were still saving to get married. I was seriously thinking of applying for a day job when out of the blue I received a letter, short and to the point, from a Mr Green who ran a small establishment in the West End – the Boley Club in Denman Street. His letter stated that he was looking for a pianist cum vocalist. It went on to say, "You have been strongly recommended by a friend of mine. If you are vacant, and are interested would you ring me at your earliest convenience to arrange a meeting. I am here from 10.00 a.m. from Monday to Saturday."

I couldn't believe my luck. A few moments ago I was abandoning the idea of climbing the ladder, and here was a letter not only offering me an engagement, but it was in the West End too – my first time ever. Playing the piano and singing in a club wasn't exactly show business, but after all it was London, and who knows, I thought, what might come of it.

I rang immediately and within ten minutes of making the appointment I had donned my best suit and was catching a No. 15 bus from Canning Town station, making my way to Piccadilly.

Mr Green, who sported a pencil moustache, was a short stocky man with dark wavy hair. Unlike many others I had dealt with in the past, he was a gentleman. If I accepted the job he could guarantee me four weeks, but over and above that he wouldn't commit himself. That, he said, depended on the success of the experiment. I agreed on five pounds a week, and on our way from his office to show me the club itself, he told me that it was really a drinking club with a pianist playing background music. Now, to make it more attractive, he had cleared a small area in the centre of the room for dancing. "And," he said pushing open the double doors, "I thought that perhaps a number or two from you every now and then would make it more entertaining . . . sort of give it that added extra."

Standing in the club room, I was more than surprised at what I saw – especially after his dingy office. To the left as you entered was a stage, not over-large but big enough to take its half-size grand piano. Red plush bench seats were against either wall, with glass-topped tables set at intervals before them; and placed around the small parquet dance floor were more glass-topped tables, each with four red plush bucket chairs. Opposite the stage, at the far end of the room, sparkling with cut glass and chrome, was a pleasantly proportioned bar. The counter had three porcelain beer pumps and the glass shelves at the back were stocked with every conceivable drink one could wish for. The whole place had been tastefully decorated; even the bar stools had red plush tops to match the rest of the furniture.

I had been impressed when I'd seen it in the daylight but at eight thirty the following Monday evening, when I arrived to start my engagement, it looked sumptuous, with its subtle wall lighting and the red ball-shaped table candles all lit. I ran my fingers over the Bechstein and was relieved to discover it was all that it looked, a beautiful piano – just as well as I was committed to playing it for the next month.

I was miles away, thinking how fortunate I'd been that through an unknown admirer's recommendation I had landed such a delightful job, when Mr Green broke into my thoughts: "You look rather splendid in your white tuxedo, and I want to thank you for your nice gesture of wearing a red carnation to go with our decor." I accepted his compliment, but omitted to tell him that the imitation carnation had been in my buttonhole ever since I bought the jacket a month ago. I was so used to it being part of my dress that until he had mentioned it I had forgotten it was there.

He was such a nice man I was determined to do all I could to help make his club a success – and I did. I sang every request asked for, but although my popularity did attract a few more to the club, I couldn't battle the threat of war. War was the only topic of conversation. Every day something was happening to remind you that a conflict with Hitler wasn't far off; so it was no surprise when towards the end of my fourth week Mr Green told me, with a very sad heart, that his experiment hadn't been successful enough to warrant keeping me on. "But it is not all bad news for you," he said, brightening up. "A friend of mine who owns the El Gaucho night club in Wardour Street is looking for an act from next Monday. I have told him all about you, and on my recommendation he would be delighted to take you on, so if you would like to go and see him after you finish here on Saturday night and fix terms, you've got the job."

The El Gaucho was different again to the Boley Club. For one thing it was downstairs and lacked the Boley's charm. However, once your eyes became adjusted to the subdued lighting you could see that money hadn't been spared when it came to its lush decor. It was certainly not a clip-joint. Its clientele was drawn from the rich upper classes, and at £10–£12 a bottle for spirits, they had to be rich. In 1939 a bottle of Scotch whisky could be bought at an off-licence for twelve and sixpence and gin was a little cheaper.

I preferred the Boley Club for its wonderful atmosphere and amiability, but then one can always draw comparisons; for instance, my hours of working, from 8.30 p.m. to midnight at the Boley Club, didn't compare with just twenty minutes at the El Gaucho. The audiences at the El Gaucho were tougher to please too, but at those prices for liquor, who wouldn't be?

I was originally booked for a two-week run for the same money as I had received at the Boley Club, but after my poor reception on the first night I was fully expecting them to terminate my contract there and then. Much to my amazement not only was I kept on for the fortnight but the contract was extended for a further two weeks. I soon learned that artistes working in night clubs were merely added attractions.

A few months earlier I had introduced a novelty into my act. I played my arrangement of "When Day Is Done" blindfolded and with the keyboard completely covered by a sheet. It looked spectacular, but having been brought up from an early age to play in the dark, for me this little stunt was comparatively easy. Nevertheless it was amusing and became quite a talking point.

One day in the middle of my last week at the El Gaucho, I was invited for a drink by one of the members, an exceptionally tall man. He introduced the other people at his table as his friends, but having just come from a brightly lit area to this near blackness, it was only their voices that told me they were male and female.

Hardly had my bottom touched the seat when he said, "Drink?" I couldn't see what drinks were on the table, but being very thirsty after just finishing my act, I said, "Oh yes please!"

Picking up a glass I could barely see he asked, "Ginger ale or soda?"

"Ginger ale would be lovely!" I answered.

I heard the fizz of the ginger ale being poured into my glass. We chinked our glasses. "Cheers!" I took a deep gulp.

I wondered what the hell had hit me. I choked and spluttered as I gasped for breath. Wheezing noises were coming from my throat as I tried my hardest to force some air down my gullet into my lungs. I was doubled over with the effort of trying to get my breath, and seeing my distress he jumped up and started vigorously slapping me on the back, repeating, "Are you all right? Are you all right?"

I didn't know which was worse – fighting for my breath, or my head hitting the table in rhythm to his thumping. Luckily for me he took it that I was nodding "Yes," and stopped.

I knew the moment the drink hit my throat that it was more than just the ginger ale, but not wanting to embarrass myself by telling him that I'd never drunk spirits before – in answer to his enquiry, "Was it too strong?" I told a white lie.

"No, it just went down the wrong way, that's all!"

He waited until I had fully recovered before telling me that his name was Alan Bristow, and that he, with his partner Alec Rose, wrote all the music and lyrics for the already famous Windmill Theatre shows. He congratulated me on my act. "I'm sure Mr Van Dam would like to hear your piano arrangements, particularly the novel treatment you give to 'When Day Is Done', so if you would like me to," he offered, "I will speak to the governor tomorrow, and if he is interested I will pop in and let you know."

Without hesitation and trying to keep my excitement under control, I thanked him profusely and accepted his offer.

"Oh there is one other thing," he said as I was about to leave. "When do you finish here?"

"This Saturday," I told him.

"That might turn out to be just right," he said.

I thanked him again, then quickly bade his guests good night before my excitement exploded in front of them.

I didn't feel too let down when Alan Bristow hadn't shown up by the Thursday night, but come Friday and Saturday when there was still no sign of him, no words could describe my disappointment. Dejectedly I made my way to the small dressing room knowing that this crushing blow was going to take a lot longer to heal than all the other disillusionments I'd had in my career.

I had changed and was halfway through making up when there came a knock on my door. "Come in," I said, fully expecting it to be the waiter with my usual soft drink, but instead of "There's your lemonade, Reggie," Alan Bristow's voice said hurriedly, "I can't stop now, but I've had a word with Mr Van Dam. Meet me at the Windmill, Monday morning, ten o'clock sharp, and I will introduce you to him."

"Oh thank you!" I said, but he didn't hear me, he was gone. I stared at the closed door thinking, as I had done so often in the past – this is the magic of show business . . . one moment you're in the depths of despair and then, with a wave of the wand, you're back on top of the world again.

On the Monday morning the walled mirrors of the rehearsal room made it look massive, when in fact it was quite small. There were just the two of us there, Vivian Van Dam and myself. I had already played him my arrangement of "You Are My Heart's Delight", the song Richard Tauber had made famous, and now with the last chord of "When Day Is Done", with great showmanship I whipped the blindfold off and sat at the old upright waiting hopefully for a favourable reaction.

He made no comment either way, just sat there with lips pursed, staring into space, deep in thought. While I waited in silence for his decision – a wait which seemed interminable – I took the sheet that covered the keyboard, folded it neatly, and put it back in my little case.

Suddenly without warning, he slapped his knees and stood up. "Yes," he said, smiling, "that was excellent and will fit perfectly into the sketch I am incorporating in my next edition. There is one thing, however. I shall be getting two showgirls to assist you with your blindfold act."

I stood up as he walked towards me explaining how it should be done. "After you have played your first number," he was saying, "the two girls will make their entrance. One will cover the piano with the sheet, while the other, at the end of your announcement, will blindfold you, and escort you back to the piano, after which they will hold the sheet for you; but as to how you want it held, you will have to explain that yourself when we rehearse with the girls later on."

He took a pencil out of his top pocket and with a "Now!" signifying a change of subject, he asked, "Have you any commitments for the next four weeks?" (This was the length of the run.)

"Nothing I can't get out of," I told him, not bothering to hide my joy.

"Good!" he said, producing a small notepad from his inside pocket. "Who's your agent?"

"I haven't got one."

"Oh!" was all he said as he returned his pencil and pad whence they had come. "Well, how much were you getting at the El Gaucho?"

"Five pounds," I told him.

He came straight back with, "I'll give you six. Is that all right?" and before I had time to say yes or no he said, "Good, now let's go and rehearse with the girls."

I remember thinking at the time that six pounds a week for five shows a day was rather a paltry sum, yet I knew that as it was the Windmill, in the heart of London, I would have done it for even less; also with not a date in my book for the next two months, I was in no position to argue.

After my rehearsal with the two showgirls, which took only a matter of minutes, he told me that as I only had my act to do in the sketch, I wouldn't be needed again until the Saturday morning run-through of the show, but of course there would be a full dress rehearsal on Sunday ready for the Monday opening.

Three other performers were involved in my scene, which followed the big musical opening: Hal Bryan, a well-known review comic and pantomime dame of those days; Dickie Hurran, a song and dance man who eventually became one of our most successful producers of the London Palladium spectaculars and summer seasons; and Eric Woodburn, who in later years played the part of Doctor Snoddy in the BBC drama series *Dr Finlay's Casebook*. The scene opened up with Hal Bryan sitting at a desk playing the part of a theatrical producer giving auditions. To his call of "Next," Dickie Hurran entered. A short comedy routine ensued, leading Dickie into his song and dance number. Eric Woodburn followed, reciting a comedy monologue as his audition piece, after which I went on and closed the scene with my piano act.

Sunday's rehearsal went smoothly and although I had been warned that applause was difficult to come by at the Windmill, I didn't realise just how difficult until I had given my first performance in Monday's new show. It soon became apparent to newcomers like myself that the famous Windmill nudes were the main attraction. By the time we reached the fourth and fifth shows each day, some signs of life were evident, but nothing to write home about. It wasn't until the last two houses of Friday and Saturday, particularly Saturday, that I got a true appraisal of my act. Nothing seemed amiss in the first week; but on the odd occasion during the second week I detected a smattering of laughter coming from the audience in the course of my act, which became more noticeable as the week wore on. This irritated me somewhat and knowing that my performance had nothing to do with comedy, I naturally came to the conclusion that Hal Bryan must be the culprit. I didn't know what he was doing, but I suspected he was using the desk as a piano and miming my actions.

It was after my last performance on the Saturday night of the fourth week that things came to a head. I had not long begun my act when the laughter started and by the time I had got to my novelty blindfold arrangement of "When Day Is Done" the audience was falling about. At the end, I whipped off the blindfold as usual – not with showmanship, but in anger. As always the two showgirls assisting me made their exit while I took my call, and hardly had the curtain closed on the sketch than I was off like a shot. I thought I had conquered my hypersensitivity, but I hadn't. The "little gypsy" fiasco of my beginnings had left a deep scar, which could easily flare up at the least provocation.

My haste to the dressing room was impeded by the rush of befeathered girls tearing down the stone stairway to the screams of "Come on, girls, you'll be off!" (Time has always been exaggerated in the theatre.) This allowed Hal Bryan to catch up with me. He didn't speak, just took me gently by the arm and ushered me towards his dressing room.

"Sit down, son," he said, closing the door behind him. He was a likeable man of medium height. Only when he removed his jacket could you see that although he wasn't what you'd call a fat man, he nevertheless could have done with shedding a few pounds. "There is something very important I have been wanting to say to you for a long time." He was taking his next change of costume off the rail. "I know that you're of the opinion that I am responsible for all the laughter going on during your act." He arched his eyebrows. "I'm right, aren't I?" He didn't ask again if I agreed, my silence was confirmation enough.

"First of all" – he was pulling another shirt over his head – "let me put you straight on one thing." He paused, then emphasised, "I am not, as you suspect, doing any funny business while you are performing. In the first place, I wouldn't dare; in the second place, Van Dam would have me out on my ear; and in the third place, it would be a complete waste of time on my part, because all the

spotlights are focused on you, whereas I am in utter darkness."
Listening to his explanation, the hostility I had felt towards him
left me completely, in fact if anything I was suffering slightly from
a guilty conscience, knowing now that my suspicions had been
unjustified.

"It's going to surprise you to know" – he was now putting on a
pair of check trousers – "that it's not me they are laughing at, it's
you!"

"Me!" I exclaimed, looking at him with eyes nearly popping out
of my head.

"Yes, you!" He slipped his arms through his braces. "I know it's
hard for you to swallow, but take it from me, son, it's true."

Bewildered, I asked, "What am I doing to make them laugh?"

"That's just it." He was buttoning his flies. "You're not doing
anything, but I can tell you why they are!" He sat down in front
of the mirror, clipped an enormous red bow on to his collar and
fluffed it up. "You possess a most wonderful gift." He turned to
me, leant forward and said earnestly, "You're a natural comedian,
and you don't know it."

I was about to speak when he put up his hand. "No, let me
finish, and tell you the reason. First, as it's a comedy scene the
audience are already in a receptive mood for laughter, so when you
come on with your little comedy face and throw yourself into your
arrangements with a great display of showmanship, the audience
naturally take it that you are burlesquing a concert pianist, and
the more you glare at them for what you think I am doing, the
more they laugh at you."

It struck me forcibly, the moment he said it, that this must have
been the quality the audience saw in me all those years ago at the
Plumstead Radical Club.

He stood up and took the check jacket off its hanger. "Now
listen, son, take my advice, the first opportunity you get to go into
comedy you take it . . . I've been around a long time, and believe
me I know what I'm talking about."

I thanked him for his advice, and as we both left his dressing
room he said, "Think nothing of it, lad, you'd have discovered it
yourself sooner or later."

I stood there thinking about what he had said, how unknowingly
I had made the audience laugh. Although from a child I had always
had the power to make my family laugh, I wondered if I would
ever have the courage to do it before an audience, knowingly. I
did, but not until many years later.

I did a second month at the Windmill Theatre, but only playing a small upright piano in a vast tropical musical scena. Being one of a group wasn't very satisfying. The only reward came from Mr Van Dam who gave me a two pounds rise, making my money up to eight pounds a week, which helped enormously.

I wasn't sad when the show came to an end, far from it. I was enriched with the knowledge of my comedy abilities, which I now accepted as true, and what's more I had been given the names of several West End agents of repute. At last, I kept telling myself, nothing can stop me now, nothing! But of course it did. Just one week after my last show at the Windmill my career in show business came to a temporary halt, at eleven o'clock on Sunday morning, September 3rd, 1939.

22

The Factory Worker

We were all (that is, Lily, her mum and dad, sister Ruby, her boy friend Bob, and myself) gathered around the loudspeaker of the Cossor wireless set, listening to Neville Chamberlain's grave declaration of war with Germany. The whole country had really known that war was inevitable when, months before, everyone was issued with gas masks, including children and babies. They came in cardboard boxes, and were made of rubber and fitted over the head with adjustable straps. You breathed in through the filtered pig-like snout, and exhaled through the rubber sides. Unfortunately, when you exhaled it made the noise of someone passing wind . . . in fact when worn they made everyone look and sound like a farting pig.

It was only a matter of minutes after Neville Chamberlain's broadcast had finished that the up-and-down wailing of the siren pierced through our stunned silence.

None of us moved for a second or two, then, suddenly realising the seriousness of our situation, terror-stricken we made a dash for the Anderson shelter that Lily's father and I had erected at the bottom of their yard. Once outside the back door it was as though the whole world had come alive simultaneously. There was pandemonium. Hysterical cries were coming from every back yard.

"Where's Maud for God's sake? Come on, Maud, get a move on . . . where the hell have you been?"

"The dog! The dog! Who's got the dog?" a woman's voice called.

A man yelled with rage, "Now where's Gran got to? Come on, Gran, what the hell have you been doing for Christ's sake?"

"I had to go to the lavatory."

With panic all around, accompanied by the constant terrifying wail of the siren, it was as if all hell had broken loose.

Then someone from our group yelled, "Gas masks! We haven't got our gas masks!"

Back to the house we fled, disappearing in all directions to look for them.

Assembled once again at the back door, Lily, looking at her father, screamed, "Where's your gas mask? You haven't got your gas mask!"

Giving his usual little sniff, he said, "I can't seem to find it anywhere, duck. I know I've seen it around somewhere."

"There!" said her mother, thrusting his gas mask at him and giving him a withering look.

It was when we were on our way to the shelter for the second time that Ruby, suddenly noticing that Bob was nowhere to be seen, shouted to us through the ear-splitting noise, "Where's Bob, has anyone seen Bob?"

It was only then that we realised none of us had seen him since Chamberlain's disturbing broadcast. She was turning to go back into the house when I quickly stopped her, saying reassuringly, "He's probably looking for his gas mask . . . he'll be with us as soon as he's found it." She accepted my explanation and we hurried with the others to the shelter. When we arrived, the steel blast door the girls' father had fitted in the opening to the shelter was wide open, and inside sat the missing Bob, with his gas mask already donned, farting away like a good 'un.

The sirens had stopped, and it had become eerily quiet – now it seemed as if the whole world had ceased to exist. We sat huddled together in the confined space of the six-foot-square Anderson shelter, suffering badly from claustrophobia. My heart was pumping away at twice its normal rate, my face felt flushed with fright, and it was becoming increasingly difficult to control my shaking limbs. I looked at the others and knew that they were as scared as I was. Not even our noisy gas masks could hide our fear.

Ten minutes from now – that's how long I calculated it would take the enemy bombers to reach us from the coast – and we would know the worst. We were convinced, as I suspect the rest of London was, that this was the end. After the ten minutes I had allotted had passed and nothing had happened, our nerves were thankfully released by the wonderful sound of the siren's "all clear".

We immediately removed our gas masks and the first words spoken came from Lily's mum: "I'll go and put the kettle on. We'll have a nice cup of tea."

We emerged from the shelter into a beautiful cloudless sunny day, and Lily, Ruby and their mum and dad made straight for the house, while Bob and I lit a fag and stood listening to the over-excited chatter of relief, and the countless number of lavatory chains being pulled up and down the street. Bob and I were no exception, we wanted to "go" as badly as everyone else, but there was no point in our making a move for the next five minutes or so, because our four had already beaten us to it.

* * *

THE FACTORY WORKER

Like everyone from the age of eighteen upwards, I had to register at the Labour Exchange for duty in the Armed Forces. We were to be called up in groups, the eighteen-year-olds going first, then the nineteen-year-olds, and so on. I was twenty-three at the outbreak of war, and as I had been informed by the officials that it would be a month or two before they got around to calling up my age group, Lily and I decided to get married, on October 1st, 1939, at St Bartholomew's Church, Barking Road, East Ham. Lily's mum and dad let us have the two front rooms of their house, since it would have been pointless for us to rent a place for such a short period of time.

Now that I was married, and since it seemed that show business had come to a complete standstill as most theatres had closed, I had to get a job to tide me over until I was called up; so without waiting for the Labour Exchange to send me God knows where, I contacted an old acquaintance of mine, a great fan of my piano-playing, Jim Palmer, who was a charge hand at a factory in Millwall.

I explained to him my situation, and without hesitation he said, "OK, I'll see what I can do" – though I must confess he did at the time express his doubts as to whether I would stand up to his type of work. I hadn't a clue as to what type of work it was; even so, I told him I was sure I would be able to cope.

So it was, the following Monday morning, I arose at six thirty (an unearthly hour for me) and by seven forty-five, on a bike borrowed from my younger brother Stanley, I was on my way from East Ham to Millwall. It couldn't have been a worse morning to start a new job. With the tiny regulation slit of light from my bicycle lamp barely showing beyond the front wheel, and the freezing cold wind driving drizzle into my face, I began to wonder if this wasn't some sort of omen. Not being a true cyclist I wasn't prepared for such atrocious weather, so within ten minutes of starting out, I was near to being soaked to the skin, and by the time I had arrived outside Westwoods I well and truly was.

Jim Palmer met me at the gate, showed me how to clock on, then took me across the road to the sheet metal department (commonly known as the 'Tin Shop'), where he was charge hand. He waited while I changed into my new set of overalls and when I'd draped my saturated trousers over a radiator, which was cold, I followed him to the drilling machine, where he showed me to the job he had obviously had lined up for me. After a few minutes, when he could see that I was quite capable of carrying out this simple task, he said, "Well, it's all yours," and went about his work leaving me to it.

From the moment I stepped into the cold and uninviting atmosphere of the place, I knew I'd made a terrible mistake and that Jim's doubts about my working there had been justified. I loathed every minute of it. Piling twenty sheets of metal, one at a time, on to a "jig", clamping a template on top and drilling the twenty sheets through the ferrules of the template hour after hour was, for me, soul-destroying. The constant lifting of the sheets of $1/16$-inch plate from the never-ending pile on the float tore my delicate hands to shreds. How I got home on my bike with such sore and bleeding hands, coupled with a back I couldn't straighten, is to me a mystery to this day.

Lily was so horrified at my physical state that for a moment she stood looking at me, stunned – what a pitiful sight I must have seemed, bent over unable to straighten up and my face screwed up in agony. And when she saw my sliced and bleeding knuckles, the result of my inexperience in lifting razor-sharp sheets of metal, she came to me and put her arms around me comfortingly. I tried to put my arms round her, but winced the moment I touched her; seeing the pain in my face, she turned my palms over. Tears coursed down her cheeks at the sight of my torn and bleeding, grimy hands. "Oh darling," she wept, "what have they done to your lovely hands?" She said it accusingly, as though someone else was responsible for their condition.

"I don't think I'll ever be able to play the piano again," I said miserably.

"Yes, you will," she cried, helping me off with my overalls. "I'll get your hands better, I've got just the thing for them."

"Yes! And I've got the very thing for your back," said her father, coming in from the scullery carrying a small bottle.

"What's that?" I moaned.

"Sloan's Liniment. It'll get your back right in no time."

They were all tremendously concerned. Her mother was buzzing around and at Lily's request brought a bowl of warm water from the scullery and put it on the kitchen table, wincing herself as she caught sight of the damage.

"You'll have to give in your notice tomorrow," Lily stressed tearfully, as she bathed my hands in the warm water with soapy cotton wool. "You're not cut out for this type of work."

She was right, of course, but I had to confess to her that, much as I loathed and hated it, having only done one day, I hadn't the courage to tell Jim Palmer that I was packing it in, especially as he had gone to so much trouble to get me the job. "Besides," I reminded her as she continued to massage each hand in turn with olive oil, "it will only be a matter of weeks before I'm called up, and as I'm sure I can stick it out until then, I don't see the point of offending him when it's not necessary."

"Yes, I suppose you're right." She continued her gentle treatment of my hands, the pain of my every "Ouch" showing on her face.

When she had finished bandaging my cuts, her father handed me the bottle of Sloan's Liniment and said, "Here, you hold this while I help you up the stairs." Once in the bedroom I stripped off (which was an agony in itself) then lay face down on the bed. I let out a few "Oohs" and "Aahs" of pain when he began his massaging of my back, but when I'd got used to his heavy hands and the heat of the Sloan's began to penetrate into the muscles, it became quite pleasant.

He warmed to his task. "Sloan's is reckoned to be the best thing for all aches and pains – all your athletes and footballers swear by it." He was steadily working his way down, and when he got to the small of my back, putting on extra pressure, he grunted with the effort. "Now this is where it gets most people." I couldn't help a big "Oooh!" escaping as I felt my spine touch my belly button.

"Did that hurt?" he asked with concern.

"A little bit" – then quickly – "but nice though." The moment I'd said it, I wished I hadn't. Now he concentrated all his efforts on that one spot. When I could stand it no longer, I said casually, "Actually, I feel it more in the region of my waist."

"Ah, that's the bending up and down that's done that! Right! I'll soon fix that!" and so saying he filled his cupped palm with the liniment and sloshed it on my waist.

Now Sloan's, being the same consistency as water, took the line of least resistance and made straight for the cheeks of my bare arse, cascading down the crevice on to my more tender parts. Often I've heard fellows discussing the excruciating pains they have endured at some time or another, all vying with each other to prove that the pain they had suffered was the worst – but I can categorically state, here and now, that until they've had their testicles drenched with a quarter of a pint of Sloan's, they don't know what pain is.

I screamed and leapt off the bed. I continued screaming in pain as, naked, with knees bent and legs apart, I jumped up and down, and round and round the bedroom, trying to get some cold air to the affected parts. When that didn't work, I bent as low as I possibly could and blew in the direction of the fire. Not being a contortionist, I found it useless. Nearly out of my mind with pain I shrieked, "Water, water!" Lily's father, immediately realising what had happened, dashed down the stairs, and within seconds was back with an enamelled bowl filled with cold water which he placed on the bedside chair. I promptly ceased my native war dance, and literally threw my bottom and genitals into the beautiful cold water. Dad looked at me with concern, which after a while turned to relief when the fire began to die away and I said, "Oh boy! What a blessing!"

Lily, having heard the hullabaloo, was knocking on the bedroom door enquiring anxiously, "Is everything all right?"

In those days, conversation about private parts, particularly with the opposite sex, was very much frowned upon, so Dad called back casually, "Yes, everything's under control! There's nothing to worry about, Nin!" "Nin" was the family's pet name for Lily. Hearing her retreating footsteps he asked, "How does it feel?"

I looked up at him from my undignified squatting position and answered, "I'm OK now."

Relieved, he walked to the mantelshelf, picked up the cap of the near-empty bottle of Sloan's, and screwing it back on said with his usual little sniff, "Well, I don't suppose you'll be wanting this any more?"

Now that we had agreed to let things stand at work, Lily, to protect my hands, bought me a pair of thick industrial gloves, which I thought would be the answer to the problem. Much to my amazement, by the end of the week the vicious sheets of metal had ripped them to pieces, rendering them useless. On the Saturday afternoon, coming home from work, I bought myself another pair, but at the end of the following week they, too, had gone the same way. As unskilled labour I was getting one and twopence an hour, and as the gloves were three and sixpence a pair, I didn't have to be a mathematician to realise the futility of this, and so, come the third week, gloves were out and cuts were back in.

It was halfway through the third week that Jim, having just shown me how to operate a notching machine, said, "I see you've given the gloves up!"

"Well, they barely lasted a week, and at three and a tanner a throw, it was ridiculous." He nodded in agreement. "Besides," I said, picking up a sheet of metal to notch, "I've only got another two or three weeks at the outside, and I'm sure I can put up with a few cuts for that long."

A puzzled expression spread across his face. "Two or three weeks for what?"

"Well," I replied, surprised that he hadn't already guessed, "they're already calling up the twenty-two group, and as I'm in the twenty-threes . . ."

"Oh," he said, cottoning on at last, "I thought you knew!"

"Knew what?" It was my turn to look puzzled now.

"Well," and a big grin split his face, "have I got good news for you!" I looked at him in amazement. Apart from sacking me, I couldn't for the life of me think of any other good news he could possibly have to tell me. "You," he emphasised, "won't be called up. We're on war work here . . . even what you are doing right now is connected with war work. You're in a reserved occupation, and that means for the duration." Then, mistaking my look of horror for astonishment, he added as he left me to notch two thousand sheets of metal stacked in piles all over the floor, "I thought that would please you!"

I stood there dumbstruck . . . it had been bad enough when I'd believed I had only a few more weeks to go – but now! The thought of being stuck in this dreadful place, forced to do this mundane, monotonous, boring work for God knows how long, was more than my mind would accept.

There was only one place to go – and I made straight for it. Out the back yard, past the site where the steel erectors were assembling the frame of a huge building, to the row of "bogs" ahead. I pulled open the door of the first one, bolted it behind me, stepped over all the old bits of newspaper littering the floor, and sat down on the grubby pan.

I had gone there to think, but what was there to think about? Whichever way I looked at it I had to accept the fact that, as Jim had said, I was here for the duration. The finality of it shattered me.

Knowing I couldn't sit there all day, I eventually stood up and was about to leave when a torn piece of newspaper on the floor caught my eye. It was the printed drawing of the bristled head of a broom that held my attention, reminding me of something, but for the life of me I couldn't think what. Suddenly the picture of the hard stone path outside our scullery door, which led to the outside lavatory, sprang to my mind. It was my Saturday morning chore, when I was a child, to take a broom similar to the one in the advert and, with a bucket of cold water heavily laced with carbolic, to scrub the said stone path.

I hated that job too, and every time I got the bucket and broom out, Dad, seeing my face as long as a kite, would say, "You don't like doing that job, do you?"

"No, Dad," I'd reply.

To which he would answer, "Well, you'd better like it!" I never understood what he meant by it. It was never, "You'd better like it, or else!" – meaning a clump round the ear. No, it was always, "Well, you'd better like it!" After a while I gave up trying to fathom its meaning, and dismissed it from my mind.

A smile gradually spread across my face as I stood there, remembering – and understanding the meaning of Dad's words for the first time. "If you've *got* to do it – you'd better like it."

I stooped down, picked up the torn advert, folded it up and put it in my overall pocket; then light of step I marched back to the workshop and got stuck into notching the two thousand sheets of metal.

Even though Dad's few words of wisdom were of great value to me, I was nevertheless determined to get off the boring, repetitious work and on to something more interesting. This I eventually did, but it took time. Every night for weeks I took home old blueprints, studied and learned to read them. After nearly a year of this, coupled with the knowledge I'd gleaned from the everyday practical side, I was ready to do my first job from the blueprint stage. It was to make twenty small steel boxes with hinged lids, and although a simple task, as it was for the Admiralty, the measurements had to be spot on.

Being a meticulous worker this suited me down to the ground; in fact I was so absorbed with what I was doing for most of the time, that it wasn't until they had shut the machinery down that I realised it was time to knock off. I was thrilled, when I had completed the job and the boxes had been inspected, to be congratulated by Jim on the accuracy and finish of my workmanship. Unfortunately, with jobs like that being few and far between, it was back to the old grind again.

One of the firm's specialities was making lockers for changing rooms, which didn't call for such care and attention, and now that the war was well under way and new factories were going up all over the place, orders for lockers came flooding in.

One morning Jim arrived with an order for seventy-five lockers. Normally all seventy-five would have been knocked out together, but on this occasion twenty-five of them had different dimensions. Jim had no alternative but to split up the job. He gave fifty to a chap known to all as "Smudger, the Locker King", and the other twenty-five to me, saying, "It's not an Admiralty job." I knew exactly what he meant by that – when it came to lockers the firm preferred speed to accuracy. Unfortunately it is impossible for me to work that way, and although I never stop for a second, I am not a speed merchant. Everything for me has to be "as per drawing – to the thou".

Not a day went by without my being questioned by Jim as to how the job was coming along. This I knew was his way of giving me the hurry-up treatment, but as there was nothing I could do about it, I tried to ignore his sarcasm. I don't know how long I'd been doing the job, but what I do know is that it was mid-afternoon on the Friday when he stormed over to me with a face like thunder, and said, "Haven't you finished that job yet?"

"Not quite," I said, trying to keep my calm, then added, "but I'm nearly finished."

"Nearly finished!" he exploded. "Gawd Blimey! Smudger finished his fifty days ago!!!"

Taking umbrage at his bawling out, I snapped back, "Maybe he did – but give 'em a push and his lot'll fall over, but mine won't!"

His immediate reply was, "Neither will Smudger's when they're screwed to the bleeding wall!"

The day after my little contretemps with Jim, Lily and I, having had our lunch, were getting ready to go to the pictures for our usual Saturday afternoon treat, when a little argument started about which picture we should see. For once our tastes differed, and neither would give way to the other's views. The outcome of this show of stubbornness was that Lily went off alone to the Coronation Cinema at Manor Park Broadway. I intended to go elsewhere, but would leave later so as not to arrive halfway through the main picture.

It was while I was sitting in the front room, waiting for the time to pass, that I got to thinking about our argument, and when I realised how stupid I had been to let such a trivial thing come between us, I decided to abandon my plans, meet her outside the Coronation Cinema when the programme had finished, and have a meal at Tony's, a lovely little restaurant, to make it up to her. It would cost me seven and sixpence, a lot of money in those days, but I considered it was worth it under the circumstances.

In the year following Chamberlain's fateful broadcast, with England remaining comparatively quiet, people got back to running their lives as normally as restrictions such as rationing, blackouts, etc., would allow. Entertainment had returned and pubs began to flourish once again.

I was inundated with offers to play the piano in several of them – one in particular, the Burnell Arms, down the hill from East Ham station, wanted me to do six nights a week from 8 to 10.30 p.m. This was impossible because now that we were compelled to do two hours' overtime each day, I wasn't getting home from work until seven forty-five. In any case, with the enormous number of hours involved, it would have been far too taxing. I did tell them, however, that I was willing to do three nights a week providing they made it from 8.30 to 10.30 p.m. They said they would consider it and get back to me.

Now that I had made up my mind to meet Lily at the cinema, I sat there in a much happier mood, and with three hours to kill before her programme finished, I thought it best to get down to some practice on the piano just in case the Burnell Arms accepted my offer.

It was a gorgeous early September day, and as I sat flexing my fingers and looking at the pattern of the lace curtains stencilled across the front panel of the piano, made by the sun streaming through the windows, I wondered how my fingers would react. My hands by now had hardened to the rough work, but as I had scarcely touched a piano since starting at Westwoods my fingers had become very stiff with the lack of playing. I was amazed to find after only half an hour's practice how supple they were becoming. An hour of this each night, I thought happily, and they would soon be back to normal.

Playing at a pub I would naturally be expected to know, apart from the latest hits, all the old evergreens as well, so I thought it wise to jot them down. I got out my notebook and started to write them down in alphabetical order. I had finished all that came to my mind under the heading of "A" and was just about to start on the "B"s, when the peace of the afternoon was suddenly shattered by the harrowing wail of the siren.

Although it was a sound that made your blood curdle, as it was daylight I couldn't imagine anything would come of it, and after about ten minutes when nothing did, I came to the conclusion that it was a false alarm like the one after Chamberlain's broadcast.

I returned to my list of "oldies". I had written down about a dozen under the heading "B" and was halfway through adding "Bye Bye Blackbird" when I heard the far-away sound of aircraft.

I sat there motionless, straining my ears, listening as the steady drone gradually grew louder and when I heard the distant but unmistakable rumble of anti-aircraft gunfire, my first thoughts went to Lily in the cinema. I dropped everything I was doing, grabbed my jacket and as I tore through the kitchen to get to the back gate, I shouted to her mum and dad, who were in a state of indecision, "I'm going to get Lily!"

As I raced down Mitcham Road to get to the bus stop, opposite the White Horse public house, the thought of how I was going to do this never entered my mind. A 101 bus going to Manor Park Broadway arrived just as I got there and as I boarded it the noise of the enemy planes, together with the constant barrage of gunfire, was coming ominously nearer. By the time I arrived at the Coronation Cinema about ten minutes later, the sound was deafening.

I rushed to the cinema but the latticed gates were drawn across barring the entrance. I was in a turmoil as to what to do next. With the gates closed, for all I knew the Management might have turned everyone out immediately the warning went. If this was the case, our paths would have crossed and Lily would already be home.

Usually the Manor Park Broadway was teeming with people, but now, with not a soul about, it looked vast, and I felt terribly alone . . . it was eerie. So it was a comforting sight to see a 101 bus going in the direction from which I had just come, pull up at the stop across the road. Hardly had it stopped before it was off again. In a panic at the thought of losing my only companion, I leapt across the road and chased after it, and although it was gathering speed all the time, I managed to catch up with it and jump on.

"Where to, mate?" the conductor shouted through the ear-splitting din, as I was heading for the top deck.

"The White Horse," I shouted back, very much out of breath.

He gave a nasal "I thank you" as he took my twopence ha'penny, and stuffing the ticket in my pocket, I continued my journey upstairs, sat down and put on a fag to steady my nerves.

The driver was changing gear in readiness to pull up at East Ham station when a piece of shrapnel from one of our own guns tore through the roof of the bus, and with a frighteningly loud crack embedded itself in the floor close to my right foot.

"Right, mate!" the conductor shouted to me from halfway up the stairs. "This is as far as we're going!"

I got off, shaking like a leaf.

No. 80 Masterman Road, where Lily and I were living with her mum and dad, was about a mile from East Ham station, and as I started my journey home, with no bus around me for protection, I felt very vulnerable. Each step took me nearer to the destruction going on ahead, which I now knew to be centred on the Woolwich Arsenal and the Royal Albert Docks. The sky was full of enemy aircraft, with our boys in their Spitfires diving in and out of the enemy formations looking like tiny silver fish as the sun caught them.

I had to put my hands over my ears to protect them from the abominable noise made by the throbbing engines of what must have been hundreds of planes, the whistling exploding bombs, and the salvos from all the anti-aircraft guns that were being driven around the side streets. The ground continually shook as stick after stick of the Luftwaffe's bombs rained down on their target. The huge pall of dense black smoke hanging over the devastated area began to drift its way towards East Ham, blackening out the perfect blue sky.

Scared stiff and with legs like jelly, I crossed over the Barking Road to the Town Hall, passed the library and continued on up the High Street north towards Woolwich.

Apart from the conductor of the bus, I hadn't seen a soul. I desperately wanted to get out of this hell and under cover, but as there was no sign of a shelter – well, not that I could see – I thought it best to get home as quickly as I possibly could.

I was about one or it may have been two hundred yards past the Town Hall when suddenly I was grabbed by a Chief Air Raid Warden in his white steel helmet with a big black "W" stencilled on the front. "Come in here, you silly little sod!" he said angrily, and added as he led me towards a flight of steps, "What were you trying to do . . . prove to everybody how brave you are?" I made no comment, but thought as he marshalled me down the stairs to the underground shelter, that with the streets deserted, it was a pretty stupid remark to make. But then had he known just how terrified I really was he most probably wouldn't have made it.

The shelter was crowded with shoppers who had been caught out by the unexpected raid. Most of the adults were seated on low forms provided, and those with children either had them on their laps or clustered round them. The vibration from the falling bombs was even more apparent underground than on top and as each stick of bombs could be heard whistling down, the mothers huddled their children to them, as a hen would protect her chicks, and when the crunch came, the rest of us cowered against the shower of fine dust that fell from the reinforced rafters. The battle raged on, growing in intensity, for what seemed like an eternity, when in fact it was only about an hour; and then as quickly as it came, it went.

Outside, the smell of cordite hung in the air, and the dense cloud of smoke that earlier had been slowly wending its way up the High Street from Woolwich, now enveloped all of East Ham, and a deep red glow could be seen through the distant smoke where the Royal Albert Docks were alight.

Lily had arrived home a little before me and it was over tea that we learned from the six o'clock news on the wireless that it was not only the Royal Albert Docks that the German planes attacked, but all the other docks and targets along the Thames east of Tower Bridge.

Warned by the radio announcer that from now on we could expect continued bombing attacks, we immediately got down to preparing our air raid shelter for longer stays. Hitherto regarded as a place just for emergencies, the shelter's only furniture had been a couple of chairs and a stool; now, within an hour, Lily, her mum and her sister Ruby had fitted it out with a mattress and bedding for themselves, while her dad and I rigged up a couple of temporary bunks.

With the docks along the Thames still burning fiercely, lighting up the sky for miles around, we fully expected a return visit that night, but owing to bad weather on the Continent, so the weather report said, all enemy aircraft were grounded, and we were spared that one night of hell. The weather must have cleared on the Sunday, because that night the Luftwaffe bombed us unmercifully, as they did every night for weeks thereafter.

Every day now thousands and thousands of women and children were being evacuated, and it was plain after that terrifying Sunday night that Lily's mum, who suffered very badly from claustrophobia and asthma, would have to be evacuated too.

Fortunately Ruby's boy friend Bob, who at that time was working at the RAF depot at Milton, near Reading, had heard of a bungalow with two bedrooms for rent in Goring, Berkshire. Lily's father and I decided that as Silvertown, where Lily and Ruby worked as secretaries, had been badly hit (and a great number of its factories razed to the ground) they should be evacuated with their mother. So it was, on the following Sunday morning, we said our goodbyes at Paddington Station telling them we would be down at the weekend.

*   *   *

With the siren going off every night immediately it got dark, Dad and I geared our lives to the shelter. In fact it wasn't uncommon for the warning to go while I was still cycling home from work. When this was the case, Lily's dad, who worked as a fitter at the East Ham Town Hall and was home by 5.30 p.m., would have my dinner ready for me in the Anderson shelter.

Life for us in the shelter was pretty grim, with heavy bombing night after night. Apart from Saturday afternoon and Sunday, when we visited our family at Goring, our working clothes also became our pyjamas. The light from our single torch was hopeless for reading, but that was of no consequence because our nights were spent in terror listening to the screaming bombs being rained down upon us and wondering if we would be emerging the next morning sound of limb, if at all.

There was one improvement, however; with only ourselves to worry about, toilet arrangements weren't a problem. When the women were there, all of us had to wait for a lull before dashing up in turn to the outside toilet; whereas now, a po was in order, kept within easy reach just outside the baffle door. But we had a strict rule . . . it was only to be used for peeing in. Nature's heavier calls had to be controlled until such time as there was a lull.

Now that the vast majority of husbands had evacuated their wives and children, they shared shelters with their neighbours or friends, so as not to suffer alone.

My elder brother Sid had arranged for his wife and baby son to be evacuated to Addlestone in Surrey, but like the rest of us, because of his work he remained in London. As Canning Town, where he still lived, was so close to the East India Docks and Silvertown, streets were being razed to the ground night after night, making the area unrecognisable next day. One Wednesday morning, after arriving at work, I heard of the terrible damage that Canning Town had received the previous night, and decided to visit Sid on my way home from work.

The night was drawing in as I turned into Cambus Road where Sid lived. In the dusk it looked quite normal, but on closer inspection you could see the appalling damage. A bomb had fallen in Heyday Road, on a row of houses that backed immediately on to Sid's road. Every window of most of the houses had been blown out, and every door too, and those that hadn't were hanging precariously on their frames. The road was strewn with glass, so I dismounted from my bike, hooked the crossbar over my shoulder and went the rest of the way on foot.

The street door of Sid's self-contained flat was halfway up the stairs, and with huge cracks in the walls and all the ceilings down, the house was virtually a write-off. Relieved at seeing his bike propped up against the porch wall, I unhooked mine from my shoulder and rested it on his. I went on up the stairs, and as I squeezed my way past the wedged street door, I called out, "It's only me, Sid!" and when I got no reply, I called again, "It's only me, Sid!" After repeating this several times more, still with no answer, a terrifying thought struck me: just because his bike was in the porch, there was no reason to conclude that he had just arrived home from work . . . it could have been there yesterday. Then, my mind raced on out of control . . . his yard backed on to Heyday Road where the bomb dropped, and if he'd been in the shelter at the time . . . "Oh, my God!" I said, as in a panic I tore up the stairs and raced through his kitchen to get to the back door, which opened on to the stairs that led down to his shelter. With a strength I didn't know I possessed, I wrenched open the jammed back door, and as I was about to descend I heard him call out, "Is that you, Reg?"

It's hard to describe my feelings on hearing his voice. I stood at the top of the wooden stairs, and as I heard him coming through the kitchen towards me, I quickly knuckled dry my tears of relief and turned to him. He looked at me, and so as not to embarrass me by asking why I'd been crying, he said, "What's up?"

"Nothing," I said, trying to sound as casual as I could. "I got a load of shit in my eyes from your ceiling trying to squeeze past that door."

Although Sid knew I was lying he didn't say anything, he just came towards me and as we embraced in a brotherly greeting he said over my shoulder, with such feeling, "God! I'm glad to see you!"

I could tell by the way he held on to me that his nerves had been shot to pieces by the terrifying experience he had suffered the night before.

"Me too, Sid," I replied, patting his back comfortingly, and before our emotions got completely out of control, I pulled away, saying, "Right, you're not staying here a moment longer . . . you're coming home with me." As we were squeezing past the wedged door on the stairs, I continued, "There's plenty of room in our shelter . . . besides, Lily's dad will be only too pleased to have you with us."

Once again, because of the broken glass everywhere, we shouldered our bikes and as we set off he started to tell me about the nightmare of the previous evening, alone in the shelter. I listened appalled at what he had been through, and he told me how families had been leaving the area every day, until eventually he was the only one left. We got to the corner of the street, unhooked the bikes from our shoulders, mounted them and just before we rode off he took one last look back down Cambus Road, and said, more to himself than to me, "And then there were none!"

When Lily's dad and I were alone in the shelter listening to the war raging overhead, there was little cause for humour, but now, with Sid sharing our nightly ordeal, it became more tolerable, and what's more our sense of humour began to return. One particular night when the bombing was exceptionally heavy in our district, Sid was counting the sticks of bombs as they were dropped. From the moment the first bomb of the stick screamed down we knew that the last one was going to be perilously close. When it landed only a few streets away, it lifted our shelter two or three inches off the ground, slamming the baffle door shut. Sid and I, white with fear, looked at each other, and when things had quietened down a little I said, "Blimey! It's a bad one tonight!"

"Yes!" said Lily's dad from his bunk, "they've certainly got no respect for a feller trying to get some sleep."

Life went on as usual. Despite the devastation of the previous night's bombing, we did what had to be done. And strangely, since Sid had joined us, our shelter became a haven for any one of the family who had to come up to London.

One night, upon arriving home from work, Sid and I were surprised to see our own father, with Lily's dad and her Uncle Harry, all merrily chatting away in the kitchen. It soon became apparent that they, because of some private matters that needed attention, would be staying with us for a few nights.

As always, as soon as Sid and I had finished our dinner, the siren went. Now, instead of our customary tray with a pot of tea and three cups, Lily's dad, I noticed, had made two pots of tea, and instead of the three cups there were now five.

Hardly had we opened the back door to make for the shelter, when the guns started up.

"Christ! They're over quick tonight," said Lily's dad. Out of habit I looked up and saw the familiar pattern of searchlights swinging across the jet black sky, seeking out their quarry; and when the Beaufort gun let off a salvo in the street just outside, frightening the life out of us, we scurried to our burrow like rabbits.

You had to admit that, with five of us housed in such a small space, there wasn't a great deal of room left in the shelter for manoeuvring. The two dads occupied the bunks, while Uncle Harry, Sid and I took possession of the ground floor, so to speak.

When we had had our tea and settled down, I told my dad and Uncle Harry about the law of the po, and how it was only for peeing in. Uncle Harry said he wouldn't dream of doing anything else. "Besides," my dad added, "I like a bit of privacy when I'm unloading."

It was quite a heavy raid that night, but even so we felt safe in one another's company. Sid and I relaxed on the floor's mattress and, in the dim light from the torch, listened to the reminiscences, some of which were very funny. In fact the whole night was hilarious.

As we had drunk two cups of tea apiece, the po was being made good use of. When it was just Lily's dad and myself, the emptying of it could easily be left until the morning, but when Sid joined us this wasn't possible, and unless there was a lull, it had to be emptied on to the garden from inside the shelter. With the shelter set down three feet below ground level, this was a very tricky operation indeed. We developed a knack; after pushing open the baffle door, you leant the upper part of your torso out of the shelter as far as you could, then, gripping the po firmly by the handle with your thumb hooked over the rim, with a straight left arm, you gave it a good "swoosh" round the baffle door on to what was laughingly known as the "lawn".

Brother Sid was an expert "po-swoosher", and when it was just the three of us we left it to him; but now with five of us at it, it was obvious that more than one or two swooshes a night would be needed. It was Uncle Harry who said that it wasn't fair to let Sid do all the emptying; he suggested, and we all agreed, that the last one to fill it up was the one to do the swooshing.

A little while later my dad slid off his bunk, saying, "It's no good, I can't hold it any longer," and when he lifted the po he muttered, "Gawd Blimey – this is heavy!" With inadequate light from the torch, he peered into it with eyes squinting. "How d'you know when this pot's full up?"

"When it comes up to your thumb," Lily's father replied.

Dad laughed. "Well, it looks as though it's my turn to do the swooshing." A few seconds went by before we heard him say, "Well, here goes!" The next minute we heard him cry out, "Oh, Jesus Christ."

"What's happened?" we said simultaneously.

"I forgot to open the bloody door!" And then he joined us in helpless laughter.

About a fortnight later the raids started to ease off – at least they did in our area. Thinking it was safe, Lily came down for the weekend, instead of my visiting her in Goring. We had a peaceful and enjoyable Saturday evening, but on the Sunday night we were both surprised by the wail of the siren. We dashed to the shelter immediately and soon after the Luftwaffe arrived and attacked the City of London itself. They saturated the City with incendiary bombs, and it wasn't long before huge fires were raging. Fire engines with their bells ringing could be heard coming from miles around, all chasing to save our precious capital, but with so many massive buildings already ablaze, despite their great effort they couldn't cope, and it wasn't long before practically the whole of the City seemed to be alight.

Fore Street in the heart of the City where my brother Sid's small typewriter repair firm was situated, was razed to the ground like the rest. So now, with nothing left in London, he found himself a job connected with the aircraft industry, and stayed in Surrey for the duration of the war.

Despite another lull soon after the near destruction of the Blitz, we had the feeling that it was not going to last, so rather than take any chances, Dad and I kept to sleeping in the Anderson shelter.

After being confined to their shelters night after night, for months on end, people once more began gradually to get out and about. With the pubs starting to do business again, the Burnell Arms contacted me, wanting to know if I was still interested in their offer. My weekly take-home pay, for the amount of hours I was working, was still appalling; so the fifty bob offered for playing piano three nights a week was most welcome.

Lily's dad was all for my earning a few extra bob, and knowing my concern about leaving him on his own for three evenings, said he would go to his club at the Town Hall and have a few games of billiards. I therefore started at the Burnell Arms the following Monday evening. When I arrived, a chap well past the age of calling up was in the process of fitting up his saxophone and clarinet. I introduced myself.

"Pleased to meet you. The name's Bob, but everyone calls me 'Lips'." It was easy to see why, by the way he wrapped his huge mouth round the mouthpiece of both his saxophone and clarinet every time he prepared himself to play.

I enjoyed my evenings at the pub, and back once more entertaining the public I was in my element. The lounge bar of the Burnell Arms, although large, had a great atmosphere, and its customers were a fabulous audience. Business grew rapidly, and with it my popularity. I was continually asked by the regulars to sing their favourites and it amazed me how they never tired of hearing the same songs, such as "The White Cliffs of Dover" and "We'll Meet Again". Songs made famous by Vera Lynn were always being requested, as were Irving Berlin's numbers of the past, particularly from one regular who always sat on the same stool at the end of the bar nearest our small but adequate stage. He was always there when I arrived and was still there when I left, so that to me he appeared to be a permanent fixture.

He wasn't a young man, neither was he old – he was one of those men who seem ageless. Immaculately dressed and never without his Homburg hat, he was always referred to by Lips as the "Toff". He was a loner. Not once did I ever see him in conversation with anyone. He drank steadily all the evening, and whenever he wanted his glass replenished, he never asked, he just nodded to the barman, as though bidding at an auction. Round about ten o'clock he went on the Scotch, and after downing a couple of these, he would call out, in a voice belying his gentlemanly looks, "Oy! Give us 'When I Leave the World Behind'."

One Wednesday, however, these cherished evenings came to an abrupt end. At about nine thirty (although the siren must have sounded long before this), Lips and I were playing a selection of oldies. Everyone in the packed pub was having a marvellous time singing along, when suddenly, with an almighty crash the back of the bar caved in, and dust seemed to come from everywhere. People dived under tables, but since it was so unexpected nobody panicked. The shudder from the wall behind the piano had pushed it towards me, and the keyboard was almost in my lap, but the strange thing was that both Lips and I continued to play . . . sheer reaction, of course. It was the Chief Air Raid Warden, who came in blowing his whistle, who stopped us.

"Now ladies and gentlemen," he said, "I don't want you to panic, but I'm afraid I must ask you to leave as there is a land mine with its parachute caught up in a tree just outside."

I've never seen people move so quickly in my life; it was like watching a reel of an early movie. Within seconds the place was empty – that is, with the exception of the Toff. Smashed out of his skull and with the aid of the bar to keep him upright, he wandered slowly along it drinking all the remaining drinks left by the customers.

I pushed the piano back to the wall and with our hair and faces absolutely smothered with dust, Lips and I followed everybody out by the back entrance of the pub. Although it wasn't a direct hit, the damage done to the Burnell Arms was extensive.

Everything came to a halt, and with no buses running, I started the mile and a half trek home with my eyes glued to the sky. Conventional bombs you could hear coming, but not bombs dropped by parachute.

On my way home I could see flashes and hear explosions coming from near and far, which meant that once again the East End was the enemy's target. I walked round the back doubles in order to make it home quicker, as I was worried about Lily's dad. He usually got home from his club about nine thirty. Had he made it home, and if so, was he in the shelter? I knew he would be out of his mind wondering if I was all right. There wasn't one street I went through where I wasn't walking on broken glass.

I was nearing the Barking Road when, still scanning the sky, I saw for the first time a white parachute dropping in the direction of Masterman Road. Panic-stricken, I ran like a bat out of hell for home. Halfway up Pulleyn's Avenue I saw a huge flash, followed by a tremendous explosion. Frantic now, I urged my legs to go faster, but they refused. My heart was pumping so fast with the exertion of running that I thought my eardrums would burst.

Out of Pulleyn's Avenue and on down Sandford Road I raced, till finally I reached our house, which stood on the corner of Masterman Road and Sandford Road. I was relieved to see the house still standing, but I guessed by the masses of glass strewn about that the blast must have caused a certain amount of damage, but to see how much we would have to wait until daylight.

At that moment my thoughts were for Lily's dad. I tore through the back gate – hanging at a crazy angle on one hinge – down the back yard to the shelter. "Dad, Dad – are you there?" Frantically I squeezed past the jammed baffle door and called into the eerie blackness, "Dad, are you there?" Receiving no answer, I rushed to the small lean-to where I kept my bike, wrenched the lamp from its bracket and dashed back to the shelter. I thrust my bike lamp into the black hole, and the light showing through the restricted slit confirmed what I already knew, but I had to be sure.

I tried to think where he could possibly be, but my mind was in a turmoil. I kept telling myself to calm down, but how could one be calm in a situation like this? I ran to the back door which opened on to the scullery, repeatedly shouting, "Dad, Dad – where are you?" When I got to the door, through the dim light from my lamp, I could see it had been blown in and was now leaning precariously against the gas stove and the clothes boiler.

On through the kitchen I rushed – momentarily wondering why I couldn't hear my footsteps – to the door leading to the passage. I turned to go up the stairs, but like my brother Sid's the street door was jammed halfway up.

Getting no response to all the shouting I was doing, I was convinced now that he was nowhere in the house. He must still be at his club, I thought. If this was the case, and I hoped it was . . . he would be safe in the Town Hall's shelter. I gave up yelling for him, there was no point. I walked aimlessly through the open doorway and out into Masterman Road itself. Once outside I could plainly hear cries and shouts coming from nearby, and although there were no fire engines or ambulances to be seen in Masterman Road, the land mine must have dropped dangerously close.

I had just set off in the direction of the commotion, when I saw Lily's father coming towards me. With a great sigh of relief I quickened my pace and went to meet him. It was too dark to see his features, but nevertheless he was obviously in a state of shock; his first words to me were, "Jesus Christ, son, I've just had the most terrifying experience."

We walked back to our battered house with the intention of making a pot of tea, then realising the damage that might have been caused by the bomb to the gas main, we decided against it and went straight into the shelter. We squeezed past the jammed baffle door and dropped inside. Lying on the floor's mattress with his back resting against the corrugated iron, he began to relive his nightmarish ordeal. To me it was a repeat of my brother Sid's awful experience, the only difference being that Sid heard his bomb coming, whereas Dad's, being a land mine, had given no warning whatsoever.

"I don't know how long I'd been sitting in the shelter after the explosion, shaking like a leaf," he said, "but eventually when everything quietened down I thought I'd better make a move, but when I went to open the baffle door, I got another shock . . . the 'buddy' thing wouldn't budge." (He never said "bloody".) "It was only by sheer brute strength that I managed to open it as far as it is now." He didn't speak for a few seconds, then right out of the blue he asked, "What was it like up your end?"

"Well," I replied, "we had our fair share." Then I proceeded to tell him my horror story, but only the humorous side. He laughed at my description of the customers and the speed with which they exited from the pub, and even more so when I told him about the Toff and the way he cleared up all the drinks on his way out. We chatted on for quite some time till eventually, exhausted from the worry of it all, sleep overcame us.

Next morning when I awoke Lily's dad was already up, and I guessed he was somewhere in the house assessing the damage. I scrambled out of the shelter and found him in the scullery putting the kettle on, and in answer to my enquiring look, he told me he had met a neighbour who had informed him, on good authority, that it was all right to use the gas.

After a cup of tea and a piece of toast we decided first of all to weigh up the damage done. One inspection was all that was needed to see that the house was no longer habitable; even so, we knew our worldly goods had to be protected from the elements, so between us we managed to screw the doors of both street and scullery back on to their frames. The kitchen floor, covered in at least an inch of soot (the reason for my not being able to hear my footsteps the night before), was our next task. Dad had earlier found the canary still in its cage on the floor, and now it was back on its stand, looking like a tiny blackbird with little beady eyes.

It took us two hours and goodness knows how many buckets of water to clean the kitchen up, and then it was by no means perfect. At least we were no longer treading soot all over the place. It was now about 8.30 a.m. and I said to Dad, "I think we ought to let the girls know the position, and if I ring Lily at Goring I shall catch her before she goes to work." This agreed, and with the kindness of the owners of the corner sweetshop, I rang Lily and put her in the picture. Her immediate response was to tell me that they would all be at Masterman Road about midday on Saturday.

When I got back from phoning, I found Uncle Harry, whose wife and boys had returned from Dovercourt some time ago and were now living at their home in Barking. He had heard how East Ham had been badly mauled by land mines and had come over to see if we were OK. Seeing that our house was no longer habitable, he told us that he knew a woman who lived only two streets from him in Barking, who was desperate to rent her place. "I'll let you know by early afternoon . . . in the meantime get yourselves a moving van lined up." Thus by Friday afternoon we, with the help of Uncle Harry and Aunt May, had moved in.

In the scullery of the Masterman Road house we had a bath – not a tin bath but a full-sized bath. It had no taps of course, and like the others had to be filled by hand. When not in use it had a wooden lid covered with a black and white check linoleum, to make it look smart. The first time I saw it I was reminded of the times when I used to go to the fair and roll pennies down a triangular slot.

On the Saturday morning, with not a stick of furniture left in the house, Lily's dad and I were sitting on the bath-top waiting for the rest of the family to arrive. They were always excellent time-keepers, and bang on the dot of twelve o'clock, with smiles of excitement, they burst through the open back door. The smiles were soon wiped off their faces on seeing the scullery, with the exception of the gas stove and the bath we were sitting on, stripped of everything. Too stunned to speak they wandered into the kitchen, and seeing just the empty shell, came back to us aghast. We told them the whole story from the beginning, and when we had finished, Lily's mother said, "But surely, Dan, the damage can't be as bad as you say!" Then Lily and Ruby, being of the same frame of mind as their mother, left Dad and me sitting on the bath-top while they made their own inspection of the house, to grasp at straws, hoping we were wrong.

Left alone, we looked at each other and shrugged, knowing that once they had seen the dreadful condition of the house, with all the ceilings down, the huge cracks in the walls, and the black felt tacked over what was left of the window frames, they would understand. And when five minutes later all three of them came down crying, we knew that they had accepted the inevitable, and that they agreed we had been right in making alternative arrangements. We slid off the bath-top as they entered the scullery, and Ruby, her face awash with tears, said to her father, "Oh Dad! What have they done to our lovely house?"

Neither of us said a word – we just let them get it out of their system. Eventually, Lily's father, after his customary little sniff, said gently, "Well come on, we'd better make a move." With that, we picked up their luggage and started the journey to our new home . . . 32 Stratton Drive, Upney, Barking.

By 1942, the country, losing battles in all areas of conflict, and now in desperate need of men, was calling on firms to release all those not directly involved with the war effort. Westwoods had already released a few men, so it was no surprise to me, upon arriving home from work one evening early in October, to see propped up against the clock on the mantelpiece a buff-coloured envelope with OHMS in black printed across the top. I opened it immediately and discovered that at such-and-such a time on a certain date in October I was to attend the Drill Hall in Romford for my medical. Soon after this, I received another buff-coloured envelope informing me that I was now a member of the Armed Forces, and on October 15th I was to catch the 10 a.m. train from King's Cross Station to Harrogate, where I would be met and taken to a Royal Artillery Establishment to begin my six weeks' primary training.

It was a cold, miserable October morning when Lily and I left home for King's Cross. All that had to be said had occupied the journey between Barking and King's Cross so now, with very little left to say, I stood on the platform in my navy blue serge suit, my Mickey Mouse gas mask slung over my shoulder with a piece of string, waiting for the special train that was to take me, along with hundreds of other young men crowding the platform, to Harrogate.

Time dragged on, and it was a relief when eventually at nine forty-five the train slowly edged its way along the platform, shrouded in clouds of steam. No sooner had the buffers touched than all the goodbyes started, accompanied by masses of tears. The guard was yelling "All aboard," when Lily suddenly said, "Oh! – I nearly forgot."

I looked at her, puzzled, as she began to search in her handbag. "What are you looking for?"

"Well, you know that little black box your mother gave me when we were married?"

"No, I don't," I answered, "but carry on."

"Yes, you do," she said, still fumbling in her handbag, "the one that had your birth certificate and penny insurance policies in it." Then taking an envelope from out of her bag, she continued, "Anyway, it doesn't matter now, I've found what I was looking for."

I was eyeing the aged envelope she held, when she said, "Open your hand!" I did as I was told, not knowing for what reason.

"Do you remember this?" she asked.

"Remember what?" I queried.

Then tipping the envelope upside down she said, "This!" and out into my hand dropped the little celluloid clown.